THE NEW HARTFORD MEMORIAL LIBRARY

D1267642

WITHDRAWN

Critical Essays on

CHARLES DICKENS'S
A Tale of Two Cities

CRITICAL ESSAYS
ON
BRITISH LITERATURE

Zack Bowen, General Editor
University of Miami

Critical Essays on
CHARLES DICKENS'S
A Tale of Two Cities

edited by

MICHAEL A. COTSELL

G. K. Hall & Co.
An Imprint of Simon & Schuster Macmillan
New York

Prentice Hall International
London   Mexico City   New Delhi   Singapore   Sydney   Toronto

Copyright © 1998 by G. K. Hall

All rights reserved. No part of this book may be reproduced or transmitted in any form or by any means, electronic or mechanical, including photocopying, recording, or by any information storage and retrieval system, without permission in writing from the Publisher.

G. K. Hall & Co.
An Imprint of Simon & Schuster Macmillan
1633 Broadway
New York, NY 10019

Library of Congress Cataloging-in-Publication Data

Critical essays on Charles Dickens's A tale of two cities / edited by
    Michael A. Cotsell.
        p. cm. — (Critical essays on British literature)
    Includes bibliographical references and index.
    ISBN 0-7838-0072-X (alk. paper)
    1. Dickens, Charles, 1812–1870. Tale of two cities. 2. France—
History—Revolution, 1789–1799—Literature and the revolution.
    I. Cotsell, Michael. II. Series.
    PR4571.C75   1998
    823'.8—dc21   98–21418
                                                           CIP

This paper meets the requirements of ANSI/NISO Z3948–1992 (Permanence of Paper).

10 9 8 7 6 5 4 3 2 1

Printed in the United States of America

Contents

◆

General Editor's Note

♦

The Critical Essays on British Literature series provides a variety of approaches to both classical and contemporary writers of Britain and Ireland. The formats of the volumes in the series vary with the thematic designs of individual editors, and with the amount and nature of existing reviews and criticism, augmented, where appropriate, by original essays by recognized authorities. It is hoped that each volume will be unique in developing a new overall perspective on its particular subject.

Michael Cotsell's reading and selection of essays draws its approach from the title of the work itself, with its assertion of the novel's fundamental structural and thematic "splitting," or division into contrasting cities, scenes, situations, characters, and ideologies, all mutually informing each other. The introduction gives ample hints of subjects for class discussion, such as the relations between history and the present, and the history of the book's genesis in Dickens's own life and in Thomas Carlyle's *The French Revolution,* excerpts from which are published as the first selection.

ZACK BOWEN
University of Miami

Publisher's Note

◆

Producing a volume that contains both newly commissioned and reprinted material presents the publisher with the challenge of balancing the desire to achieve stylistic consistency with the need to preserve the integrity of works first published elsewhere. In the Critical Essays series, essays commissioned especially for a particular volume are edited to be consistent with G. K. Hall's house style; reprinted essays appear in the style in which they were first published, with only typographical errors corrected. Consequently, shifts in style from one essay to another are the result of our efforts to be faithful to each text as it was originally published.

Introduction

MICHAEL COTSELL

After a typical period of uneasy gestation, Dickens began work on *A Tale of Two Cities* in March 1859 (he had finished *Little Dorrit* in May 1857). The new novel was to begin publication in the first number of his new weekly journal, *All the Year Round,* and run for 31 short weekly installments between 30 April and 26 November 1859. Dickens's *Book of Memoranda,* a notebook of ideas for novels he kept in 1855, contains the notions of the Lion and Jackal relationship of Stryver and Carton and the idea of a man who objects to his wife praying, used with Jerry and Mrs. Cruncher. There also Dickens considered a number of titles: "What do you say to the title, ONE OF THESE DAYS? . . . What do you think of *this* name for my story—BURIED ALIVE? Or, THE DOCTOR OF BEAUVAIS?"[1]

In his "Preface to the First Edition," Dickens mentions two sources for the novel. One is the play he wrote with his friend, the younger novelist Wilkie Collins, entitled *The Frozen Deep* (discussed at length in Leonard Manheim's essay "A Tale of Two Characters: Studies in Multiple Projection).[2] The other is simply identified as "Mr. Carlyle's wonderful book." Of course, Dickens's readers knew he was referring to Thomas Carlyle's *The French Revolution* (1837). Carlyle's influence and the whole subject of the French Revolution are discussed later in this introduction.

For Dickens, a catalyst for the composition and production of the play *The Frozen Deep* had been reports from "Eskimos" that the members of the ill-fated Arctic expedition of Sir John Franklin had resorted to cannibalism in their last struggles for life. Dickens had long interested himself in the search for the lost expedition, and this scandalous suggestion shocked his idealism. He wrote two articles in his journal *Household Words,* published in December 1854, in which he argued that no English gentleman could do what members of Franklin's expedition were now accused of doing ("The Lost Arctic Voyagers," reprinted in two parts in *Miscellaneous Papers*). In the first of these, Dickens asked his readers to consider a "supposititious case" of extreme duress:

> [I]f they had undergone such fatigue, exposure, and disaster, that scarcely power remained to them to crawl . . . if they could not bear the contemplation of their "filth and wretchedness, each other's emaciated figures, ghastly countenances, dilated eyeballs, and sepulchral voices"; if they had eaten their shoes, such outer clothes as they could part with and not perish of cold, the scraps of acrid marrow yet remaining in the dried and whitened spines of dead wolves; if they had wasted away to skeletons, on such fare, and on bits of putrid skin, and bits of hides and the covers of guns, and pounded bones; if they had passed through all the pangs of famine, had reached that point of starvation where there is little or no pain left, and had descended so far into the valley of the shadow of Death, that they lay down side by side, calmly and even cheerfully awaiting their release from this world; if they had suffered such dire extremity, and yet lay where the bodies of their dead companions lay unburied, within a few paces of them; and yet never dreamed at the last gasp of resorting to this said "last resource"; would it not be strong presumptive evidence against an incoherent Esquimaux story. . . ?

Dickens's point was that this had already been the case on a previous Franklin expedition. The force of his evocation of the experience of near starvation, with a forbidden source of nourishment lying at hand, is remarkable. Also noticeable is the emphasis on hide and shoe leather, which anticipates Dr. Manette's obsessive business of repairing shoes (a kind of reversing of the gnawing work of hunger). As well, this passage contains the fantasy of dying to a peace beyond appetite.

In mid-September 1856 Dickens and Collins completed a draft of *The Frozen Deep*. The story turns on the rivalry of two members of a polar expedition, Richard Wardour and Frank Aldersley, for the love of Clara Burnham. Unbeknownst to Frank, Richard, his unsuccessful rival for Clara's love, is obsessed by thoughts of murdering him. For much of the play the audience thinks that Richard has indeed murdered Frank. Instead, at the play's climax it is revealed that Richard has rescued Frank, carrying him across the "frozen deep," at the cost of his own life. He dies of this self-sacrifice, asking only for a kiss from his "sister," Clara. In production, Dickens himself played the part of Richard. (This theme of noble self-sacrifice is also found in the Christmas story "Perils of Certain English Prisoners" (1859), a little imperialist tale set in Belize, in which a heroic Captain Carton is a central character.)

In "The Lost Arctic Voyagers" Dickens warned that charges of cannibalism had often been used by Europeans to discredit non-Europeans or were a misunderstanding of native rites and customs. Indeed, cannibalism—though it has an objective existence—is one of the great fantasies of the West. Harry Stone has shown how pervasive the fantasy is in Dickens's own writings: "He was not simply strong on, he was obsessed by the subject of cannibalism—the unpardonable sin, that 'dreadful,' 'horrible,' 'wolfish,' 'last resource,' as he later called it."[3] The dimensions of this subject are too broad for the present study; it is enough perhaps to notice the obvious aggressive oral character of cannibalism. More directly to the point, it is ironic how in *The Frozen Deep* this lurid image of appetite is so readily transferred to sexuality. It is also ironic, and evidence of the psyche's natural life, that, having staged this sexual self-sacrifice in the person of Richard Wardour, Dickens promptly fell in love with one of the young actresses playing opposite him, Ellen Lawless Ternan. This led to separation from his wife, public scandal, and a relationship with Ellen that did not conclude till Dickens's death in 1870.

The Frozen Deep is clearly germane to *A Tale of Two Cities,* in which Dickens celebrates the self-sacrifice of " 'It is a far, far better thing.' " Traditionally, this staging of self-sacrifice has been felt to be one of the novel's great merits, and indeed it provides one of Dickens's most memorable lines. The novel has always been felt to be weaker in other respects than Dickens's mature works: "[s]o little humor and so few remarkable figures," is how Forster summarized the criticism. What in Forster's view saved the book was its theme of "heroic sacrifice": "Dickens speaks of his design to make impressive the dignity of Carton's death, and in this he succeeded even beyond his expectation."[4] Modern criticism has not taken the heroism of this self-sacrifice for granted (see the discussion in Manheim, Lawrence Frank's essay "Dicken's *A Tale of Two Cities:* The Poetics of Impasse," and "Dickens and the Catastrophic Continuum of History in *A Tale of Two Cities*" by J. M. Rignall). However, it has found the politics of the novel more interesting, particularly the representation of the French Revolution; the doubling of the heroes and other psychologically expressionistic features; and the intensity of Dickens's evocation of isolated, repressed, and inflamed states of mind (matched only by Poe among his contemporaries).

If a great work of literature is in a deep sense the product of a writer's entire life, then the gestation of *A Tale of Two Cities* in Dickens's mind began not in the late 1850s, but in childhood. Since Edmund Wilson's seminal essay in *The Wound and the Bow* (1947), it has been customary to see the imprisonment for debt of Dickens's father and the surrounding circumstances as a primary influence on the novelist's view of the world. To review this episode (which is given in full in Dickens's words in Forster and other biographies): While his father languished in the Marshalsea prison for debtors, Dickens was put to a work in a small factory, washing bottles and pasting on labels for boot blacking. Here, clearly, is one source of Manette's shoemending. At one time Dickens's employers even displayed him in a street window, an experience that may lie behind Defarge showing Manette off to the Jacques. When his father was released from debtor's prison, Dickens begged to be let out of the factory, and in the family discussion that followed, his mother argued that he should stay on. At this point in his account Dickens's tone is implacable: "I never afterwards forgot, I never shall forget, I never can forget, that my mother was warm for my being sent back." The episode as a whole (and we do not know everything about it) left Dickens scarred and traumatized: "[N]o word of that part of my childhood . . . has passed my lips to any human being. . . . I never had the courage to go back to the place where my servitude began. I never saw it. I could not endure to go near it."[5]

The prison became the most frequently used of Dickens's great symbols and is, of course, a primary symbol in *A Tale of Two Cities*. But, rather than going directly to what has often been taken as a great image of repression,[6] it is important for interpretation of *A Tale of Two Cities* to establish a deeper organizing psychic structure. This structure is powerful and regressive enough to suggest very early stages of psychic organization, but it is undoubtedly also a consequence of the blacking-factory trauma.

I am referring to the fact that *A Tale of Two Cities* is marked by massive splitting, or, rather, deep splitting underneath superficial ambivalence or rapprochement, which is ultimately a kind of sleight of hand (for an extended discussion of splitting, see Albert Hutter's essay "Nation and Generation in *A Tale of Two Cities*"). Splitting is a concept found in Freud but much developed by Melanie Klein. As Klein presents it, splitting is the most primitive of defenses, an attempt to preserve an all-good parent figure and ego by attributing all that is unsatisfactory to a repressed bad ego and internalized parent. Klein associates it strongly with infant rage in the pre-Oedipal stages; she is the first figure in what became the English school of psychoanalysis called Object Relations and the first to emphasize the processes of psychic construction prior to Freud's Oedipal moment. In Object Relations, the mother becomes the great formative influence, not, as in Freud, the father. Along with splitting, Klein also talks about the oral character, violence, incoherence, and fragmentation of early imagery. Rather than simply accepting Kleinian attribution of these darker fantasies to infant envy and vehemence, we need also to recall the later blacking-factory trauma and Dickens's hurt and anger at that time. Trauma is regressive in its effects, as the novel's violent images of part objects attest; for trauma of this degree affects the core self.

Such violently fragmented imagery is characteristic of *A Tale of Two Cities*. For instance, in the novel's first chapter, large heads and jaws float free (disembodied and devouring parental objects); there are bizarre spiritual apparitions and tappings; hands are cut off; tongues of youths are torn out with pincers; and there are dirty monks, mire, pigs, blunderbusses, shot and ball, snipped-off diamond crosses, hangings, and burnings. Finally, "those two of the large jaws," the parental objects, return as the Woodman Fate and the Farmer Death.

As well, Dickens's famous swinging, unstable opening to the novel is about splitting:

> It was the best of times, it was the worst of times, it was the age of wisdom, it was the age of foolishness, it was the epoch of belief, it was the epoch of incredulity, it was the season of Light, it was the season of darkness, it was the spring of hope, it was the winter of despair, we had everything before us, we

had nothing before us, we were all going direct to Heaven, we were all going direct the other way. (bk. 1, chap. 1)

Dickens is being ironic about this kind of polarization, and thereby prefiguring, from the beginning, a solution in the reform politics practiced in England at crucial junctures since the French Revolution had declared the beginning of modern history. Even the more roller-coaster political processes of France will, as Carton prophecies at the novel's end, lead "a brilliant people" to "rise from the abyss" becoming through "triumphs and defeats" (like the revolution of 1848, and the coup d'état of Louis Napoleon in 1851) "truly free" (bk. 1, chap. 15). (For Dickens's reaction to the revolution of 1848, see "Carlyle, Dickens, and the Revolution of 1848" by Michael Goldberg. On the coup d'état, see the excerpt from "Letters on the French *Coup d'état* of 1851" by Walter Bagehot.) Nevertheless, there is an obvious persistence of splitting in that very vision of a "brilliant people" rising from an abyss.

Central to the novel's splitting is, of course, the use of the doubled hero, Carton-Darnay (see especially the discussion in Manheim), which was anticipated in *The Frozen Deep*. Carton is a striking early example of what Jung was to call the Shadow, an aspect of the self repressed by the ego that may yet embody considerable vital energies. Jung's answer to the challenge represented by the Shadow was to recommend that it be integrated into consciousness and the larger self's life project. This involves the dissolution and reformation of both Ego and Shadow, which otherwise remain polarized and mutually consuming: It is the reversal of splitting. Dickens may have been influenced by Edgar Alan Poe's story of a dark double, "William Wilson" (1839), but by the end of the century the Shadow was to become ubiquitous, as in Wilde's *The Picture of Dorian Gray* (1891) and Stevenson's *The Strange Case of Dr. Jekyll and Mr. Hyde* (1886) and *The Master of Ballantrae* (1889).

Carton's noble death, we are led to understand, somehow brings him into reconciliation with Darnay's possession of Lucy and therefore gives him a presence in it, a solution in which the exiled Englishman lives on in the domestic bliss of the exiled Frenchman—a reasonably chastened view of fulfillment. On the other hand, splitting persists: One hero survives in an idyll cut off from history, while another goes to his execution amidst the bloodthirsty crowd. He is accompanied at his death only by a little French stranger. Of course, insofar as the novel's energies run with Carton—as, certainly, the more interesting of the young men—we see a reflection of Dickens's French idyll with the actress Ellen Ternan. (Dickens kept a home in Boulogne in these later years and was also much in Paris.) In Carton's exaltation we may discern a glad rejection of the English world of domestic virtue. In nobly giving up Lucy by dying for her, it might be said that Dickens finally found a way to get away from those relentless little figures of feminine virtue—little Nell, Florence Dombey, Little Dorrit—who had held him in their tiny grips ever since his sister-in-law Mary Hogarth died in his arms in 1837. Unlike

Arthur Clennam at the end of *Little Dorrit,* Sydney Carton does not escape the "uproar" of the "froward and the vain" to pass into an idyll of domestic bliss (bk. 2, chap. 34). His destiny is the lurch of the tumbril, the roaring crowds, the sudden shock of the guillotine. He escapes both disapproving English virtue and his own lassitude in the thrilling intrigues of revolutionary Paris. This is much more *exciting,* though it can only be enjoyed/feared as a kind of death (*la Guillotine*). This produces a further splitting, as a martyred Christlike Sidney rises up above the bloodthirsty mob even as he descends into its maw. To identify with Christ in this fashion might be seen as the most extreme kind of splitting, a choice for purity that can only serve to confirm the Shadow over what Jung was to argue for, wholeness, integration, what he called individuation. Sidney's death is dissociative, or, if you like, ecstasy as self-abnegation.

Splitting therefore underlies the novel. It is *A Tale of Two Cities,* one revolutionary, the other not. Despite the Anglo-French rapprochement of this period, and despite Dickens's own affection for France, he falls back into the deep English tradition of seeing France as the Other. ("They hate us," Thackeray had succinctly put it, implying that the feeling was as sincerely returned [*The Paris Sketch-Book,* 1841].) In the 1830s, revolution in Paris had hurried on reform in London, but by the revolutions of 1848 most English commentators saw difference, not likeness, between the two countries. Walter Bagehot's provocative series of letters on Louis Napoleon's coup d'état is a sophisticated example of the argument based on national character. The coup d'état brought an end to the short-lived Second Republic, which had been founded by the revolution of 1848, ushering in the Second Empire. Bagehot went on from this comparison to work out his *English Constitution* (1867), one of the most influential works of British political theory of the century. Nicholas Rance discusses how Dickens "takes refuge in the dogma of national characteristics" in his essay "Charles Dickens: *A Tale of Two Cities*" (1859).

Like Bagehot, Dickens found the English stupid and also lacking in passion: in comparison to the French art in the Paris Exposition of 1855, Dickens thought English painting "small, shrunken, insignificant, 'niggling' "[7] (art for Little Dorrit, as it were). If one thinks of Manet's or Degas's women compared to the anaemic pre-Raphaelite heroines—let alone their academic counterparts—one is inclined to agree. France, after all, is always sexually wicked to English minds, hence interesting. The French write novels of adultery, the English of marriage, or, as Virginia Woolf was to suggest, for children—perhaps novels of marriage for children. Some of Dickens's contemporaries thought he was too like the French, a sensation novelist like the French novelist Eugene Sue, bringing the scandalous Mysteries of Paris to the Mysteries of London (to conflate the titles of novels by Sue and George Reynolds). In *A Tale of Two Cities,* Tellson's Bank and Mr. Lorry are admirable but stupid. Miss Pross, a repressive guardian of English femininity and a typically stupid

English tourist, defeats Mme. Defarge, but, although Dickens chooses the good English woman over the devouring French woman, Miss Pross is rendered deaf in the struggle, an evident comment on Mrs. Dickens's mother's failure to hear her son's distress. In *A Tale of Two Cities* Dickens is engaged in trying to face the noise of the negative mother, part of what had kept him trapped in Little Nelldom. Madame Defarge is luridly scary and masculine, but Dickens senses her essential energy and justice.

The scene where the maternal is most present and significant in the novel is partially unseen: it is the scene when Dr. Manette makes his first appearance (bk. 1, chap. 5). The gruff Defarge leads another father figure, Lorry, and Lucy up those back stairs: "Through such an atmosphere, by a deep dark shaft of dirt and poison, the way lay." There they pass members of the novel's revolutionary secret society (an importation from sensationalized accounts of the later Italian Rissorgimento),[8] the Jacques, looking at the prisoner. Lorry objects to Defarge making a spectacle of Manette. Indeed, we will never see what the Jacques see, the imprisoned Manette. Now Lucy comes to her father, like light, a breast on which he can rest his head, "trembling with eagerness to lay the spectral face upon her warm young breast, and love it back to life and hope." Dickens had used the same image in *Little Dorrit* (bk. 1, chap. 19, bk. 2, chap. 29; see as well, Elizabeth Gaskell, *North and South,* bk. 2, chap. 5). It is derived from the classical story known as "Roman Charity" in which the daughter breast-feeds the imprisoned father: Dickens knew paintings of the subject in English and Roman galleries.[9] Steinbeck used the motif to conclude another epic of class struggle, *The Grapes of Wrath* (1939). Here the breast is at its most idealized, the feminine as that idealized breast. " 'I bring back the remembrance of a Home long desolate, while you're away, weep for it, weep for it!' " (bk. 1, chap. 6), Lucy cries. In speaking of the infant's splitting of the mother figure, Klein utilizes the terms the Good and Bad Breasts, a terminology that is helpful for this novel, and that is manifest in the contrasts between French scenes of foaming and castrating feminine rage, and the extremely idyllic sexless world of the Manettes in England. The implications for the presentation of women characters are discussed in Lisa Robson's essay "The 'Angels' in Dickens's House: Representations of women in *A Tale of Two Cities.*"

Perhaps it will seem contradictory to suggest that in *A Tale of Two Cities* Dickens in part longs to be rid of Lucy. How can this be so if she is this idealized breast? The answer is, simply, the price you pay for virtue, or for the idealized relationship of self and object, in which Dickens had invested deeply (as at Tellson's). This is the other castration (to match that of the *vagina denta* guillotine), making the hero into a Manette. Carton's choice, however concealed, is for death with *jouissance,* a Dionysian choice, and though filled with panicky antifeminine noise, it is, in a degree, also a renunciation of a patriarchal self. Consider the description of the revolutionary dance, the *Carmagnole,* that Dickens chooses to present from the point of view of Lucy:

They danced to the popular revolution song, keeping a ferocious time that was like a gnashing of teeth in unison. Men and women danced together, women danced together, men danced together, as hazard had brought them together. . . . It was so emphatically a fallen sport—a something once innocent, delivered all over to devilry—a healthy pastime changed into the means of angering the blood, bewildering the senses and steeling the heart. . . . The maidenly bosom bared to this, the pretty almost child's head thus distracted, the delicate foot mincing in the slough of blood and dirt, were types of the disjointed time. (bk. 2, chap. 5)

Passages like this teeter on the edge of giving in to the Dionysian urge of demos.

Splitting is crucial with the Defarge's. That episode provides a symbolic fable of two aspects of a psychic response represented as two political traditions. The Jacques have seen the trauma, that is they look into the place of Manette's imprisonment. In "Nation and Generation in *A Tale of Two Cities*," Albert Hutter has said that "Manette's story is the narrative equivalent of a trauma." Manette is not an image of repression. Rather he is an image of a dissociation consequent on trauma. In fact, he is doubly connected to trauma. As a figure of prolonged agony, out of a "living grave" he is himself traumatizing. Similarly, in *Barnaby Rudge,* the condemned prisoners the mob releases from Newgate are appalling to the beholders: "The crowd fell off, as if they had been laid out for burial, and had risen in their shrouds; and many were seen to shudder, as though they had been actually dead men" (chap. 65). In these scenes there is an image of the shock to the young Dickens of his father's imprisonment. The Jacques here represent that which can see the imprisoned father but not save him. But in the imprisoned Manette we can also see Dickens himself, laboring at the blacking bottles. The Jacques are also the witnesses to all his trauma. In their hurried and appalled responses, they are that which has seen the trauma of the split-off self. Their reaction is, of course, violent upheaval, rage. It is quite interesting to think of Defarge as that part of the adult ego that regulates this rage.

Rage is directed primarily at the novel's bad father (actually uncle) figure, Monsieur Le Marquis, whose selfish way, in an appropriate detail, kills a child. Dickens's images of the tenacities of revenge (the shadow figure under the carriage; the frozen stillness surrounding the murder; the revenger imprisoned, starving in a suspended cage; the slow exploding of the chateau) wonderfully elaborate this bad son–bad father dyad. Monsieur Le Marquis is reminiscent of the bad father Chester in Dickens's other novel of insurrection, *Barnaby Rudge.* Chester is founded on the Lord Chesterfield who insulted Dr. Johnson, for Dickens a representative figure of the evils of aristocracy (though amid so much faux earnestness there is a certain relish to be had from these coolly selfish types).

It is Monsieur Le Marquis who, representing the system of the lettres de cachet—a Lacanian image—is held responsible for Manette's imprisonment, though I have been suggesting another chain of causes. Here Manette is the *traumatized*. He has been imprisoned for witnessing the melodrama of the rape of a peasant woman and murder of her husband by the novel's Corsican brothers. Manette has a record of this hidden in the Bastille that the lettre de cachet cannot block. This act of witnessing places Manette at the source of much of the justified anger and defiance in the novel. But he is *not* that anger, only a witness to it, and the action never allows him to identify with it, even in the telling: "A terrible sound arose when the reading of this document was done. A sound of craving and eagerness in it that had nothing articulate in it but blood. The narrative called on the most revengeful passions of the time" (bk. 3, chap. 10).

The young peasant husband worked to death hauling a cart like an animal; his dying, raped wife; her brother killed in a duel in his angry defiance of power; these are the traumatizing images that Manette has seen, which have lead to his imprisonment. This recognition is the origin of the splitting and accounts for all that shaping of leather. But why this denial/distance? Is it simply a matter of bourgeois politics? That would be to put the fable before the trauma. Rather it is alienation from a certain energy associated with trauma (*droits de seigneur*), the equation of energy with the abuse of power, at some level a blaming of part of the self that is a typical defense in trauma.

George Bernard Shaw once observed that Dickens knew about the political role of the big aristocratic houses, like the Chesney Wold of *Bleak House:* "Trollope and Thackeray could see Chesney Wold; but Dickens could see through it. And this was no joke to Dickens. He was deeply concerned about it, and understood how revolutions begin with burning the chateaux."[10]

But Dickens was not Marx or Michael Collins, and though the big houses were burned in France, and a century later in Ireland, they remained untouched in England. In his lifetime Dickens was often a guest in them. In *Bleak House* the big house has a kind of pathos: it is the site of a kind of projection of the weary self into the aristocratic father, as with Trooper George and Sir Leicester Deadlock. It is certain that in *Bleak House* Dickens modeled the Lady Deadlock story on another tale of the French Revolution, Alexander Dumas's *The Queen's Necklace* (1849–1850), as Manette's imprisonment owes something to Dumas's *The Man in the Iron Mask* (in *Le Vicomte de Bragelonne,* 1848–1850). But in *A Tale of Two Cities,* there are none of these plots of Oedipal transgression and it is not the castrating father who will cut off Sydney Carton but, rather, the splitting described above. In the Evrémond family the son offends the "father" (already once removed) by *not* seeking to be his heir, both a refusal and a subtle undermining of the Law of the Father, a prurient move with a latent Dionysian potential. But Darnay only challenges the bad French father. His renunciation of expectations and decision to go to work make England the scene of the good Oedipal structure. There, we find Lorry, the positive father figure who brings the fantasy of healing to the passive and thankful prisoner, the bride to the good son (recollect his response to Stryver's intentions in respect of Lucy). The bad Oedipal son is the *louche* Sydney. These son–father structures are discussed more fully in Hutter's essay.

It might be said that to formulate the splitting in *A Tale of Two Cities,* Dickens took advantage of that originary image of modern history, the storming of the Bastille. For that scene, which heralded in a new age, was not one of prisoners escaping from the inside, but of a mob storming a prison *from the outside.* Thus the imprisoned and the forces of release are never completely united. In fact, the number of prisoners in the Bastille at that time was very small and those released were almost lost in the confusion, an irony much-labored by conservative commentators (see excerpted passages from *The French Revolution* by Thomas Carlyle). In *Barnaby Rudge,* at the storming of the prison, Dickens had emphasized the confusion and strange apathy of the prisoners the mob releases from Newgate (ch. 67). This idea is developed in *A Tale of Two Cities* in the refrain of the first book, repeatedly sounded in the mind of the good father Lorry:

> "I hope you care to live?"
> "I can't say." (bk. 1, chap. 3)

Manette provides a masterly image of the persistence of dissociation, but, of course, he must persist because he is cut off from the transforming energies, which are *confined to the outside* (thus England becomes a prison). Prisoner and mob ought to be united, Manette is a hero of the French Revolution, but it does not happen. He is on the other side of the novel's fundamental split. There is only that strange image of his shoemaking to express how he weaves his own imprisonment, work without reward or hope. He is an old man because it has been forever: behind him is the child Dickens washing those blacking bottles with no hope of release. Resurrection, true resurrection, is outlawed, confined to the comic presence of Jerry Cruncher. Cruncher is understandably annoyed with the virtuous feminine, as represented by his wife's flopping. She goes for the postponed resurrection, Jerry wants its rewards now.

It is worth thinking for a moment about the novel's two trial scenes, neither of which can stage justice (in fact, to Dickens's Victorian eyes, this is a world before the institution of justice). In these, the rule of the father, the negative Oedipus, may seem apparent, but in fact Dickens makes both scenes not so much trial by the repressive social order as trial by the eyes of the mob (at the novel's end, Carton and his French female friend exposed to the crowd is surely an image informed by the scandal over Dickens's separation from his wife). In these trial scenes splitting is fundamental and its relation to judgment is clear. Carton saves Evrémond at the first trial, an instance of the Shadow's unifying capacities. Of course, he will save him again: the Shadow is always saving the ideal self, just as it is Sydney's work that underlies all strivings (we never see Darnay *work*). At the second trial Darnay is unjustly condemned, but there some cogency must be given to the accusers: in the reading we are making, Darnay's virtue is the problem. To the mob he represents that which has kept them hungry, kept the lifeblood or wine from them (it must be drunk from the mud, as Carton knows). We see again the price of a virtue founded on splitting. It is noticeable that faced with this judgment, Manette again retreats into dissociation.

I have included here extracts from George Lukács's seminal work *The Historical Novel.* Lukács's influential, and in many respects convincing, analysis of nineteenth-century politics and culture rests on the argument that after 1848 the European bourgeoisie began to perceive itself not as revolutionary, as it had fondly wished to be—for that road led to the empowerment of the working class—but subtly reactionary. Lukács sees this as the moment when the integrated world of character and history in the realist novel becomes the world of naturalism in which the little lives of characters are set against the evocation of the gigantic forces of history and the environment, as the Manette household is set against the backdrop of the French Revolution. (See also the fuller discussion in Lukács's *Studies in European Realism.*)[11] This kind of ideological splitting points to a moment when psychological and historical junctures meet to create a really characteristic work. Lukács sees the kind of historical novel that Dickens writes as particularly liable to this evasion of the real situation of the middle class. In *A Tale of Two Cities,* Dickens reverts to a heroic time when the villains were aristocrats and the middle class the heroic alternative. In a wiser mood, at length in *Little Dorrit,* he had shown he knew the inherent tendency of the middle class to either ally with or ape the aristocracy.

Certainly *A Tale of Two Cities* cannot be understood without some sense of the institutions and events of its time. The prison, for instance, has a very personal history in Dickens, but his experience also made him a lifelong examiner of prisons and cognate institutions. One of the great influences on the presentation of Manette was Dickens's visit to the Eastern Penitentiary in Philadelphia, described in the excerpt from *American Notes.* Michael Foucault's influential work *Discipline and Punish* (*Surveiller et punir,* 1975) contrasts the brutalities of punishment under the ancien regime with the new systematics of surveillance and discipline most vividly represented by the Panopticon building envisaged by the utilitarian philosopher Jeremy Bentham (who Dickens had satirized in *Hard Times*). The prison in Philadelphia, now open to visitors, is one of the few remaining panopticon structures in the world. It is ironic, and telling in the way that Foucault's work is, to see that although Dickens berates the appalling punishments of the older penal code in *A Tale of Two Cities,* the reformed order has its own hideousness. Just as Foucault opens his work by describing the barbarous punishments inflicted on a would-be regicide under the old regime, so Dickens has Darnay threatened with the hanging, drawing, and quartering, and these punishments are inflicted on the murderer of the Marquis. Yet Dickens's vision is shaped by a new order of cruelty: "I hold this slow and daily tampering with the mysteries of the brain, to be immeasurably worse than any torture of the body," he wrote in *American Notes*. His depiction of the horrors of that symbol of the old order, the Bastille, owes much to his experience of a progressive institution in a New World city of brotherly love.

But, as has been said, the Bastille cannot be thought of without its other half, the revolutionary crowd. Here Dickens drew heavily on Carlyle, as evidenced in the excerpt from *The French Revolution* reprinted in this collection. Carlyle's influence is pervasive and is fully discussed in Andrew Sanders's authoritative *The Companion to "A Tale of Two Cities"*.[12] The significance of Carlyle's tempestuous genius for Dickens is discussed by Nicholas Rance and others in this volume, and indeed it is the subject of books.[13] The passages from Carlyle given here enable the reader to compare Carlyle's depiction of two scenes of revolutionary violence, the storming of the Bastille and the murder of Foulon, with Dickens's handling of these scenes (*A Tale of Two Cities*, bk. 2, chaps. 21 and 22). In the comparison, Dickens will not seem less extreme than his mentor.

Dickens's portrayal of the revolutionary crowd in *A Tale of Two Cities* is intense and important and one suspects that it goes a long way to explain the influence of the novel and its frequent presence in the classroom (see also the essay by Manheim). There is a challenge here to the educator to provide a considered evaluation of Dickens's material. David Craig, in an article entitled "The Crowd in Dickens," has given an indication of how Dickens misrepresents events:

> The terror which Dickens makes climactic in his novel was in fact the last stage of an escalation whose pace was forced relentlessly by successive governments and their troops, Town Guards, and so on. The stages in this blur beneath Dickens's lurid imagery of a blood-curse working itself out. They are further obscured by the plot with its jumps in time and from Paris to London and back again. Finally he distorts the record by the propaganda device of mentioning the atrocities done by one side only: e.g., during the siege of the Bastille at least 150 citizens were killed against seven of the garrison, but the only blood-letting Dickens brings fully onto camera is the beheading of the governor.[14]

One recalls a remark of Edmund Wilson's: there are two histories, the history of those who remember the heads that rolled in the Reign of Terror of the French Revolution (or who, as Thomas Paine said of Edmund Burke, "pity the plumage and forget the dying bird"), and the history of those who remember the vastly larger number of Parisian proletarians killed by the army of the bourgeois Third Republic at the suppression of the Paris Commune of 1870.

I have included here, along with passages from Carlyle, a passage from the seminal study of the revolutionary crowd, George Rudé's classic *Paris and*

London in the Eighteenth Century: Studies in Popular Protest. Rudé's work clearly shows that Dickens's bloodthirsty depiction is a tremendous caricature. Michael Goldberg's discussion of Dickens's response to the revolution of 1848 is also relevant here, partly because it shows how different Dickens's response to revolution in France could be.

Indeed, the question arises: why was Dickens writing about revolution in 1859, when the revolutionary tradition was seemingly more and more a thing of the past? (For an opposing view, see the essay by Nicholas Rance.) What *was* recent was the so-called Indian Mutiny of 1857. English people had been shocked by the grossly sensationalized tales of brutalities committed in the Sepoy Rebellion, shock that was to be used to justify merciless retaliation. Here, for instance, is the sometime radical Charles Kingsley:

> I can think of nothing but these Indian massacres. The moral problems they invoke make me half wild. Night and day the heaven seems black to me. . . . I can hardly bear to look at a woman or child. . . . they raise such horrible images. . . . Show me the security I have that my wife, my children should not suffer, from some unexpected outbreak of devils.[15]

Kingsley's passage suggests the strong tendency to racism in excited characterizations of uprisings and the strong element of confused and projected sexuality.

We can certainly see Dickens's expressionist mob as a vehicle of rage and other inchoate energies, and thus we can see the logic that leads him to emphasize the fate of the unfortunate Foulon. Hungry for blood, like those sensational cannibals, the mob forces grass into the mouth of the decapitated head that denied them. Psychically, this is the revenge of the life starved of true nourishment on the representative of a denying economy.

The mob must also be considered within a political framework. Dickens's splitting-off of violence onto another nation (France) and class (the poor), in order to preserve the fantasy of domestic idyll, is still with us, always liable in a society divided between the ideal order of the suburbs and the abandoned inner cities. It is always possible, for instance, to argue that the violence of crime, or of the Los Angeles riots, has its origin only in the place of its containment. Studied in these ways, Dickens's great but flawed work can still have a very significant life in the classroom.

The essays that follow explore Dickens's dark and dynamic irresolutions from a number of perspectives and in greater depth than here. Lawrence Frank, discussing what he calls "the poetics of impasse," concludes that

> In the closing pages of *A Tale of Two Cities,* impasse reigns. Allusions to the filial heroism of Christ's atonement, muted parallels to the mythology of twins, do not convincingly depict that passing on of authority from father to son that Dickens wishes to effect. . . . The broken Manette, the quintessential Double in the novel, suggests the fate of every son, of every father.

In his essay "The Purity of Violence: *A Tale of Two Cities*," Joseph Kucich suggests that in Carton's death Dickens presents us with "an image of an explicitly desired violation of human limits, one that is presented as the only possible escape from the twin mechanisms of rivalry and repressed violence." J. M. Rignall argues that

> As oppression is shown to breed oppression, violence to beget violence, evil to provoke evil, a pattern emerges that is too deterministic to owe much to Carlyle and profoundly at odds with the conventional complacencies of Whig history.

Sacrifice in the novel is dubious, Rignall argues, and Dickens presents "a grimly determinist view of history."

Cates Baldridge takes a more optimistic view in the essay "Alternatives to Bourgeois Individualism in *A Tale of Two Cities*," arguing not so much for splitting as for Dickens's "ambivalance towards the Revolution": "The aspect I refer to is the Revolution's assertion that the group, the class, the Republic—and *not* the individual—comprise, or should comprise, the basic unit of society." Baldridge sees Lorry and Carton embodying "well-disguised escapes from the constricting confines of bourgeois individualism." In his essay, the theme of heroic sacrifice reemerges.

The language of sacrifice is also examined in the essays by Tom Lloyd and Lisa Robson. In "Language, Love and Identity: *A Tale of Two Cities*," Lloyd makes use of Romantic models, particularly the thought of Schiller, to examine questions of identity and communication. This leads him to a significant exploration of the language of Sydney's sacrifice and of the novel's larger mysteries. Robson explores the polarization, or splitting, of the depiction of the feminine in the novel into emasculating maenads on the one hand and idealized "angels" on the other. How does the idea of sacrifice play in a novel in which sacrifice is routinely expected of women? Though Dickens bemoaned the Philadelphia solitary system for men he argued that it refined women.

It remains to place *A Tale of Two Cities* in a tradition of fiction that explores the violence of revolutionary politics, a tradition in which an author's own violences are often projected into the imagined material. Dickens's novel owes something not only to Carlyle but to Sir Walter Scott's insurrectionary scenes in *The Heart of Midlothian* (1818). In *Little Dorrit,* Dickens had begun to assemble an international cast of restless alienated figures in revolt against all order (Miss Wade, for instance), and he goes a step further in the later parts of *A Tale of Two Cities,* with its spies, plots, and counterplots. Leftist conspiracy was soon to become a fashionable subject in the European novel, primarily represented in depictions of Bakunin's anarchists. This specter indeed haunted the mind of Europe, out of all proportion to its political significance. Relevant works here are Dostoevsky's *The Possessed* or *The Devils* (1871–1872); Turgenev's *Rudin* (1857); Zola's *Germinal* (1885); Henry James's *The Princess Casamassima* (1886); Stevenson's *The Dynamiter* (1885); and Conrad's *The Secret Agent* (1907) and *Under Western Eyes* (1911). There are too many works on this subject in the twentieth century to continue this list. Three that have seemed important to this writer have been Christopher Isherwood's *Goodbye to Berlin* (1939); Doris Lessing's *The Good Terrorist* (1985); and Don DeLillo's *Mao II* (1991).

Notes

1.   John Forster, *The Life of Charles Dickens,* ed. J. W. T. Ley (London: Cecil Palmer, 1928), 729.

2.   Unless otherwise cited, essays referenced in this introduction are included in this volume.

3.   Harry Stone, *The Night Side of Dickens: Cannibalism, Passion, Necessity* (Columbus: 1994), 3. Stone provides a brilliant extended discussion. See especially the section on *A Tale of Two Cities,* 162f.

4.   Forster, 732.

5.   Forster, 35.

6.   See, for instance, Lionel Trilling, *"Little Dorrit," Kenyon Review* 15 (1953): 577–90. Trilling refers to the picture of a prisoner that is the frontispiece to Freud's *Collected Works.*

7.   *The Letters of Charles Dickens,* Pilgrim edition, vol. 17, eds. Graham Storey, Kathleen Tillotson, and Angus Easson (Clanendon, U.K.: Oxford, 1993), 742–43.

8.   Dickens knew the exiled Mazzini through the Carlyles.

9.   See Martin Meisal, *Realizations: Narrative, Pictorial and Theatrical Arts in Nineteenth-century England* (Princeton, N.J.: Princeton University Press, 1983), 302–21, especially 315.

10.   From the foreword to 1937 edition of *Great Expectations,* reprinted in *Charles Dickens: A Critical Anthology,* ed. Stephen Wall (Harmondsworth, U.K.: Penguin, 1970), 287.

11.   Lucáks, George, *Studies in European Realism* (London: Hillary, 1959).

12.   Andrew Sanders, *The Companion to "A Tale of Two Cities"* (London: Unwin Hyman, 1988).

13.   See Michael Goldberg, *Carlyle and Dickens* (Athens: University of Georgia Press, 1972), and William Oddie, *Dickens and Carlyle* (London: Centenary, 1972).

14.   In Robert Giddings, ed., *The Changing World of Charles Dickens* (London and Totowa, N.J.: Vision and Barnes and Noble, 1983), 86.

15.   Charles Kingsley, *Charles Kingsley, His Letters and Memoirs* (New York: J. F. Taylor, 1900), 2:70.

[Two Passages From *The French Revolution*]

Thomas Carlyle

["The Fall of the Bastille"]

And now, to the Bastille, ye intrepid Parisians! There grapeshot still threatens: thither all men's thoughts and steps are now tending.

Old De Launay, as we hinted, withdrew "into his interior" soon after midnight of Sunday. He remains there ever since, hampered, as all military gentlemen now are, in the saddest conflict of uncertainties. The Hôtel-de-Ville "invites" him to admit National Soldiers, which is a soft name for surrendering. On the other hand, His Majesty's orders were precise. His garrison is but eighty-two old Invalides, reinforced by thirty-two young Swiss; his walls indeed are nine feet thick, he has cannon and powder; but, alas, only one day's provision of victuals. The city too is French, the poor garrison mostly French. Rigorous old De Launay, think what thou wilt do!

All morning, since nine, there has been a cry everywhere: To the Bastille! Repeated "deputations of citizens" have been here, passionate for arms; whom De Launay has got dismissed by soft speeches through portholes. Towards noon, Elector Thuriot de la Rosière gains admittance; finds De Launay indisposed for surrender; nay disposed for blowing up the place rather. Thuriot mounts with him to the battlements: heaps of paving-stones, old iron and missiles lie piled; cannon all duly levelled; in every embrasure a cannon,— only drawn back a little! But outwards, behold, O Thuriot, how the multitude flows on, welling through every street: tocsin furiously pealing, all drums beating the *générale:* the Suburb Saint-Antoine rolling hitherward wholly, as one man! Such vision (spectral yet real) thou, O Thuriot, as from thy Mount of Vision, beholdest in this moment: prophetic of what other Phantasmagories, and loud-gibbering Spectral Realities, which thou yet beholdest not, but shalt! "*Que voulez-vous?*" said De Launay, turning pale at the sight, with an air of reproach, almost of menace. "Monsieur," said Thuriot, rising into the moral-sublime, "what mean *you?* Consider if I could not precipitate *both* of us from this height,"—say only a hundred feet, exclusive of the walled ditch. Whereupon De Launay fell silent. Thuriot shows himself from some pinnacle, to comfort the multitude becoming suspicious, fremes-

From Thomas Carlyle, *The French Revolution* (1837), Book 5, Chapters 6, 7, and 9 cent: then descends; departs with protest; with warning addressed also to the Invalides,—on whom, however, it produces but a mixed indistinct impression. The old heads are none of the clearest; besides, it is said, De Launay has been profuse of beverages (*prodigua des buissons*). They think, they will not fire,—if not fired on, if they can help it; but must, on the whole, be ruled considerably by circumstances.

Wo to thee, De Launay, in such an hour, if thou canst not, taking some one firm decision, *rule* circumstances! Soft speeches will not serve; hard grapeshot is questionable; but hovering between the two is *un*questionable. Ever wilder swells the tide of men; their infinite hum waxing ever louder, into imprecations, perhaps into crackle of stray musketry,—which latter, on walls nine feet thick, cannot do execution. The Outer Drawbridge has been lowered for Thuriot; new *deputation of citizens* (it is the third, and noisiest of all) penetrates that way into the Outer Court: soft speeches producing no clearance of these, De Launay gives fire; pulls up his Drawbridge. A slight sputter;—which has *kindled* the too combustible chaos; made it a roaring fire-chaos! Bursts forth Insurrection, at sight of its own blood (for there were deaths by that sputter of fire), into endless rolling explosion of musketry, distraction, execration;—and over head, from the Fortress, let one great gun, with its grapeshot, go booming, to show what we *could* do. The Bastille is besieged!

On, then, all Frenchmen, that have hearts in your bodies! Roar with all your throats, of cartilage and metal, ye Sons of Liberty; stir spasmodically whatsoever of utmost faculty is in you, soul, body, or spirit; for it is the hour! Smite, thou Louis Tournay, cartwright of the Marais, old-soldier of the Regiment Dauphiné; smite at that Outer Drawbridge chain, though the fiery hail whistles round thee! Never, over nave or felloe, did thy axe strike such a stroke. Down with it, man; down with it to Orcus: let the whole accursed Edifice sink thither, and Tyranny be swallowed up forever! Mounted, some say, on the roof of the guardroom, some "on bayonets stuck into joints of the wall," Louis Tournay smites, brave Aubin Bonnemère (also an old soldier) seconding him: the chain yields, breaks; the huge Drawbridge slams down, thundering (*avec fracas*). Glorious: and yet, alas, it is still but the outworks. The Eight grim Towers, with their Invalide musketry, their paving-stones and cannon-mouths, still soar aloft intact;—Ditch yawning impassable, stone-faced; the inner Drawbridge with its *back* towards us: the Bastille is still to take!

To describe this Siege of the Bastille (thought to be one of the most important in History) perhaps transcends the talent of mortals. Could one but, after infinite reading, get to understand so much as the plan of the building! But there is open Esplanade, at the end of the Rue Saint-Antoine; there are such Forecourts, *Cour Avancé, Cour de l'Orme,* arched Gateway (where Louis Tournay now fights); then new drawbridges, dormant-bridges, rampart-bastions, and the grim Eight Towers: a labyrinthic Mass, high-frowning there, of all ages from twenty years to four hundred and twenty;—beleaguered, in this its last hour, as we said, by mere Chaos come again! Ordnance of all calibers; throats of all capacities; men of all plans, every man his own engineer: seldom since the war of Pygmies and Cranes was there seen so anomalous a thing. Half-pay Elie is home for a suit of regimentals; no one would heed him in coloured clothes: half-pay Hulin is haranguing Gardes Françaises in the Place de Grève. Frantic Patriots pick up the grapeshots; bear them, still hot (or seem-ingly so), to the Hôtel-de-Ville:—Paris, you perceive, is to be burnt! Flesselles is "pale to the very lips"; for the roar of the multitude grows deep. Paris wholly has got to the acme of its frenzy; whirled, all ways, by panic madness. At every street barricade, there whirls simmering a minor whirlpool,—strengthening the barricade, since God knows what is coming; and all minor whirlpools play distractedly into that grand Fire-Mahlstrom which is lashing round the Bastille.

And so it lashes and it roars. Cholat the wine-merchant has become an impromptu cannoneer. See Georget, of the Marine Service, fresh from Brest, ply the King of Siam's cannon. Singular (if we were not used to the like): Georget lay, last night, taking his ease at his inn; the King of Siam's cannon also lay, knowing nothing of *him,* for a hundred years. Yet now, at the right instant, they have got together, and discourse eloquent music. For, hearing what was toward, Georget sprang from the Brest Diligence, and ran. Gardes Françaises also will be here, with real artillery: were not the walls so thick!—Upwards from the Esplanade, horizontally from all neighbouring roofs and windows, flashes one irregular deluge of musketry, without effect. The In-valides lie flat, firing comparatively at their ease from behind stone; hardly through portholes show the tip of a nose. We fall, shot; and make no impres-sion!

Let conflagration rage; of whatsoever is combustible! Guardrooms are burnt, Invalides mess-rooms. A distracted "Perukemaker with two fiery torches" is for burning "the saltpetres of the Arsenal";—had not a woman run screaming; had not a Patriot, with some tincture of Natural Philosophy, in-stantly struck the wind out of him (butt of musket on pit of stomach), over-turned barrels, and stayed the devouring element. A young beautiful lady, seized escaping in these Outer Courts, and thought falsely to be De Launay's daughter, shall be burnt in De Launay's sight; she lies swooned on a paillasse: but again a Patriot, it is brave Aubin Bonnemère the old soldier, dashes in, and rescues her. Straw is burnt; three cartloads of it, hauled thither, go up in white smoke: almost to the choking of Patriotism itself; so that Elie had, with singed brows, to drag back one cart; and Réole the "gigantic haberdasher" another. Smoke as of Tophet; confusion as of Babel; noise as of the Crack of Doom!

Blood flows; the aliment of new madness. The wounded are carried into houses of the Rue Cerisaie; the dying leave their last mandate not to yield till the accursed Stronghold fall. And yet, alas, how fall? The walls are so thick! Deputations, three in number, arrive from the Hôtel-de-Ville; Abbé Fauchet (who was of one) can say, with what almost superhuman courage of benevolence. These wave their Town-flag in the arched Gateway; and stand, rolling their drum; but to no purpose. In such Crack of Doom, De Launay cannot hear them, dare not believe them: they return, with justified rage, the whew of lead still singing in their ears. What to do? The Firemen are here, squirting with their fire-pumps on the Invalides cannon, to wet the touchholes; they unfortunately cannot squirt so high; but produce only clouds of spray. Individuals of classical knowledge propose *catapults.* Santerre, the sonorous Brewer of the Suburb Saint-Antoine, advises rather that the place be fired, by a "mixture of phosphorus and oil-of-turpentine spouted up through forcing-pumps": O Spinola-Santerre, hast thou the mixture *ready?* Every man his own engineer! And still the fire-deluge abates not: even women are firing, and Turks; at least one woman (with her sweetheart), and one Turk. Gardes Françaises have come: real cannon, real cannoneers. Usher Maillard is busy; half-pay Elie, half-pay Hulin rage in the midst of thousands.

How the great Bastille Clock ticks (inaudible) in its Inner Court there, at its ease, hour after hour; as if nothing special, for it or the world, were passing! It tolled One when the firing began; and is now pointing towards Five, and still the firing slakes not.—Far down, in their vaults, the seven Prisoners hear muffled din as of earthquakes; their Turnkeys answer vaguely.

Wo to thee, De Launay, with thy poor hundred Invalides! Broglie is distant, and his ears heavy: Besenval hears, but can send no help. One poor troop of Hussars has crept, reconnoitering, cautiously along the Quais, as far as the Pont Neuf. "We are come to join you," said the Captain; for the crowd seems shoreless. A large-headed dwarfish individual, of smoke-bleared aspect, shambles forward, opening his blue lips, for there is sense in him; and croaks: "Alight then, and give up your arms!" The Hussar-Captain is too happy to be escorted to the Barriers, and dismissed on parole. Who the squat individual was? Men answer, It is M. Marat, author of the excellent pacific *Avis au Peuple!* Great truly, O thou remarkable Dogleech, is this thy day of emergence and new-birth: and yet this same day come four years—!—But let the curtains of the Future hang.

What shall De Launay do? One thing only De Launay could have done: what he said he would do. Fancy him sitting, from the first, with lighted taper, within arm's-length of the Powder-Magazine; motionless, like old Roman Senator, or Bronze Lampholder; coldly apprising Thuriot, and all men, by a slight motion of his eye, what his resolution was:—Harmless he sat there, while unharmed; but the King's Fortress, meanwhile, could, might, would, or should in nowise be surrendered, save to the King's Messenger: one old man's life is worthless, so it be lost with honour; but think, ye brawling *canaille,* how will it be when a whole Bastille springs skyward!—In such statuesque, taper-holding attitude, one fancies De Launay might have left Thuriot, the red

Clerks of the Basoche, Curé of Saint-Stephen and all the tagrag-and-bobtail of the world, to work their will.

And yet, withal, he could not do it. Hast thou considered how each man's heart is so tremulously responsive to the hearts of all men; hast thou noted how omnipotent is the very sound of many men? How their shriek of indignation palsies the strong soul; their howl of contumely withers with unfelt pangs? The Ritter Gluck confessed that the ground-tone of the noblest passage, in one of his noblest Operas, was the voice of the Populace he had heard at Vienna, crying to their Kaiser: Bread! Bread! Great is the combined voice of men; the utterance of their *instincts,* which are truer than their *thoughts:* it is the greatest a man encounters, among the sounds and shadows which make up this World of Time. He who can resist that, has his footing somewhere *beyond* Time. De Launay could not do it. Distracted, he hovers between two; hopes in the middle of despair; surrenders not his Fortress; declares that he will blow it up, seizes torches to blow it up, and does not blow it. Unhappy old De Launay, it is the death-agony of thy Bastille and thee! Jail, Jailoring and Jailor, all three, such as they may have been, must finish.

For four hours now has the World-Bedlam roared: call it the World-Chimæra, blowing fire! The poor Invalides have sunk under their battlements, or rise only with reversed muskets: they have made a white flag of napkins; go beating the *chamade,* or seeming to beat, for one can hear nothing. The very Swiss at the Portcullis look weary of firing; disheartened in the fire-deluge: a porthole at the drawbridge is opened, as by one that would speak. See Huissier Maillard, the shifty man! On his plank, swinging over the abyss of that stone Ditch; plank resting on parapet, balanced by weight of Patriots,—he hovers perilous: such a Dove towards such an Ark! Deftly, thou shifty Usher: one man already fell; and lies smashed, far down there, against the masonry! Usher Maillard falls not: deftly, unerring he walks, with outspread palm. The Swiss holds a paper through his porthole; the shifty Usher snatches it, and returns. Terms of surrender: Pardon, immunity to all! Are they accepted?—*"Foi d'officier,* On the word of an officer," answers half-pay Hulin,—or half-pay Elie, for men do not agree on it,—"they are!" Sinks the drawbridge,—Usher Maillard bolting it when down; rushes-in the living deluge: the Bastille is fallen! *Victoire! La Bastille est prise!*

Along the streets of Paris circulate Seven Bastille Prisoners, borne shoulder-high; seven Heads on pikes; the Keys of the Bastille; and much else. See also the Gardes Françaises, in their steadfast military way, marching home to their barracks, with the Invalides and Swiss kindly enclosed in hollow square. It is one year and two months since these same men stood unparticipating, with Brennus d'Agoust at the Palais de Justice, when Fate overtook D'Espréménil; and now they have participated; and will participate. Not Gardes Françaises henceforth, but *Centre Grenadiers of the National Guard:* men of iron discipline and humour,—not without a kind of thought in them!

Likewise ashlar stones of the Bastille continue thundering through the dusk; its paper archives shall fly white. Old secrets come to view; and long-buried Despair finds voice. Read this portion of an old Letter: "If for my consolation Monseigneur would grant me, for the sake of God and the Most Blessed Trinity, that I could have news of my dear wife; were it only her name on a card, to show that she is alive! It were the greatest consolation I could receive; and I should forever bless the greatness of Monseigneur." Poor Prisoner, who namest thyself *Quéret-Démery,* and hast no other history,—she is *dead,* that dear wife of thine, and thou art dead! 'Tis fifty years since thy breaking heart put this question; to be heard now first, and long heard, in the hearts of men.

["THE DEATH OF FOULON"]

Nevertheless, as is natural, the waves still run high, hollow rocks retaining their murmur. We are but at the 22d of the month, hardly above a week since the Bastille fell, when it suddenly appears that old Foulon is alive; nay, that he is here, in early morning, in the streets of Paris: the extortioner, the plotter, who would make the people eat grass, and was a liar from the beginning!—It is even so. The deceptive "sumptuous funeral" (of some domestic that died); the hiding-place at Vitry towards Fontainebleau, have not availed that wretched old man. Some living domestic or dependent, for none loves Foulon, has betrayed him to the Village. Merciless boors of Vitry unearth him; pounce on him, like hell-hounds: Westward, old Infamy; to Paris, to be judged at the Hôtel-de-Ville! His old head, which seventy-four years have bleached, is bare; they have tied an emblematic bundle of grass on his back; a garland of nettles and thistles is round his neck: in this manner; led with ropes; goaded on with curses and menaces, must he, with his old limbs, sprawl forward; the pitiablest, most unpitied of all old men.

Sooty Saint-Antoine, and every street, musters its crowds as he passes;—the Hall of the Hôtel-de-Ville, the Place de Grève itself, will scarcely hold his escort and him. Foulon must not only be judged righteously, but judged there where he stands, without any delay. Appoint seven judges, ye Municipals, or seventy-and-seven; name them yourselves, or we will name them: but judge him! Electoral rhetoric, eloquence of Mayor Bailly, is wasted, for hours, explaining the beauty of the Law's delay. Delay, and still delay! Behold, O Mayor of the People, the morning has worn itself into noon: and he is still unjudged!—Lafayette, pressingly sent for, arrives; gives voice: This Foulon, a known man, is guilty almost beyond doubt; but may he not have accomplices? Ought not the truth to be cunningly pumped out of him,—in the Abbaye Prison? It is a new light! Sansculottism claps hands;—at which handclapping, Foulon (in his fairness, as his Destiny would have it) also claps.

"See! they understand one another!" cries dark Sansculottism, blazing into fury of suspicion.—"Friends," said "a person in good clothes," stepping forward, "what is the use of judging this man? Has not he been judged these thirty years?" With wild yells, Sansculottism clutches him, in its hundred hands: he is whirled across the Place de Grève, to the "*Lanterne,*" Lamp iron which there is at the corner of the *Rue de la Vannerie;* pleading bitterly for life,—to the deaf winds. Only with the third rope—for two ropes broke, and the quavering voice still pleaded—can he be so much as got hanged! His Body is dragged through the streets; his Head goes aloft on a pike, the mouth filled with grass: amid sounds as of Tophet, from a grass-eating people.

Surely if Revenge is a "kind of Justice," it is a "wild" kind! O mad Sansculottism, hast thou risen, in thy mad darkness, in thy soot and rags; unexpectedly, like an Enceladus, living-buried, from under his Trinacria? They that would make grass be eaten do now eat grass, in *this* manner? After long dumb groaning generations, has the turn suddenly become thine?—To such abysmal overturns, and frightful instantaneous inversions of the centre-of-gravity, are human Solecisms all liable, if they but knew it; the more liable, the falser (and topheavier) they are!

["The Solitary Prisoner" from *American Notes*]

CHARLES DICKENS

In the outskirts [of Philadelphia], stands a great prison, called the Eastern Penitentiary: conducted on a plan peculiar to the state of Pennsylvania. The system here, is rigid, strict, and hopeless solitary confinement. I believe it, in its effects, to be cruel and wrong.

In its intention, I am well convinced that it is kind, humane, and meant for reformation; but I am persuaded that those who devised this system of Prison Discipline, and those benevolent gentlemen who carry it into execution, do not know what it is that they are doing. I believe that very few men are capable of estimating the immense amount of torture and agony which this dreadful punishment, prolonged for years, inflicts upon the sufferers; and in guessing at it myself, and in reasoning from what I have seen written upon their faces, and what to my certain knowledge they feel within, I am only the more convinced that there is a depth of terrible endurance in it which none but the sufferers themselves can fathom, and which no man has a right to inflict upon his fellow-creature. I hold this slow and daily tampering with the mysteries of the brain, to be immeasurably worse than any torture of the body: and because its ghastly signs and tokens are not so palpable to the eye and sense of touch as scars upon the flesh; because its wounds are not upon the surface, and it extorts few cries that human ears can hear; therefore I the more denounce it, as a secret punishment which slumbering humanity is not roused up to stay. I hesitated once, debating with myself, whether, if I had the power of saying "Yes" or "No," I would allow it to be tried in certain cases, where the terms of imprisonment were short; but now, I solemnly declare, that with no rewards or honours could I walk a happy man beneath the open sky by day, or lie me down upon my bed at night, with the consciousness that one human creature, for any length of time, no matter what, lay suffering this unknown punishment in his silent cell, and I the cause, or I consenting to it in the least degree.

I was accompanied to this prison by two gentlemen officially connected with its management, and passed the day in going from cell to cell, and talking with the inmates. Every facility was afforded me, that the utmost courtesy could suggest. Nothing was concealed or hidden from my view, and

From Charles Dickens, *American Notes* (1842), Chapter 7.

every piece of information that I sought, was openly and frankly given. The perfect order of the building cannot be praised too highly, and of the excellent motives of all who are immediately concerned in the administration of the system, there can be no kind of question.

Between the body of the prison and the outer wall, there is a spacious garden. Entering it, by a wicket in the massive gate, we pursued the path before us to its other termination, and passed into a large chamber, from which seven long passages radiate. On either side of each, is a long, long row of low cell doors, with a certain number over every one. Above, a gallery of cells like those below, except that they have no narrow yard attached (as those in the ground tier have), and are somewhat smaller. The possession of two of these, is supposed to compensate for the absence of so much air and exercise as can be had in the dull strip attached to each of the others, in an hour's time every day; and therefore every prisoner in this upper story has two cells, adjoining and communicating with, each other.

Standing at the central point, and looking down these dreary passages, the dull repose and quiet that prevails, is awful. Occasionally, there is a drowsy sound from some lone weaver's shuttle, or shoemaker's last, but it is stifled by the thick walls and heavy dungeon-door, and only serves to make the general stillness more profound. Over the head and face of every prisoner who comes into this melancholy house, a black hood is drawn; and in this dark shroud, an emblem of the curtain dropped between him and the living world, he is led to the cell from which he never again comes forth, until his whole term of imprisonment has expired. He never hears of wife or children; home or friends; the life or death of any single creature. He sees the prison-officers, but with that exception he never looks upon a human countenance, or hears a human voice. He is a man buried alive; to be dug out in the slow round of years; and in the mean time dead to everything but torturing anxieties and horrible despair.

His name, and crime, and term of suffering, are unknown, even to the officer who delivers him his daily food. There is a number over his cell-door, and in a book of which the governor of the prison has one copy, and the moral instructor another: this is the index to his history. Beyond these pages the prison has no record of his existence: and though he live to be in the same cell ten weary years, he has no means of knowing, down to the very last hour, in what part of the building it is situated; what kind of men there are about him; whether in the long winter nights there are living people near, or he is in some lonely corner of the great jail, with walls, and passages, and iron doors between him and the nearest sharer in its solitary horrors.

Every cell has double doors: the outer one of sturdy oak, the other of grated iron, wherein there is a trap through which his food is handed. He has a Bible, and a slate and pencil, and, under certain restrictions, has sometimes other books, provided for the purpose, and pen and ink and paper. His razor, plate, and can, and basin, hang upon the wall, or shine upon the little shelf.

Fresh water is laid on in every cell, and he can draw it at his pleasure. During the day, his bedstead turns up against the wall, and leaves more space for him to work in. His loom, or bench, or wheel, is there; and there he labours, sleeps and wakes, and counts the seasons as they change, and grows old.

The first man I saw, was seated at his loom, at work. He had been there six years, and was to remain, I think, three more. He had been convicted as a receiver of stolen goods, but even after this long imprisonment, denied his guilt, and said he had been hardly dealt by. It was his second offence.

He stopped his work when we went in, took off his spectacles, and answered freely to everything that was said to him, but always with a strange kind of pause first, and in a low, thoughtful voice. He wore a paper hat of his own making, and was pleased to have it noticed and commended. He had very ingeniously manufactured a sort of Dutch clock from some disregarded odds and ends; and his vinegar-bottle served for the pendulum. Seeing me interested in this contrivance, he looked up at it with a great deal of pride, and said that he had been thinking of improving it, and that he hoped the hammer and a little piece of broken glass beside it "would play music before long." He had extracted some colours from the yarn with which he worked, and painted a few poor figures on the wall. One, of a female, over the door, he called "The Lady of the Lake."

He smiled as I looked at these contrivances to while away the time; but when I looked from them to him, I saw that his lip trembled, and could have counted the beating of his heart. I forget how it came about, but some allusion was made to his having a wife. He shook his head at the word, turned aside, and covered his face with his hands.

"But you are resigned now!" said one of the gentlemen after a short pause, during which he had resumed his former manner. He answered with a sigh that seemed quite reckless in its hopelessness, "Oh yes, oh yes! I am resigned to it." "And are a better man, you think?" "Well, I hope so: I'm sure I hope I may be." "And time goes pretty quickly?" "Time is very long, gentlemen, within these four walls!"

He gazed about him—Heaven only knows how wearily!—as he said these words; and in the act of doing so, fell into a strange stare as if he had forgotten something. A moment afterwards he sighed heavily, put on his spectacles, and went about his work again.

In another cell, there was a German, sentenced to five years' imprisonment for larceny, two of which had just expired. With colours procured in the same manner, he had painted every inch of the walls and ceiling quite beautifully. He had laid out the few feet of ground, behind, with exquisite neatness, and had made a little bed in the centre, that looked by-the-by like a grave. The taste and ingenuity he had displayed in everything were most extraordinary; and yet a more dejected, heart-broken, wretched creature, it would be difficult to imagine. I never saw such a picture of forlorn affliction and distress of mind. My heart bled for him; and when the tears ran down his cheeks, and he took one of the visitors aside, to ask, with his trembling hands nervously clutching at his coat to detain him, whether there was no hope of his dismal sentence being commuted, the spectacle was really too painful to witness. I never saw or heard of any kind of misery that impressed me more than the wretchedness of this man.

In a third cell, was a tall, strong black, a burglar, working at his proper trade of making screws and the like. His time was nearly out. He was not only a very dexterous thief, but was notorious for his boldness and hardihood, and for the number of his previous convictions. He entertained us with a long account of his achievements, which he narrated with such infinite relish, that he actually seemed to lick his lips as he told us racy anecdotes of stolen plate, and of old ladies whom he had watched as they sat at windows in silver spectacles (he had plainly had an eye to their metal even from the other side of the street) and had afterwards robbed. This fellow, upon the slightest encouragement, would have mingled with his professional recollections the most detestable cant; but I am very much mistaken if he could have surpassed the unmitigated hypocrisy with which he declared that he blessed the day on which he came into that prison, and that he never would commit another robbery as long as he lived.

There was one man who was allowed, as an indulgence, to keep rabbits. His room having rather a close smell in consequence, they called to him at the door to come out into the passage. He complied of course, and stood shading his haggard face in the unwonted sunlight of the great window, looking as wan and unearthly as if he had been summoned from the grave. He had a white rabbit in his breast; and when the little creature, getting down upon the ground, stole back into the cell, and he, being dismissed, crept timidly after it, I thought it would have been very hard to say in what respect the man was the nobler animal of the two.

There was an English thief, who had been there but a few days out of seven years: a villainous, low-browed, thin-lipped fellow, with a white face; who had as yet no relish for visitors, and who, but for the additional penalty, would have gladly stabbed me with his shoemaker's knife. There was another German who had entered the jail but yesterday, and who started from his bed when we looked in, and pleaded, in his broken English, very hard for work. There was a poet, who after doing two days' work in every four-and-twenty hours, one for himself and one for the prison, wrote verses about ships (he was by trade a mariner), and "the maddening wine-cup," and his friends at home. There were very many of them. Some reddened at the sight of visitors, and some turned very pale. Some two or three had prisoner nurses with them, for they were very sick; and one, a fat old negro whose leg had been taken off within the jail, had for his attendant a classical scholar and an accomplished surgeon, himself a prisoner likewise. Sitting upon the stairs, engaged in some slight work, was a pretty coloured boy. "Is there no refuge for young criminals in Philadelphia, then?" said I. "Yes, but only for white children." Noble aristocracy in crime!

There was a sailor who had been there upwards of eleven years, and who in a few months' time would be free. Eleven years of solitary confinement!

"I am very glad to hear your time is nearly out." What does he say? Nothing. Why does he stare at his hands, and pick the flesh upon his fingers, and raise his eyes for an instant, every now and then, to those bare walls which have seen his head turn grey? It is a way he has sometimes.

Does he never look men in the face, and does he always pluck at those hands of his, as though he were bent on parting skin and bone? It is his humour: nothing more.

It is his humour too, to say that he does not look forward to going out; that he is not glad the time is drawing near; that he did look forward to it once, but that was very long ago; that he has lost all care for everything. It is his humour to be a helpless, crushed, and broken man. And, Heaven be his witness that he has his humour thoroughly gratified!

There were three young women in adjoining cells, all convicted at the same time of a conspiracy to rob their prosecutor. In the silence and solitude of their lives they had grown to be quite beautiful. Their looks were very sad, and might have moved the sternest visitor to tears, but not to that kind of sorrow which the contemplation of the men awakens. One was a young girl; not twenty, as I recollect; whose snow-white room was hung with the work of some former prisoner, and upon whose downcast face the sun in all its splendour shone down through the high chink in the wall, where one narrow strip of bright blue sky was visible. She was very penitent and quiet; had come to be resigned, she said (and I believe her); and had a mind at peace. "In a word, you are happy here?" said one of my companions. She struggled—she did struggle very hard—to answer, Yes; but raising her eyes, and meeting that glimpse of freedom overhead, she burst into tears, and said, "She tried to be; she uttered no complaint; but it was natural that she should sometimes long to go out of that one cell: she could not help *that*," she sobbed, poor thing!

I went from cell to cell that day; and every face I saw, or word I heard, or incident I noted, is present to my mind in all its painfulness. But let me pass them by, for one, more pleasant, glance of a prison on the same plan which I afterwards saw at Pittsburgh.

When I had gone over that, in the same manner, I asked the governor if he had any person in his charge who was shortly going out. He had one, he said, whose time was up next day; but he had only been a prisoner two years.

Two years! I looked back through two years of my own life—out of jail, prosperous, happy, surrounded by blessings, comforts, and good fortune—and thought how wide a gap it was, and how long those two years passed in solitary captivity would have been. I have the face of this man, who was going to be released next day, before me now. It is almost more memorable in its happiness than the other faces in their misery. How easy and how natural it was for him to say that the system was a good one; and that the time went "pretty quick—considering"; and that when a man once felt that he had offended the law, and must satisfy it, "he got along, somehow": and so forth!

"What did he call you back to say to you, in that strange flutter?" I asked of my conductor, when he had locked the door and joined me in the passage.

"Oh! That he was afraid the soles of his boots were not fit for walking, as they were a good deal worn when he came in; and that he would thank me very much to have them mended, ready."

Those boots had been taken off his feet, and put away with the rest of his clothes, two years before!

I took that opportunity of inquiring how they conducted themselves immediately before going out; adding that I presumed they trembled very much.

"Well, it's not so much a trembling," was the answer—"though they do quiver—as a complete derangement of the nervous system. They can't sign their names to the book; sometimes can't even hold the pen; look about 'em without appearing to know why, or where they are; and sometimes get up and sit down again, twenty times in a minute. This is when they're in the office, where they are taken with the hood on, as they were brought in. When they get outside the gate, they stop, and look first one way and then the other; not knowing which to take. Sometimes they stagger as if they were drunk, and sometimes are forced to lean against the fence, they're so bad:— but they clear off in course of time."

As I walked among these solitary cells, and looked at the faces of the men within them, I tried to picture to myself the thoughts and feelings natural to their condition. I imagined the hood just taken off, and the scene of their captivity disclosed to them in all its dismal monotony.

At first, the man is stunned. His confinement is a hideous vision; and his old life a reality. He throws himself upon his bed, and lies there abandoned to despair. By degrees the insupportable solitude and barrenness of the place rouses him from this stupor, and when the trap in his grated door is opened, he humbly begs and prays for work. "Give me some work to do, or I shall go raving mad!"

He has it; and by fits and starts applies himself to labour; but every now and then there comes upon him a burning sense of the years that must be wasted in that stone coffin, and an agony so piercing in the recollection of those who are hidden from his view and knowledge, that he starts from his seat, and striding up and down the narrow room with both hands clasped on his uplifted head, hears spirits tempting him to beat his brains out on the wall.

Again he falls upon his bed, and lies there, moaning. Suddenly he starts up, wondering whether any other man is near; whether there is another cell like that on either side of him: and listens keenly.

There is no sound, but other prisoners may be near for all that. He remembers to have heard once, when he little thought of coming here himself, that the cells were so constructed that the prisoners could not hear each other, though the officers could hear them. Where is the nearest man—upon the right, or on the left? or is there one in both directions? Where is he sitting now—with his face to the light? or is he walking to and fro? How is he dressed? Has he been here long? Is he much worn away? Is he very white and spectre-like? Does *he* think of his neighbour too?

Scarcely venturing to breathe, and listening while he thinks, he conjures up a figure with its back towards him, and imagines it moving about in this next cell. He has no idea of the face, but he is certain of the dark form of a stooping man. In the cell upon the other side, he puts another figure, whose face is hidden from him also. Day after day, and often when he wakes up in the middle of the night, he thinks of these two men, until he is almost distracted. He never changes them. There they are always as he first imagined them—an old man on the right; a younger man upon the left—whose hidden features torture him to death, and have a mystery that makes him tremble.

The weary days pass on with solemn pace, like mourners at a funeral; and slowly he begins to feel that the white walls of the cell have something dreadful in them: that their colour is horrible: that their smooth surface chills his blood: that there is one hateful corner which torments him. Every morning when he wakes, he hides his head beneath the coverlet, and shudders to see the ghastly ceiling looking down upon him. The blessed light of day itself peeps in, an ugly phantom face, through the unchangeable crevice which is his prison window.

By slow but sure degrees, the terrors of that hateful corner swell until they beset him at all times; invade his rest, make his dreams hideous, and his nights dreadful. At first, he took a strange dislike to it; feeling as though it gave birth in his brain to something of corresponding shape, which ought not to be there, and racked his head with pains. Then he began to fear it, then to dream of it, and of men whispering its name and pointing to it. Then he could not bear to look at it, nor yet to turn his back upon it. Now, it is every night the lurking-place of a ghost: a shadow:—a silent something, horrible to see, but whether bird, or beast, or muffled human shape, he cannot tell.

When he is in his cell by day, he fears the little yard without. When he is in the yard, he dreads to re-enter the cell. When night comes, there stands the phantom in the corner. If he have the courage to stand in its place, and drive it out (he had once: being desperate), it broods upon his bed. In the twilight, and always at the same hour, a voice calls to him by name; as the darkness thickens, his Loom begins to live; and even that, his comfort, is a hideous figure, watching him till daybreak.

Again, by slow degrees, these horrible fancies depart from him one by one: returning sometimes, unexpectedly, but at longer intervals, and in less alarming shapes. He has talked upon religious matters with the gentleman who visits him, and has read his Bible, and has written a prayer upon his slate, and hung it up as a kind of protection, and an assurance of Heavenly companionship. He dreams now, sometimes, of his children or his wife, but is sure that they are dead or have deserted him. He is easily moved to tears; is gentle, submissive, and broken-spirited. Occasionally, the old agony comes back: a very little thing will revive it; even a familiar sound, or the scent of summer flowers in the air; but it does not last long, now: for the world without, has come to be the vision, and this solitary life, the sad reality.

If his term of imprisonment be short—I mean comparatively, for short it cannot be—the last half year is almost worse than all; for then he thinks the prison will take fire and he be burnt in the ruins, or that he is doomed to die within the walls, or that he will be detained on some false charge and sentenced for another term: or that something, no matter what, must happen to prevent his going at large. And this is natural, and impossible to be reasoned against, because, after his long separation from human life, and his great suffering, any event will appear to him more probable in the contemplation, than the being restored to liberty and his fellow-creatures.

If his period of confinement have been very long, the prospect of release bewilders and confuses him. His broken heart may flutter for a moment, when he thinks of the world outside, and what it might have been to him in all those lonely years, but that is all. The cell-door has been closed too long on all its hopes and cares. Better to have hanged him in the beginning than bring him to this pass, and send him forth to mingle with his kind, who are his kind no more.

On the haggard face of every man among these prisoners, the same expression sat. I know not what to liken it to. It had something of that strained attention which we see upon the faces of the blind and deaf, mingled with a kind of horror, as though they had all been secretly terrified. In every little chamber that I entered, and at every grate through which I looked, I seemed to see the same appalling countenance. It lives in my memory, with the fascination of a remarkable picture. Parade before my eyes, a hundred men, with one among them newly released from this solitary suffering, and I would point him out.

The faces of the women, as I have said, it humanises and refines. Whether this be because of their better nature, which is elicited in solitude, or because of their being gentler creatures, of greater patience and longer suffering, I do not know; but so it is. That the punishment is nevertheless, to my thinking, fully as cruel and as wrong in their case, as in that of the men, I need scarcely add.

My firm conviction is that, independent of the mental anguish it occasions—an anguish so acute and so tremendous, that all imagination of it must fall far short of the reality—it wears the mind into a morbid state, which renders it unfit for the rough contact and busy action of the world. It is my fixed opinion that those who have undergone this punishment, MUST pass into society again morally unhealthy and diseased. There are many instances on record, of men who have chosen, or have been condemned, to lives of perfect solitude, but I scarcely remember one, even among sages of strong and vigorous intellect, where its effect has not become apparent, in some disordered train of thought, or some gloomy hallucination. What monstrous phantoms, bred of despondency and doubt, and born and reared in solitude, have stalked upon the earth, making creation ugly, and darkening the face of Heaven!

Suicides are rare among these prisoners: are almost, indeed, unknown. But no argument in favour of the system, can reasonably be deduced from this circumstance, although it is very often urged. All men who have made diseases of the mind their study, know perfectly well that such extreme depression and despair as will change the whole character, and beat down all its powers of elasticity and self-resistance, may be at work within a man, and yet stop short of self-destruction. This is a common case.

That it makes the senses dull, and by degrees impairs the bodily faculties, I am quite sure. I remarked to those who were with me in this very establishment at Philadelphia, that the criminals who had been there long, were deaf. They, who were in the habit of seeing these men constantly, were perfectly amazed at the idea, which they regarded as groundless and fanciful. And yet the very first prisoner to whom they appealed—one of their own selection—confirmed my impression (which was unknown to him) instantly, and said, with a genuine air it was impossible to doubt, that he couldn't think how it happened, but he *was* growing very dull of hearing.

That it is a singularly unequal punishment, and affects the worst man least, there is no doubt. In its superior efficiency as a means of reformation, compared with that other code of regulations which allows the prisoners to work in company without communicating together, I have not the smallest faith. All the instances of reformation that were mentioned to me, were of a kind that might have been—and I have no doubt whatever, in my own mind, would have been—equally well brought about by the Silent System. With regard to such men as the negro burglar and the English thief, even the most enthusiastic have scarcely any hope of their conversion.

It seems to me that the objection that nothing wholesome or good has ever had its growth in such unnatural solitude, and that even a dog or any of the more intelligent among beasts, would pine, and mope, and rust away, beneath its influence, would be in itself a sufficient argument against this system. But when we recollect, in addition, how very cruel and severe it is, and that a solitary life is always liable to peculiar and distinct objections of a most deplorable nature, which have arisen here, and call to mind, moreover, that the choice is not between this system, and a bad or ill-considered one, but between it and another which has worked well, and is, in its whole design and practice, excellent; there is surely more than sufficient reason for abandoning a mode of punishment attended by so little hope or promise, and fraught, beyond dispute, with such a host of evils.

As a relief to its contemplation, I will close this chapter with a curious story arising out of the same theme, which was related to me, on the occasion of this visit, by some of the gentlemen concerned.

At one of the periodical meetings of the inspectors of this prison, a working man of Philadelphia presented himself before the Board, and earnestly requested to be placed in solitary confinement. On being asked what motive could possibly prompt him to make this strange demand, he answered that he had an irresistible propensity to get drunk; that he was constantly indulging it, to his great misery and ruin; that he had no power of resistance; that he wished to be put beyond the reach of temptation; and that he could think of no better way than this. It was pointed out to him, in reply, that the prison was for criminals who had been tried and sentenced by the law, and could not be made available for any such fanciful purposes; he was exhorted to abstain from intoxicating drinks, as he surely might if he would; and received other very good advice, with which he retired, exceedingly dissatisfied with the result of his application.

He came again, and again, and again, and was so very earnest and importunate, that at last they took counsel together, and said, "He will certainly qualify himself for admission, if we reject him any more. Let us shut him up. He will soon be glad to go away, and then we shall get rid of him." So they made him sign a statement which would prevent his ever sustaining an action for false imprisonment, to the effect that his incarceration was voluntary, and of his own seeking; they requested him to take notice, that the officer in attendance had orders to release him at any hour of the day or night, when he might knock upon his door for that purpose; but desired him to understand, that once going out, he would not be admitted any more. These conditions agreed upon, and he still remaining in the same mind, he was conducted to the prison, and shut up in one of the cells.

In this cell, the man, who had not the firmness to leave a glass of liquor standing untasted on a table before him—in this cell, in solitary confinement, and working every day at his trade of shoemaking, this man remained nearly two years. His health beginning to fail at the expiration of that time, the surgeon recommended that he should work occasionally in the garden; and as he liked the notion very much, he went about this new occupation with great cheerfulness.

He was digging here, one summer day, very industriously, when the wicket in the outer gate chanced to be left open: showing, beyond, the well-remembered dusty road and sun-burnt fields. The way was as free to him as to any man living, but he no sooner raised his head and caught sight of it, all shining in the light, than, with the involuntary instinct of a prisoner, he cast away his spade, scampered off as fast as his legs would carry him, and never once looked back.

["The National Character of the French" from "Letters on the French *Coup d'Etat* of 1851"]

Walter Bagehot

Letter III

Burke first taught the world at large that politics are made of time and place—that institutions are shifting things, to be tried by and adjusted to the shifting conditions of a mutable world—that, in fact, politics are but a piece of business—to be determined in every case by the exact exigencies of that case: in plain English—by sense and circumstances.

This was a great step in political philosophy—though it *now* seems the events of 1848 have taught thinking persons (I think) further. They have enabled us to say that of all these circumstances so affecting political problems, by far and out of all question the most important is *national character.* In that year the same experiment—the experiment, as its friends say, of Liberal and Constitutional Government—as its enemies say of Anarchy and Revolution—was tried in every nation of Europe—with what varying futures and differing results! The effect has been to teach men—not only speculatively to know, but practically to feel, that no absurdity is so great as to imagine the same species of institutions suitable or possible for Scotchmen and Sicilians, for Germans and Frenchmen, for the English and the Neapolitans. With a well-balanced national character (we now know) liberty is a stable thing. A really practical people will work in political business, as in private business, almost the absurdest, the feeblest, the most inconsistent set of imaginable regulations. Similarly, or rather reversely, the best institutions will not keep right a nation that *will* go wrong. Paper is but paper, and no virtue is to be discovered in it to retain within due boundaries the undisciplined passions of those who have never set themselves seriously to restrain them. In a word—as people of "large roundabout common sense" will (as a rule) somehow get on in life—(no matter what their circumstances or their fortunes)—so a nation which applies good judgment, forbearance, a rational and compromising habit to the management of free institutions, will certainly succeed; while the more eminently gifted national character will but be a source and germ of endless and disastrous failure, if, with whatever other eminent qualities, it be deficient in these plain, solid, and essential requisites.

The formation of *this* character is one of the most secret of marvelous mysteries. Why nations have the character we see them to have is, speaking generally, as little explicable to our shallow perspicacity, as why individuals, our friends or our enemies, for good or for evil, have the character which they have; why one man is stupid and another clever—why another volatile and a fourth consistent—this man by instinct generous, that man by instinct niggardly. I am not speaking of actions, you observe, but of tendencies and temptations. These and other similar problems daily crowd on our observation in millions and millions, and only do not puzzle us because we are too familiar with their difficulty to dream of attempting their solution. Only this much is most certain, all men and all nations have a character, and that character, when once taken, is, I do not say unchangeable—religion modifies it, catastrophe annihilates it—but the least changeable thing in this ever-varying and changeful world. Take the soft mind of the boy, and (strong and exceptional aptitudes and tendencies excepted) you may make him merchant, barrister, butcher, baker, surgeon, or apothecary. But once make him an apothecary, and he will never afterwards bake wholesome bread—make him a butcher, and he will kill too extensively, even for a surgeon—make him a barrister, and he will be dim on double entry, and crass on bills of lading. Once conclusively form him to one thing, and no art and no science will ever twist him to another. Nature, says the philosopher, has no Delphic daggers!—no men or maids of all work—she keeps one being to one pursuit—to each is a single choice afforded, but no more again thereafter for ever. And it is the same with nations. The Jews of to-day are the Jews in face and form of the Egyptian sculptures; in character they are the Jews of Moses—the negro is the negro of a thousand years—the Chinese, by his own account, is the mummy of a million. "Races and their varieties," says the historian, "seem to have been created with an inward *nisus* diminishing with the age of the world." The people of the South are yet the people of the South, fierce and angry as their summer sun—the people of the North are still cold and stubborn like their own North wind—the people of the East "mark not, but are still"—the people of the West "are going through the ends of the earth, and walking up and down in it." The fact is certain, the cause beyond us. The subtle system of obscure causes, whereby sons and daughters resemble not only their fathers and mothers, but even their great-great-grandfathers and their great-great-grandmothers, may very likely be destined to be very inscrutable. But, as the fact is so, so moreover, in history, nations have one character, one set of talents, one list of temptations, and one duty, to use the one and get the better of the other. There are breeds in the animal man just as in the animal dog. When you hunt with greyhounds and course with beagles, then, and not till then, may you expect the inbred habits of a thousand years to pass away, that Hindoos can be free, or that Englishmen will be slaves.

I need not prove to you that the French *have* a national character. Nor need I try your patience with a likeness of it. I have only to examine whether it be a fit basis for national freedom. I fear you will laugh when I tell you what I conceive to be about the most essential mental quality for a free people, whose liberty is to be progressive, permanent, and on a large scale; it is much *stupidity*. I see you are surprised—you are going to say to me, as Socrates did to Polus, "My young friend, *of course* you are right; but will you explain what you mean—as yet you are not intelligible." I will do so as well as I can, or endeavour to make good what I say—not by an *a priori* demonstration of my own, but from the details of the present, and the facts of history. Not to begin by wounding any present susceptibilities, let me take the Roman character—for, with one great exception,—I need not say to whom I allude—they are the great political people of history. Now, is not a certain dullness their most visible characteristic? What is the history of their speculative mind?—a blank. What their literature?—a copy. They have left not a single discovery in any abstract science; not a single perfect or well-formed work of high imagination. The Greeks, the perfection of narrow and accomplished genius, bequeathed to mankind the ideal forms of self-idolising art—the Romans imitated and admired; the Greeks explained the laws of nature—the Romans wondered and despised; the Greeks invented a system of numerals second only to that now in use—the Romans counted to the end of their days with the clumsy apparatus which we still call by their name; the Greeks made a capital and scientific calendar—the Romans began their month when the Pontifex Maximus happened to spy out the new moon. Throughout Latin literature, this is the perpetual puzzle—Why are we free and they slaves? we prætors and they barbers? Why do the stupid people always win, and the clever people always lose? I need not say that, in real sound stupidity, the English are unrivalled. You'll hear more wit, and better wit, in an Irish street row than would keep Westminster Hall in humour for five weeks. Or take Sir Robert Peel—our last great statesman, the greatest member of parliament that ever lived, an absolutely perfect transacter of public business—the type of the nineteenth century Englishman as Sir Robert Walpole was of the eighteenth. Was there ever such a dull man? Can any one, without horror, foresee the reading of his memoirs? A *clairvoyante,* with the book shut, may get on; but who now, in the flesh, will ever endure the open *vision* of endless recapitulation of interminable Hansard. Or take Mr. Tennyson's inimitable description:—

> No little lily-handed baronet he,
> A great broad-shouldered genial Englishman,
> A lord of fat prize oxen and of sheep,
> A raiser of huge melons and of pine
> A patron of some thirty charities
> A pamphleteer on guano and on grain,
> A quarter-sessions chairman, abler none.

Whose company so soporific? His talk is of truisms and bullocks; his head replete with rustic visions of mutton and turnips, and a cerebral edition of

Burn's "Justice!" Notwithstanding, he is the salt of the earth, the best of the English breed. Who is like him for sound sense? But I must restrain my enthusiasm. You don't want me to tell you that a Frenchman—a real Frenchman—can't be stupid; *esprit* is his essence, wit is to him as water, *bons-mots* as *bon-bons.* He reads and he learns by reading; levity and literature are essentially his line. Observe the consequence. The outbreak of 1848 was accepted in every province in France; the decrees of the Parisian mob were received and registered in all the municipalities of a hundred cities; the Revolution ran like the fluid of the telegraph down the *Chemin de fer du Nord;* it stopped at the Belgian frontier. Once brought into contact with the dull phlegm of the stupid Fleming, the poison was powerless. You remember what the Norman butler said to Wilkin Flammock, of the fulling mills, at the castle of the Garde Doloureuse, "that draught which will but warm your Flemish hearts, will put wildfire into Norman brains; and what may only encourage your countrymen to man the walls, will make ours fly over the battlements." *Les braves Belges,* I make no doubt, were quite pleased to observe what folly was being exhibited by those very clever French, whose tongue they want to speak, and whose literature they try to imitate. In fact, what we opprobriously call stupidity, though not an enlivening quality in common society, is nature's favourite resource for preserving steadiness of conduct and consistency of opinion. It enforces concentration; people who learn slowly, learn only what they must. The best security for people's doing their duty is that they should not know anything else to do; the best security for fixedness of opinion is that people should be incapable of comprehending what is to be said on the other side. These valuable truths are no discoveries of mine. They are familiar enough to people whose business it is to know them. Hear what a dense and aged attorney says of your peculiarly promising barrister:—"Sharp! oh yes, yes! he's too sharp by half. He is not *safe;* not a minute, isn't that young man." "What style sir," asked of an East India Director some youthful aspirant for literary renown, "is most to be preferred in the composition of official dispatches?" "My good fellow," responded the ruler of Hindostan, "the style *as we* like is the Humdrum." I extend this, and advisedly maintain that nations, just as individuals, may be too clever to be practical, and not dull enough to be free.

How far this is true of the French, and how far the gross deficiency I have indicated is modified by their many excellent qualities, I hope at a future time to inquire.

I am, my dear sir, yours truly,

AMICUS.

LETTER IV.—ON THE APTITUDE OF THE FRENCH CHARACTER FOR NATIONAL SELF-GOVERNMENT

Paris, January 29, 1852.

My Dear Sir,—There is a simple view of the subject on which I wrote to you last week that I wish to bring under your notice. The experiment (as it is called) of establishing political freedom in France is now sixty years old; and the best that we can say of it is, that it is an experiment still. There have been perhaps half-a-dozen new beginnings—half-a-dozen complete failures. I am aware that each of these failures can be excellently explained—each beginning shown to be quite necessary. But there are certain reasonings which, though outwardly irrefragable, the crude human mind is always most unwilling to accept. Among these are different and subtle explications of several apparently similar facts. Thus, to choose an example suited to the dignity of my subject, when a gentleman from town takes a day's shooting in the country, and should chance (as has happened) at first going off, to miss some six times running, how luminously soever he may "explain" each failure as it occurs, "however expanded a view" he may take of the whole series, whatever popular illustrations of projectile philosophy he may propound to the bird-slaying agriculturists—the impression on the crass intelligence of the gamekeeper will quite clearly be "He beint noo shot homsoever—aint thicker." Similarly, to compare small things with great, when I myself read in Thiers and the many other philosophic historians of this literary country, various and excellent explanations of their many mischances;—of the failure of the Constitution of 1791—of the Constitution of the year 3—of the Constitution of the year 5—of the *charte*—of the system of 1830—and now we may add, of the second republic—the annotated constitution of M. Dupin,—I can't help feeling a suspicion lingering in my crude and uncultivated intellect—that some common principle is at work in all and each of these several cases—that over and above all odd mischances, so many bankruptcies a little suggest an unfitness for the trade; that besides the ingenious reasons of ingenious gentlemen—there is some lurking quality, or want of a quality, in the national character of the French nation which renders them but poorly adapted for the form of freedom and constitution which they have so often, with such zeal and so vainly, attempted to establish.

In my last letter I suggested that this might be what I ventured to call a "want of stupidity." I will now try to describe what I mean in more accurate, though not, perhaps, more intelligible words.

I believe that I am but speaking what is agreed on by competent observers, when I say that the essence of the French character is a certain mobility; that is, as it has been defined, a certain "excessive sensibility to *present* impressions," which is sometimes "levity,"—for it issues in a postponement of seemingly fixed principles to a momentary temptation or a transient whim; sometimes "impatience"—as leading to an exaggerated sense of existing evils; often "excitement,"—a total absorption in existing emotion; oftener "inconsistency"—the sacrifice of old habits to present emergencies; and yet other unfavourable qualities. But it has also its favourable side. The same man who is drawn aside from old principles by small pleasures, who can't bear pain, who forgets his old friends when he ceases to see them, who is liable in time of excitement to be a one-idea-being, with no conception of anything but the one exciting object; yet who nevertheless is apt to have one idea to-day and quite another to-morrow (and this, and more than this, may I fancy be said of the ideal Frenchman) may and will have the subtlest perception of existing niceties, the finest susceptibility to social pleasure, the keenest tact in social politeness, the most consummate skilfulness in the details of action and administration,—may in short be the best companion, the neatest man of business, the lightest *homme de salon* [club man; literary type], the acutest diplomat of the existing world.

It is curious to observe how this reflects itself in their literature. "I will believe," remarks Montaigne, "in anything rather than in any man's consistency." What observer of English habits—what person inwardly conscious of our dull and unsusceptible English nature would ever say so. Rather in our country obstinacy is the commonest of the vices, and perseverance the cheapest of the virtues. Again, when they attempt history, the principal peculiarity (a few exceptions being allowed for) is an utter incapacity to describe graphically a long-passed state of society. Take, for instance—assuredly no unfavourable example—M. Guizot. His books, I need not say, are nearly unrivalled for eloquence, for philosophy and knowledge; you read there, how in the middle age there were many "principles," the principle of Legitimacy, the principle of Feudalism, the principle of Democracy; and you come to know how one grew, and another declined, and a third crept slowly on; and the mind is immensely edified, when perhaps at the 315th page a proper name occurs, and you mutter, "Dear me, why if there were not *people* in the time of Charlemagne! Who would have thought that?" But in return for this utter incapacity to describe the people of past times, a Frenchman has the gift of perfectly describing the people of his own. No one knows so well—no one can tell so well—the facts of his own life. The French memoirs, the French letters are, and have been, the admiration of Europe. Is not now Jules Janin unrivalled at pageants and *prima donnas?*

It is the same in poetry. As a recent writer excellently remarks, "A French Dante, or Michael Angelo, or Cervantes, or Murillo, or Goethe, or Shakespeare, or Milton, we at once perceive to be a mere anomaly; a supposition which may indeed be proposed in terms, but which in reality is inconceivable and impossible." Yet in requital as it were of this great deficiency, they have a

wonderful capacity for expressing and delineating the poetical and volup-
tuous element of every day life. We know the biography of De Béranger. The
young ladies whom he has admired—the wine that he has preferred—the fly
that buzzed on the ceiling, and interrupted his delicious and dreaming solitude, are as well-known to us as the recollections of our own lives. As in their
common furniture, so in their best poetry. The materials are nothing; reckon
up what you have been reading, and it seems a *congeries* of stupid trifles; begin
to read,—the skill of the workmanship is so consummate, the art so high and
so latent, that while time flows silently on, our fancies are enchanted and our
memories indelibly impressed. How often, asks Mr. Thackeray, have we read
De Béranger—how often Milton. Certainly, since Horace, there has been no
such manual of the philosophy of this world.

I will not say that the quality which I have been trying to delineate is exactly the same thing as "cleverness." But I do allege that it is sufficiently near
it for the rough purposes of popular writing. For this *quickness* in taking in—so
to speak—the present, gives a corresponding celerity of intellectual apprehension, an amazing readiness in catching new ideas and maintaining new theories, a versatility of mind which enters into and comprehends everything as it
passes, a concentration in what occurs, so as to use it for every purpose of illustration, and consequently, (if it happen to be combined with the least fancy),
quick repartee on the subject of the moment, and *bon-mots* also without stint
and without end—and these qualities are rather like what we style cleverness.
And what I call a proper stupidity keeps a man from all the defects of this
character; it chains the gifted possessor mainly to his old ideas; it takes him
seven weeks to comprehend an atom of a new one; it keeps him from being led
away by new theories—for there is nothing which bores him so much; it re-
strains him within his old pursuits, his well-known habits, his tried expedients,
his verified conclusions, his traditional beliefs. He is not tempted to "levity," or
"impatience," for he does not see the joke, and is thick-skinned to present evils.
Inconsistency puts him out,—"What I says is this here, as I was a saying yesterday," is his notion of historical eloquence and habitual discretion. He is very
slow indeed to be "excited,"—his passions, his feelings, and his affections are
dull and tardy strong things, falling in a certain known direction, fixing on
certain known objects, and for the most acting in a moderate degree, and at a
sluggish pace. You always know where to find his mind.

Now this is exactly what, in politics at least, you do not know about a
Frenchman. I like—I have heard a good judge say—to hear a Frenchman
talk. He strikes a light, but what light he will strike it is impossible to pre-
dict. I think he doesn't know himself. Now, I know you see at once how this
would operate on a parliamentary government, but I give you a gentle illustration. All England knows Mr. Disraeli, the witty orator, the exceedingly
clever *littérateur,* the versatile politician; and all England has made up its mind
that the stupidest country gentleman would be a better Home Secretary than
the accomplished descendant of the "Caucasian race." Now suppose, if you

only can, a House of Commons all Disraelis, and do you imagine that Parliament would work? It would be what M. Proudhon said of some French assemblies, "a box of matches."

The same quality acts in another way, and produces to English ideas a most marvellous puzzle, both in their philosophical literature and their political discussion. I mean their passion for logical deduction. Their habitual mode of argument is to get hold of some large principle or principles; to begin to deduce immediately; and to reason down from them to the most trivial details of common action. *Il faut être conséquent avec soi-même* [you have to be consistent with yourself]—is their fundamental maxim; and in a world, the essence of which is compromise, they could not well have a worse. I hold, metaphysically perhaps, that this is a consequence of that same impatience of disposition to which I have before alluded. Nothing is such a bore as looking for your principles—nothing so pleasant as working them out. People who have thought, know that enquiry is suffering. A child a-stumbling timidly in the dark is not more different from the same child playing on a sunny lawn, than is the philosopher groping, hesitating, doubting and blundering about his primitive postulates, from the same philosopher proudly deducing and commenting on the certain consequences of his established convictions. On this account mathematics have been called the paradise of the mind. In Euclid at least, you have your principles, and all that is required is acuteness in working them out. The long annals of science are one continued commentary on this text. Read in Bacon, the beginner of intellectual philosophy in England, and every page of the "Advancement of Learning" is but a continued warning against the tendency of the human mind to start at once to the last generalities from a few and imperfectly observed particulars. Read in the "Méditations" of Descartes, the beginner of intellectual philosophy in France, and in every page (once I read five) you will find nothing but the strictest, the best, the most lucid, the most logical deduction of all things actual and possible, from a few principles obtained without evidence, and retained in defiance of probability. Deduction is a game, and induction a grievance. Besides, clever impatient people want not only to learn, but to teach. And instruction expresses at least the alleged possession of knowledge. The obvious way is to shorten the painful, the slow, the tedious, the wearisome process of preliminary inquiry—to assume something pretty—to establish its consequences—discuss their beauty—exemplify their importance—extenuate their absurdities. A little vanity helps all this. Life is short—art is long—truth lies deep—take some side—found your school—open your lecture-rooms—tuition is dignified—learning is low.

I do not know that I can exhibit the way these qualities of the French character operate on their opinions, better than by telling you how the Roman Catholic Church deals with them. I have rather attended to it since I came here; it gives sermons almost an interest, their being in French—and to those curious in intellectual matters it is worth observing. In other times, and even now in out-of-the way Spain, I suppose it may be true that the Catholic Church was opposed to inquiry and reasoning. But it is not so now, and here. Loudly—from the pens of a hundred writers—from the tongues of a thousand pulpits—in every note of thrilling scorn and exulting derision, she proclaims the contrary. Be she Christ's workman, or Anti-Christ's, she knows her work too well.—"Reason, Reason, Reason"—exclaims she to the philosophers of this world—Put in practice what you teach, if you would have others believe it; be consistent; do not prate to us of private judgment when you are but yourselves repeating what you heard in the nursery—ill-mumbled remnants of a Catholic tradition. No! exemplify what you command, enquire and make search—seek, though we warn you that ye will never find—yet do as ye will. Shut yourself up in a room—make your mind a blank—go down (as ye speak) into the 'depths of your consciousness'—scrutinise the mental structure—inquire for the elements of belief—spend years, your best years, in the occupation—and at length—when your eyes are dim, and your brain hot, and your hand unsteady—then reckon what you have gained: see if you cannot count on your fingers the certainties you have reached: reflect which of them you doubted yesterday, which you may disbelieve to-morrow; or rather make haste—assume at random some essential *credenda*—write down your inevitable postulates—enumerate your necessary axioms—toil on, toil on— spin your spider's web—adore your own souls—or, if ye prefer it, choose some German nostrum—try the intellectual intuition, or the 'pure reason,' or the 'intelligible' ideas, or the mesmeric *clairvoyance*—and when so or somehow you have attained your results, try them on mankind. Don't go out into the highways and hedges—it's unnecessary. Ring the bell—call in the servants—give them a course of lectures—cite Aristotle—review Descartes— panegyrize Plato—and see if the *bonne* will understand you. It is you that say '*Vox populi—Vox dei*' [the people's voice is the voice of God]; but you see the people reject you. Or suppose you succeed—what you call succeeding—your books are read; for three weeks, or even a season, you are the idol of the *salons;* your hard words are on the lips of women; then a change comes—a new actress appears at the Théâtre Français or the Opéra—her charms eclipse your theories; or a great catastrophe occurs—political liberty (it is said) is annihilated—*il faut se faire mouchard* [you have to become an informer] is the observation of scoffers. Anyhow, *you* are forgotten—fifty years may be the gestation of a philosophy, not three its life—before long, before you go to your grave, your six disciples leave you for some newer master, or to set up for themselves. The poorest priest in the remote region of the *Basses Alpes* has more power over men's souls than human cultivation; his ill-mouthed masses move women's souls—can you? Ye scoff at Jupiter. Yet he at least was believed in—you never have; idol for idol the *de*throned is better than the *un*thorned. No, if you would reason—if you would teach—if you would speculate, come to us. We have our *premises* ready; years upon years before you were born, intellects whom the best of you delight to magnify, toiled to systematise the creed of ages; years upon years after you are dead, better heads than yours will find new matter there to define, to divide, to arrange. Consider the 100 volumes of Aquinas—which of you desire a higher life than that. To deduce, to subtilise discriminate, systematise, and decide the highest truth, and to be believed. Yet such was his luck, his enjoyment. He was what you would be. No, no—*Credite, credite.* Ours is the life of speculation—the cloister is the home for the student. Philosophy is stationary—Catholicism progressive. You call—we are heard, &c., &c., &c. So speaks each preacher according to his ability. And when the dust and noise of present controversies have passed away, and in the silence of the night, some grave historian writes out the tale of half-forgotten times, let him not forget to observe that profoundly as the mediæval Church subdued the superstitious cravings of a painful and barbarous age—in after years she dealt more discerningly still with the feverish excitement—the feeble vanities—and the dogmatic impatience of an over-intellectual generation.

And as in religion—so in politics: we find the same desire to teach rather than to learn—the same morbid appetite for exhaustive and original theories. It is as necessary for a public writer to have a system as it is for him to have a pen. His course is obvious; he assumes some grand principle—the principle of Legitimacy, or the principle of Equality, or the principle of Fraternity—and thence he reasons down without fear or favour to the details of every-day politics. Events are judged of, not by their relation to simple causes, but by their bearing on a remote axiom. Nor are these speculations mere exercises of philosophic ingenuity. Four months ago, hundreds of able writers were debating with the keenest ability and the most ample array of generalities, whether the country should be governed by a Legitimate Monarchy, or an illegitimate; by a Social, or an old-fashioned Republic, by a two-chambered Constitution, or a one-chambered Constitution; on 'Revision' or Non-revision; on the claims of Louis Napoleon, or the divine right of the national representation. Can any intellectual food be conceived more dangerous or more stimulating for an over-excitable population? It is the same in parliament. The description of the Church of Corinth may stand for a description of the late Assembly: every one had a psalm, had a doctrine, had a tongue, had a revelation, had an interpretation. Each member of the Mountain had his scheme for the regeneration of mankind; each member of the vaunted majority had his scheme for newly consolidating the government; Orleanist hated Legitimist, Legitimist Orleanist; moderate Republican detested undiluted Republican; scheme was set against scheme, and theory against theory. No two Conservatives would agree what to conserve; no Socialist could practically associate with any other. No deliberative assembly can exist with every member wishing to lead, and no one wishing to follow. Not the meanest Act of Parliament could be carried without more compromise than even the best French statesmen were willing to use on the most important and critical affairs of their country. Rigorous reasoning would not manage a parish-vestry, much less a great nation. In

England to carry half your own crotchets, you must be always and everywhere willing to carry half another man's. Practical men must submit as well as rule; concede as well as assume. Popular government has many forms, a thousand good modes of procedure; but no one of those modes can be worked, no one of those forms will endure, unless by the continual application of sensible heads and pliable judgments, to the systematic of stiff axioms, rigid principles, and incarnated propositions.

I am, &c.,

AMICUS.

P.S.—I was in hopes that I should have been able to tell you of the withdrawal of the decree relative to the property of the Orleans family. It was announced in the *Constitutionnel,* of yesterday; but I regret to add was contradicted in the *Patrie* last evening. I need not observe to you that it is an act for which there is no defence, moral or political. It has immensely weakened the government.

The change of Ministry is also a great misfortune to Louis Napoleon. M. de Morny, said to be a son of Queen Hortense (if you believe the people in the *salons,* the President is not the son of his father, and everybody else is the son of his mother), was a statesman of the class best exemplified in England by the late Lord Melbourne,—an acute, witty, fashionable man, acquainted with Parisian persons and things, and a consummate judge of public opinion, M. Persigny was in exile with the President, is said to be much attached to him, to repeat his sentiments and exaggerate his prejudices. I need not point out which of the two is just now the sounder counsellor.

[Two Passages on the Crisis of Bourgeois Realism from *The Historical Novel*]

George Lukács

I.

For the countries of Western and Central Europe the Revolution of 1848 means a decisive alteration in class groupings and in class attitudes to all important questions of social life, to the perspectives of social development. The June battle of the Paris proletariat in 1848 constitutes a turning-point in history on an international scale. Despite Chartism, despite sporadic uprisings in France during the "bourgeois monarchy," despite the rising of the German weavers in 1844, here for the first time a decisive battle is carried out by force of arms between proletariat and bourgeoisie, here for the first time the proletariat enters upon the world-historical stage as an armed mass, resolved upon the final struggle; during these days the bourgeoisie for the first time fights for the naked continuance of its economic and political rule. One has only to trace closely the history of events in Germany in 1848 to see the significant turn which the proletarian uprising and defeat in Paris gave to the development of the bourgeois revolution in Germany. Of course, anti-democratic tendencies as well as a disposition to turn bourgeois-democratic revolutionary trends into a rotten compromise with the feudal-absolutist régime were already present before then in German middle-class circles. Immediately after the March days they became much more pronounced. Nevertheless it is the June battle of the Paris proletariat which produces a decisive change in the bourgeois camp, accelerating to an extraordinary degree the inner process of differentiation which is to transform revolutionary democracy into compromising liberalism.

This change affects all spheres of bourgeois ideology. It would be altogether superficial and wrong to suppose that, when a class turns its back so radically upon its earlier political aims and ideals, the spheres of ideology, the fates of science and art can remain untouched. Marx repeatedly showed in great detail how significant the class struggles between bourgeoisie and proletariat were for the classical social science of bourgeois development, political

Reprinted from *The Historical Novel* (Boston: Beacon Press, 1962) by permission.

economy. And today, particularly in the light of the recently published works of Marx and Engels of the pre-1848 period, if we follow attentively the process of dissolution of Hegelian philosophy, we can see that the philosophical struggles of the various trends and nuances within Hegelianism were in essence nothing but partisan struggles of the period preparatory to the coming bourgeois-democratic Revolution of 1848. It is only in the light of these connections that it becomes clear why Hegelian philosophy, which from the middle twenties had dominated the entire intellectual life of Germany, "suddenly" disappeared after the defeat of the Revolution as a result of the betrayal by the German bourgeoisie of its own earlier bourgeois revolutionary aims. Hegel, earlier the central figure in Germany's intellectual life, was "suddenly" forgotten, became a "dead dog."

. In his analyses of the Revolution of 1848, Marx writes at great length about this change, about its causes and consequences. He also provides formulations of extraordinary intellectual depth, summing up this change and its effect upon all spheres of bourgeois ideological activity. "The bourgeoisie," writes Marx, "had a true insight into the fact that all the weapons which it had forged against feudalism turned their points against itself, that all the means of education which it had produced rebelled against its own civilization, that all the gods which it had created had fallen away from it. It understood that all the so-called liberties and organs of progress attacked and menaced its class rule at its social foundation and its political summit simultaneously, and had therefore become *socialistic*."

We can only examine this change briefly here with respect to its effects on historical feeling and on the sense and understanding of history; only in relation to those aspects, therefore, which are of immediate and vital importance to our problem.

1. Changes in the Conception of History after the Revolution of 1848.

Here, as in our introductory remarks to this work, we are concerned not with an internal affair of history *qua* science, not with a scholars' dispute over method, but with the mass experience of history itself, with an experience shared by the widest circles of bourgeois society, by those even who were not in the least interested in the science of history or aware that a change had taken place within it. In the same way the awakening of a more conscious sense of history had influenced the experience and ideas of the broadest masses without their necessarily knowing that their new feeling for the historical connections of life had produced a Thierry in historical science and a Hegel in philosophy etc.

The nature of this relationship must therefore be specially emphasized so that, when we speak of a change in the conception of history among authors of historical novels, it is not thought that we mean that their writing was necessarily directly affected by the changes in historical science. We can of course find influences of this kind. Flaubert, for instance, was not only acquainted with Taine, Renan etc. through their works, but also knew them very well personally. The influence of Jakob Burckhardt on Conrad Ferdinand Meyer is well known; the immediate influence of Nietzsche's conception of history on writers perhaps extends even further, and so on. However it is not this philologically demonstrable influence which is important, but rather the *common character of the reactions to reality* which in history and literature produce analogous subjects and forms of historical consciousness. These reactions have their roots in the briefly sketched change in the entire political and intellectual life of the middle class. If individual historians or philosophers achieved a notable influence in these questions, this influence is not a primary cause, but itself a consequence of the new ideological tendencies among both writers and readers, produced by the social-historical development. If then, in the following, we cite a number of leading ideologists of this new attitude to history, we regard them as representatives of general social currents which they have simply formulated in the most effective literary manner.

There is, however, one more introductory remark to be made. In the pre-1848 period the bourgeoisie was also the ideological leader of social development. Its new, historical defence of progress blazes the trail for the whole ideological development of this period. The proletariat's conception of history matures upon this basis, extending the last great phase of bourgeois ideology by means of criticism and struggle and by overcoming its limitations. The important forerunners of socialism who did not absorb these ideas were, in this respect, mystical or retrograde. This situation is very radically altered by the change which 1848 brings about.

The division of every people into "two nations" took place—in tendency, at least—in the field of ideology, too. The class struggles of the first half of the nineteenth century had already led, on the eve of the 1848 Revolution, to the scientific formulation of Marxism. The latter contained all progressive views on history in a "sublated" form, that is in the threefold Hegelian sense of the word: they were not only criticized and annulled, but also preserved and raised to a higher level.

The fact that in this period we find strong influences of general bourgeois ideology in both the working-class movement and the democratic currents allied to it, does not contradict the fundamental fact of the "two nations." The working-class movement does not develop in a vacuum, but surrounded by all the ideologies of decline of bourgeois decadence, and the "historic mission" of opportunism within the working-class movement consists here in "mediating," in smoothing out the sharp division and guiding it onto a bourgeois path. But all these complex inter-relations should not obscure the fundamental fact that the ideologies of the bourgeoisie analysed here are no longer the leading ideologies of a whole epoch, but simply class ideologies in a much narrower sense.

The central problem in which the change of attitude to history is manifested is that of *progress*. We saw that the most notable writers and thinkers of the period before 1848 made their most important step forward by giving an historical formulation to the idea of progress: they advanced to a concept of the contradictory character of human progress, even if it was only relatively correct and never complete. However, the events of the class struggle presented to the ideologists of the bourgeoisie so threatening a prospect for the future of their society and class, that the disinterested courage with which the contradictions of progress had been disclosed and declared was bound to disappear. How closely the attitude to progress connects with the future perspective of bourgeois society, can best be studied by glancing at the intelligent opponents of the idea of progress in the pre-1848 period. The latter still stated their ideas fairly uninhibitedly, since the social dangers to which they alluded and which determined their thinking were not yet so menacingly immediate as to provoke apologetic falsifications. Such is the way, for example, the Romantic reactionary, Théophile Gautier, writes about this question even in the thirties. He derides all ideas of progress as shallow and foolish; he treats Fourier's utopias with irony, but at the same time adds that if progress is at all possible, then only by this means; everything else is a bitter mockery, a spiritless harlequinade: "The phalanstery is truly an advance on the abbey of Thelème."

In these circumstances the idea of progress undergoes a regression. Classical economics, which in its day had boldly admitted certain contradictions in captitalist economy, changes into the smooth and mendacious harmony of vulgar economics. The fall of Hegelian philosophy in Germany means the disappearance of the idea of the contradictory character of progress. So far as an ideology of progress continues to prevail—it is for a long time still the leading ideology of the liberal bourgeoisie—every element of contradiction is extinguished from it, history is conceived as a smooth straightforward evolution. On a European scale and for a long period this is increasingly the central idea of the new science of sociology, which replaces the attempts to master the contradictions of historical progress dialectically.

Admittedly, this change is bound up with a renunciation of the high-flown idealism of Hegelian philosophy and, here and there, even with an at least partial return to the ideology of the Enlightenment and mechanical materialism (e.g. in Germany in the 50's and 60's). But it is precisely the weakest and most unhistorical tendencies of the Enlightenment which are revived, quite apart from the fact that certain currents of thought, which in the middle of the eighteenth century contained seeds of the right conception, in this renewed form inevitably became obstacles to the adequate scientific comprehension of history. . . .

Let us illustrate this with two examples which are of the greatest importance for the conception of history in this period. It was a great and important historical advance when the Enlighteners of the eighteenth century started to investigate the natural conditions surrounding social development and attempted to apply the categories and results of the natural sciences directly to the knowledge of society. Naturally, this gave rise to much that was perverse and unhistorical, but in the struggle with the traditional theological conception of history it signified a very considerable advance at the time. It was quite different in the second half of the nineteenth century. If historians or sociologists now attempted to make Darwinism, for example, the immediate basis of an understanding of historical development, this could only lead to a perversion and distortion of historical connections. Darwinism becomes an abstract phrase and the old reactionary Malthus normally appears as its sociological "core." In the course of later development the rhetorical application of Darwinism to history becomes a straightforward apology for the brutal dominion of capital. Capitalist competition is swollen into a metaphysical history-dissolving mystique by the "eternal law" of the struggle for existence. The most telling historical conception of this kind is the philosophy of Nietzsche, which makes a composite mythology out of Darwinism and the Greek contest, Agon.

II.

The special character of the historical novel in this period may be stated as follows: the false intentions of the writer are less easily corrected by life in the historical novel than in the novel which deals with the present. In the historical novel the false theories, literary prejudices etc. of the author cannot be, or are much less easily, corrected by a wealth of living material such as is contained in contemporary themes. What Engels described as the "triumph of realism" in Balzac—the triumph of an honest and complete reflection of the real facts and connections of life over the social, political or individual prejudices of a writer, is much more difficult in the new historical novel than in the contemporary social novel.

We dealt very briefly with two important realist writers of this period, Maupassant and Jacobsen. Maupassant approaches *Bel Ami* in the same way as he does *Une Vie*, Jacobsen *Niels Lhyne* in the same way as *Marie Grubbe*. In *Bel Ami* and *Niels Lhyne*, despite the general "problematic" of the new realism, social reality is richly nuanced. In both cases there occurs a "triumph of realism." Why? Because it was impossible for Maupassant and Jacobsen, as talented and honest observers of life, to pay no attention to the big social problems of their time when portraying a character in the present. It may have been the inner psychological development of the hero or heroine which primarily interested them, but whatever their conscious intentions the social life of the present flowed into their novels from every side, filling them with a rich and articulated life.

This happened much less readily in the historical novel. Feuchtwanger . . . was quite right to say that a subject removed in time can be more easily managed than the material of the present. His only mistake is to see this as an advantage and not a disadvantage. For the post-1848 writer historical material is less resistant, the subjective aim of the writer may be more easily imposed upon it. Hence that abstractness, that subjectivist arbitrariness, that almost dreamlike "timelessness" which we have seen in Maupassant's and Jacobsen's historical novels and which sets them off very much to their disadvantage from the more powerful and more clearly outlined social novels of the two authors.

Even with a writer of Dickens's rank the weaknesses of his petty bourgeois humanism and idealism are more obvious and obtrusive in his historical novel on the French Revolution (*A Tale of Two Cities*) than in his social novels. The between-the-classes position of the young Marquis Saint Evremonde—his disgust with the cruel methods used for maintaining feudal exploitation and his solution of this conflict by escape into bourgeois private life—does not receive its due weight in the composition of the story. Dickens, by giving pre-eminence to the purely moral aspects of causes and effects, weakens the connection between the problems of the characters' lives and the events of the French Revolution. The latter becomes a romantic background. The turbulence of the times is used as a pretext for revealing human-moral qualities. But neither the fate of Manette and his daughter, nor of Darnay-Evremonde, and least of all of Sidney Carton, grows organically out of the age and its social events. Here again any social novel of Dickens, say *Little Dorrit* or *Dombey and Son,* will show how much more closely and organically these relations are portrayed than in *A Tale of Two Cities.*

Yet Dickens's historical novel is still relatively grounded on classical traditions. *Barnaby Rudge,* where the historical events are more episodic, preserves entirely the concrete manner of portrayal of the contemporary novels. But the limitations of Dickens's social criticism, his sometimes abstract-moral attitude towards concrete social-moral phenomena inevitably come out much more strongly here. What otherwise was only an occasional blurring of line becomes here an essential defect in the entire composition. For in the historical novel this tendency of Dickens must necessarily take on the character of modern privateness in regard to history. The historical basis in *Barnaby Rudge* is much more of a background than in *A Tale of Two Cities.* It provides purely accidental circumstances for "purely human" tragedies, and this discrepancy emphasizes what is otherwise only a slight and latent tendency in Dickens to separate the "purely human" and "purely moral" from their social basis and to make them, to a certain degree, autonomous. In Dickens's best novels on the present this tendency is corrected by reality itself, by its impact upon the writer's openness and receptivity. In the historical novel this kind of correction is inevitably weaker. That this is so with as great a writer as Dickens, a classic of the novel who is affected only peripherally by the decline, serves as a particularly vivid illustration of our argument.

[The Fall of the Bastille, 14 July 1789]

George Rudé

The storming of the Bastille, though commemorated on France's National Day, is still the object of bitter controversy. The legendary valour of the "men of 14 July" has become part of the Republican tradition and most Frenchmen might be inclined to accept Michelet's verdict that the Bastille was taken as "an act of faith" and that its capture symbolised the overthrow of age-old tyrannies. Yet some Frenchmen—and there have been prominent historians among them—have denounced the "legend" of the Bastille as a propagandist stunt and have claimed that its captors were prompted by the basest motives. It has been argued that the Bastille, far from being a symbol of despotism, was a credit to the humanity of its administrators; that it was gradually being abandoned as a State prison (at the time of its capture no more than seven prisoners were released from its cells); and that the common people of Paris could, in any case, have had little interest in its fall, as it had long ceased to be a place of detention for men of humble station.

While there is more than a grain of truth in this argument, much of it is really beside the point in so far as it invites us to see the storming of the Bastille as a single, isolated event, divorced from the circumstances in which it took place and from the passions which the onset of the Revolution had already aroused. To present a faithful picture, it would therefore seem necessary to place this episode in its proper setting; and, in so doing, not merely to relate it to the political events of July 1789, but to attempt to see it from the viewpoint of the many thousands of Parisians who played a part in the drama of which it was the climax.

In one sense at least it is indisputable that the Bastille had become an anachronism. Built by Charles V in the fourteenth century as a fortress to defend the eastern approaches of the capital, it still stood, four hundred years later, as a grim reminder of a turbulent past. The awe inspired by its eight towers and eighty-foot walls was enhanced by the jealousy with which the Government guarded its secrets and the pledge of silence imposed on its prisoners as a condition of their release. Meanwhile, the face of the city was being

Reprinted from *Paris and London in the Eighteenth Century* by George Rudé. Copyright 1952, 1953, 1954, 1955, 1956, 1957, 1959, 1966, 1969, 1970 by George Rudé. Used by permission of Viking Penguin, a division of Penguin Books USA Inc.

rapidly transformed. While the Temple and Châtelet prisons vied with the Bastille as survivals from a feudal past, and the medieval splendours of Notre Dame and the Sainte Chapelle still dominated the approaches to the Cité, the work of reconstruction, begun under Louis XV and actively supported by the nobility and wealthy *bourgeoisie,* went on apace. The houses on the old bridges were being pulled down; work on the Pont Louis XVI—the present Pont de la Concorde—had been begun, and the Pont Neuf, though only completed in 1600, was, by the time of the Revolution, second only to the Pont Notre Dame in point of age. Medieval cemeteries were being cleared from the centre and pavements were beginning to appear, in imitation of London. In 1788 Sébastien Mercier was able to write that, in the last thirty years, 10,000 houses had been constructed and that one-third of Paris had been rebuilt. In the fashionable Marais, the aristocratic quarter of the Right Bank, the new town houses of the Rohans and the Soubises eclipsed the former splendours of the Hôtels de Bourgogne and de Sens. Further west, at the entrance to the elegant Faubourg St. Honoré, the Duke of Orleans, wealthiest and most popular of the Princes of the Blood and a near claimant to the throne, built the magnificent arcades and gardens of the Palais Royal, shortly to become a centre of lavish entertainment and a meeting place of journalists, pamphleteers and political gossips. On the Boulevards, the Théâtre Italien was erected in the gardens of the Duc de Choiseul; on the Left Bank, the Théâtre Français (the later Odéon) was built in 1789 on the site of the Hôtel de Condé, recently purchased for 3 million *livres.* Regiments of building workers had been enrolled from outlying provinces and the speed of construction was often phenomenal: the Opéra was built in seventy-five days and the Château de Bagatelle in six weeks!

It was not only the walls of the Bastille that stood out in sharp contrast against this feverish progress of modernisation; so did the old tenements, workshops and lodging houses in which the bulk of the Parisian population still lived and worked. It would be wrong, however, to define them—as some historians have done—in terms of a distinctive working class: while already accounting for nearly half the population of Paris, the wage-earners and their families did not as yet form a clearly defined social group, identifiable by their dress, method of living or social outlook. There was as yet no factory system or industrial "belt," though enterprising textile manufacturers had set up establishments that, on occasion, employed up to 400 or 500, or even 800, workpeople under one roof. Apart from the multifarious petty trades plied in the markets, on the riverside, in the Place de Grève or on the Pont Neuf, the prevailing mode of production was still that of the traditional workshop in which the journeyman, though his prospects of promotion were becoming ever more remote, still shared the work and gossip, and often the board and lodging, of his master. This mixed, yet closely related, population of craftsmen, petty traders, shopkeepers, journeymen and labourers—the later *sans-culottes* of the Revolution—must, in 1789, have already accounted for five out of every six inhabitants of a city of over 600,000 souls. They lived closely packed in the older quarters of the capital—in the central market area adjoining the Louvre (the most densely populated of all), on the island of the Cité and in the *faubourgs* of the north, south and east. Among these, though not the poorest, the traditional centre of popular agitation and disturbance, even before the Revolution, was the Faubourg St. Antoine, where a closely knit community of craftsmen, petty workshop masters and their journeymen lived within easy range of the walls and guns of the Bastille.

Although writers like Sébastien Mercier considered that the common people of Paris were incapable of committing the excesses witnessed in London during the Gordon Riots, there had been precedents for the great social disorders of the year 1789. Paris had, it is true, an international reputation for being well "policed"; yet diarists and the reports of the Châtelet have recorded the periodic outbursts of popular anger, usually aroused by a shortage or the high price of bread, which alarmed the respectable *bourgeois* and fashionable society of the times: the outbreaks at the time of the Law scandal in 1720; the food riots during Fleury's Ministry in 1740; the violent outcry against the kidnapping of children in 1750; the burning of the Abbé Terray in effigy in the Faubourg St. Antoine after the death of Louis XV; and, above all, the bread riots of May 1775, when every baker's shop and stall in the *faubourgs* and city centre was sacked by angry crowds. More recently, in the autumn of 1787 and 1788, when the Paris Parlement was still able to pose as the popular champion of ancient liberties, the journeymen and labourers of the city centre and southern *faubourgs* had joined with the clerks of the Palais de Justice in violent demonstrations on the Pont Neuf and in the Place Dauphine to demand the withdrawal of unpopular Ministers.

In the winter of 1788–9, as so often in the past, famine and high prices gave the initial stimulus to the popular movement. Throughout the eighteenth century the shortage and high cost of bread—which, even in normal times, accounted for half the household budget—had been endemic. Prices had far outstripped the level of wages. It has been calculated that, between the two periods 1726–41 and 1771–89, wages all over France had risen by only 22 per cent, while prices had risen by 65 per cent. This tendency became more marked in the last three years of the Old Régime. In Paris, the normal price of a 4-lb. loaf was 8 or 9 *sous* (8*d*. or 9*d*.). Between August and September 1788, it rose from 9 to 11 *sous;* and Hardy, the bookseller-diarist, who lived within a stone's throw of the great popular market of the Place Maubert, wrote: "In the markets and among the people all the talk is of future revolutions." Worse was to come: on 28 November the price of bread rose to 13 *sous,* and a bitterly cold winter, that was to throw thousands out of work, began. Early in December the price rose to 14 *sous* and Hardy reported that there were 80,000 unemployed. As the cold weather ended in the last days of January, the price of bread reached its peak at 14½ *sous;* it was to remain at this level until the week after the storming of the Bastille. We can get some idea of what this meant in terms of hardship and suffering to the ordinary Parisian when it is realised that, at prevailing rates of wages, a builder's labourer, in order to maintain his normal diet, would, between February and July 1789, have had to spend four-fifths of his earnings on bread.

Yet hunger was not the only stimulus to popular unrest. A new hope had been born—French historians have called it "la grande espérance"—with the Government's promise to summon the States General to meet in Versailles in May. At last something would be done to relieve the sufferings of the poor! The words "Third Estate" and "nation" were beginning to gain currency among the people; and, in the riots which shook the Faubourg St. Antoine at the end of April, demonstrators who raided foodshops and burned down the properties of the manufacturers Henriot and Réveillon shouted, "Vive le Tiers Etat!" But, as the conflict sharpened between the Third Estate and the Privileged Orders, it appeared that the hopes centred on Versailles would be dashed to the ground by aristocratic intrigue. From mid-summer, foreign troops were being concentrated on the outskirts of Paris: already on 3 June, Hardy had noted the arrival of German and Hungarian regiments, brought in on the pretext of preventing a renewed outburst of rioting in the Faubourg St. Antoine. The intentions of the Court Party, grouped around Marie-Antoinette and the King's younger brother, the Comte d'Artois, were becoming clear: on the night of 22 June the King was persuaded to dismiss Necker, his popular Finance Minister, and to overawe the National Assembly by a display of military force. The plot miscarried: thousands invaded the courtyard of the Palace to demand that Necker be retained in office; soldiers under the command of the Prince de Conti would not obey the command to fire; and the deputies, rallied by Mirabeau in an historic speech, refused to disperse. The King was compelled to yield.

Up to now, the insurrectionary temper developing in Paris, fed on economic hardship and rumours of "aristocratic plots," had been without effective leadership. With the latest news from Versailles, however, the professional and commercial classes, who had hitherto been prepared to wait passively on events and had viewed the simmerings in the *faubourgs* and markets without sympathy, began to give a direction to affairs without which the July revolution could not have taken place. From this date, the pamphleteers and journalists in the entourage of the Duke of Orleans (who had himself gone over to the Third Estate at Versailles) began to establish a permanent headquarters at the Palais Royal; here thousands congregated nightly and acquired the slogans and directives—and, possibly, too, the funds—of what Hardy called "the extreme revolutionary party." Also at this time, the 407 Electors of the Paris Third Estate, whose original task it had been to appoint the Parisian deputies to the Third Estate at Versailles, began to meet regularly at the Hôtel de Ville in the heart of the capital. These two bodies were to play distinctive, yet complementary, parts in the events of July. In the early days, however, it was the Palais Royal alone that gave a positive direction to the popular movement. Whereas the Hôtel de Ville contented itself with drafting paper schemes for the institution of a *milice bourgeoise,* or citizens' militia, the Palais Royal took effective measures, by public agitation and liberal expenditure, to win over the Gardes Françaises, the main body of troops stationed in Paris, from their loyalty to the Court. On 30 June, crowds directed from the Palais Royal forcibly released from the Abbaye prison eleven Guardsmen who had been jailed for refusing to fire on the people at Versailles on the night of 22–23 June; while on 10 July, eighty artillerymen, who had broken out of their barracks in the Hôtel des Invalides, were publicly fêted in the Palais Royal and the Champs Elysées.

Reacting to these developments, the Court Party attempted a new show-down: on 11 July Necker was sent into exile and replaced by the Baron de Breteuil. This proved to be the spark that touched off the insurrection in Paris. The news reached the capital at noon on the 12th. During the afternoon, Parisians flocked in their thousands to the Palais Royal, where orators—the young journalist Camille Desmoulins among them—gave the call to arms. Groups of marchers quickly formed; the busts of Necker and the Duke of Orleans were paraded on the Boulevards; theatres were compelled to close as a sign of public mourning; in the Place Louis XV demonstrators clashed with cavalry commanded by the Prince de Lambesc, who had been ordered to clear the Tuileries gardens. Besenval, commander of the Paris garrison, withdrew to the Champ de Mars; the capital was in the hands of the people. Barricades were manned and the tocsin was sounded. Bands of insurgents joined those who had already two days earlier—on their own initiative or on that of the Palais Royal—begun to burn down the hated *barrières,* or internal customs posts, that ringed the city. While the Palais Royal probably had a direct hand in this operation—it was reported that two posts belonging to the Duke of Orleans were deliberately spared by the incendiaries—the common people of Paris had their own account to settle with an institution which levied a toll on all wines, meat, vegetables and firewood that entered the capital. During the night, too, armed civilians, Gardes Françaises and local poor broke into the monastery of St. Lazare on the northern fringe of the city, searched it for arms, released prisoners and removed fifty-two cartloads of corn and flour to the central grain market.

But the main feature of the night of 12–13 July was the search for arms; religious houses were visited and gunsmiths, armourers and harness-makers were raided all over the capital. A number of statements drawn up in support of their claims for compensation have come down to us. Thus, Marcel Arlot, master gunsmith of the Rue Grenéta in the parish of St. Leu, reported that his shop was broken into at 2 a.m. by a crowd headed by a journeyman armourer of the Rue Jean Robert; muskets, pistols, sabres and swords to the value of 24,000 *livres* (£2,000) were removed. A harness-maker of the Pont St. Michel reported the theft of belts and shoulder-straps to the value of 390 *livres;* while a sword-cutler of the parish of St. Séverin, on the Left Bank, complained that his shop had been invaded several times on 12 and 13 July and that a very considerable quantity of sabres, swords and unmounted blades had been forcibly removed by numerous persons who had refused to pay for them "on the pretext that they would serve for the defence of the capital"; he had suffered a loss of 6,684 *livres* (nearly £600). The total losses eventually submitted to the National Assembly by the Parisian gunsmiths amounted to more than 115,000 *livres* (over £9,000).

Of considerable interest, too, is the eye-witness account of the events of that night given by Jean Nicolas Pepin, a tallow chandler's labourer, who, as a subpoenaed witness in the St. Lazare affair, later told the story of how he was caught up in the milling throngs of civilians and French Guards that, all night long, surged through the streets, shouting slogans, ringing the tocsin and searching for arms. From his account it is doubly clear that, at this time, the guiding centre of the revolutionary movement lay in the Palais Royal to which, rather than to the Hôtel de Ville, the angry, bewildered masses looked for leadership and guidance.

On the morning of the 13th, however, the Electors made a firm bid to gain control of the situation. They formed a Permanent Committee to act as a provisional government of the city and determined to put a stop to the indiscriminate arming of the whole population. They had been alarmed by the burning of the *barrières* and the sacking of the monastery of St. Lazare. To them the bands of unemployed and homeless, who had played some part in these operations, were as great a menace as the Privileged Orders conspiring at Versailles. Accordingly, a regular citizens' militia was hastily mobilised for the dual purpose of defending the capital from the military threat without and the danger of "anarchy" within. Each of the 60 Electoral Districts was to contribute 200 (later 800) men. While each District drew up its own conditions of enrolment, in most cases property and residential qualifications were imposed that virtually debarred a large part of the wage-earning population; certainly all unemployed and vagrants were excluded. All "irregulars" were to be immediately disarmed. According to Dr. Rigby, an English observer, this process had already begun during the afternoon of the 13th; yet it is doubtful if it went far as long as the insurrection lasted. Crowds besieged the Hôtel de Ville, demanding arms and powder. Jacques de Flesselles, *prévôt des marchands* and acting head of the provisional city government, being anxious to limit the distribution of arms, made vague promises and sent parties off on fruitless expeditions to the Arsenal and the Carthusian monastery; this "treachery" was to cost him his life on the morrow. During the night, the insistence of half-armed crowds surging round the Hôtel de Ville compelled an Elector, the Abbé Lefebvre, to distribute eighty barrels of gun-powder that had been placed in his safe-keeping.

On the next morning, 14 July, the quest for arms and ammunition continued: a spectacular raid was made on the Hôtel des Invalides across the river. According to Salmour, the Saxon ambassador, who witnessed the affair,

7,000–8,000 citizens took part. The Governor, the Marquis de Sombreuil, was abandoned by his troops and forced to open his gates. He later reported the removal of more than 30,000 muskets, of which 12,000 at least were "in dangerous hands." Meanwhile, the cry had gone up, "To the Bastille!"

Royalist historians have scoffed at the picture of thousands of Parisians hurling themselves at the Bastille in order to release seven prisoners. Such criticism falls wide of its mark. The immediate aim was to find the powder which was known to have been sent there from the Arsenal. Other motives no doubt played a part. It was believed that the fortress was heavily manned; its guns, which that morning were trained on the Rue St. Antoine, could play havoc among the crowded tenements. In the night it had been rumoured that 30,000 Royalist troops had marched into the Faubourg St. Antoine and had begun to slaughter its citizens. Besides, though it had ceased to harbour more than a trickle of State prisoners, the Bastille was widely hated as a symbol of "ministerial despotism": the *cahiers de doléances* of the Paris Districts bear witness to this fact. Yet there was no intention of taking it by storm (such a notion seemed preposterous, anyway), least of all on the part of the Permanent Committee of Electors who directed operations, with fumbling uncertainty, from the Hôtel de Ville. They made their intentions clear from the start: to negotiate with de Launay, the Governor, for the surrender of the gunpowder in his keeping and for the withdrawal of the guns from his battlements. That this plan failed, and that the Bastille fell only after the threat of a frontal assault, was due to circumstances outside their control.

Numerous eyewitness accounts of the siege of the Bastille, or accounts purporting to be such, have come down to us. Fact and fiction are often richly blended in them. Among the most trustworthy, perhaps, are those left by the Electors themselves, both in the form of the official minutes of their Assembly and in that of individual memoirs. From these it appears that the first deputation sent to parley with de Launay arrived at the Bastille at 10 o'clock. Having received a friendly welcome and an invitation to dine, they did not emerge for some time. The dense crowds waiting outside, fearing a trap, now raised a shout for the surrender or capture of the fortress. To allay suspicions, a second delegation, sent by the neighbouring District of La Culture, urged the Governor to surrender. Its leader, Thuriot de la Rozière, brought back word to the Permanent Committee that the Governor, while refusing to surrender, had withdrawn his cannon and had promised not to fire unless attacked. Up to this point, the crowds surging in from the Rue St. Antoine had penetrated only into the outer of the two courtyards leading to the main drawbridge and gate of the Bastille. This outer courtyard was, as usual, unguarded; it was separated from the inner Cour du Gouvernement by a wall and a drawbridge which de Launay had, unaccountably, left raised but undefended. Half an hour after Thuriot's departure, two men climbed the wall from a neighbouring building and lowered the drawbridge. Believing a frontal attack to be imminent, de Launay gave the order to fire. In the affray that followed, the besiegers lost ninety-eight dead and seventy-three wounded; only one of the defenders was struck. Two further deputations, sent to the Bastille in the course of this affray, were fired on and failed to gain admittance.

The worthy Electors were now at their wits' end. Their policy of peaceful negotiations had proved a complete failure. Had it not been for the angry insistence of the bands of armed citizens who swarmed in the rooms of the Hôtel de Ville, in the Place de Grève outside and along all the approaches to the Bastille, calling for vengeance for blood spilt and suspected treachery, they would certainly have abandoned their efforts. Meanwhile, two detachments of Gardes Françaises, drawn up outside the Hôtel de Ville, responded to the summons of Hulin, a former noncommissioned officer, who marched them off to the Bastille with five cannon removed from the Invalides that morning. Joined at the fortress by a few hundred armed civilians, they fought their way under fire to the inner courtyard and trained their cannon on the main gate. This proved to be decisive. The Governor offered to surrender provided that the garrison were spared; but the angry crowds would not hear of conditions and the siege continued. At this point, de Launay seems to have lost his head and threatened to blow up the fortress. He was, however, dissuaded by his garrison and, in desperation, gave orders for the main drawbridge to be lowered. So the Bastille fell.

It is perhaps surprising that the angry and triumphant crowds, pouring through the open gates of the Bastille, did not exact a more complete and indiscriminate vengeance. They had lived through days of nervous tension, continuously subject to the fear of sudden attack and disaster; they had been betrayed, they believed, by some of their leaders; over 150 of their fellows had been killed and wounded. Of 110 members of the defending garrison, six were slaughtered; de Launay, though promised a safe-conduct to the Hôtel de Ville, was struck down on the way and his head severed with a butcher's knife. De Flesselles, who had aroused popular fury by his reluctance to distribute arms, met a similar fate as he followed his accusers from the Hôtel de Ville.

Meanwhile, the seven prisoners of the Bastille had been released from their cells. Among them, there were four persons charged with forging bills of exchange, locked up without trial since January 1787; and two lunatics, of whom one had been confined for the past forty years as a would-be regicide and the other had lost his reason before his transfer to the Bastille from Vincennes prison five years earlier. The seventh, the Comte de Solages, was a young rake who, in accordance with the custom of the times, had been committed by *lettre de cachet* at his father's request "pour cause de dissipation et de mauvaise conduite." In fact, while the arbitrary manner of their confinement—without formal charge or trial—was no great credit to the prevailing system of justice, as victims of tyranny the prisoners made a decidedly poor showing. And so, after the initial toasts and celebrations which the occasion demanded, little serious effort was made to dress them up in a heroic guise. The two lunatics, at least, enjoyed neither fame nor freedom for long: after a short interval, they were despatched to the Charenton asylum.

Among the many "legends" of the Bastille, there have been few as persistent as that which represents its captors as vagabonds, criminals, or a mercenary rabble hired in the wine-shops of the St. Antoine quarter. Yet not only is there is no evidence to support this view, but the available evidence directly refutes it. From lists of the accredited captors of the Bastille, the so-called *vainqueurs de la Bastille,* drawn up by the National Assembly, we know the occupations and addresses of the great majority of those—some 700–800 in number—who played a direct part in its surrender. Most of them, far from being vagrants or down-and-outs, were settled residents of the Faubourg St. Antoine and the adjoining parishes of St. Gervais and St. Paul; most, again, were members of the citizens' militia, from which such elements were rigorously excluded. Among them appear the names of some who were to distinguish themselves in the course of the Revolution—Jean Rossignol, goldsmith of the Faubourg St. Antoine and, later, general of the Republic; Antoine Joseph Santerre, wealthy brewer and commander-in-chief of the citizens' battalions that overthrew the monarchy in August 1792; Stanislas Maillard, who played a big part in the surrender of the Bastille and, a few months later, led the market women on their historic march to Versailles. But most of them were men of no particular distinction, drawn from the typical crafts and occupations of the Faubourg and adjacent Districts: joiners and cabinet-makers, locksmiths and cobblers—these alone accounting for more than a quarter of the civilian captors—shopkeepers, gauzemakers, sculptors, riverside workers and labourers. Among them small masters and independent craftsmen, rather than journeymen or wage-earners, predominate, thus faithfully reflecting the social structure of the Faubourg.

Yet, in a wider sense, we may agree with Michelet that the capture of the Bastille was not the affair of a few hundred citizens of the St. Antoine quarter alone, but of the people of Paris as a whole. It has been said that, on that day, between 180,000 and 300,000 Parisians were under arms; and, taking an even broader view, we should not ignore the part played by the great mass of Parisian petty craftsmen, tradesmen and wage-earners—in the Faubourg St. Antoine and elsewhere—whose revolutionary temper had been moulded over many months by the rise in living costs and, as the crisis deepened, by the growing conviction that the great hopes raised by the calling of the States General were being thwarted by an "aristocratic plot."

Of little importance in itself, the capture of the Bastille had far-reaching consequences, and the news of it echoed round the world. The National Assembly was saved and received Royal recognition. The Court Party began to disintegrate and the Comte d'Artois went into voluntary exile. In the capital, power passed firmly into the hands of the Committee of Electors, who set up a City Council with Bailly as mayor. On 17 July, the King himself made the journey to Paris, was received at the Hôtel de Ville by the victors and, in token of acquiescence in the turn of events, donned the red, white and blue cockade of the Revolution. As it turned out, the Revolution was far from completed, but a decisive step had been taken. To many—and not in France alone—it seemed the dawn of Liberty. In distant St. Petersburg, we are told, at the news of the fall of the Bastille, strangers embraced in the street and wept for joy.

A Tale of Two Characters:
A Study in Multiple Projection

Leonard Manheim

Dickens scholars have never been able to forgive *A Tale of Two Cities* its pop-ularity—its very special kind of popularity. *Pickwick Papers* has survived the adulation of the special Pickwick cult; *David Copperfield* has survived the sen-timental biography-hunting of the Dickensians; even *Great Expectations* may survive its selection as the Dickens work to be presented in "service courses" on the lower college level. But *A Tale of Two Cities* will never wholly live down the fact that it has received a kiss of death by its almost universal adoption as the Dickens work to be presented to secondary school students, usually dur-ing the tenth year of their formal education. Several factors have contributed to the persistence of the high-school syllabus-makers in prescribing the read-ing of *A Tale of Two Cities*. The first reason seems to be its compactness; it is not as long as most other Dickens works. In my own experience, it has been preferred even when *David Copperfield* was permitted as an alternative, purely because *David Copperfield* was so much longer. A second reason, which stems from the era when all novels were suspect, is the fact that *A Tale of Two Cities* is an historical novel, and the curse was considered removed from the "novel" because of the "history." But the factor which probably loomed largest in the minds of the syllabus-makers was the "purity" of *A Tale of Two Cities*. It is wholly without the taint of immorality; it seems to be practically free of sexu-ality. (Can the account of the rape of Madame Defarge's sister in Doctor Manette's secret narrative be called sexuality? It is easy enough to pass over it—it is so hazily referred to; and in any event, it is a story of an occurrence in a benighted foreign country and hence a horrible example of "foreign" moral-ity.) There is no Little Em'ly, no Martha Endell. There is no Hetty Sorrel; in-deed *Adam Bede* was never permitted to sully the adolescent mind. Silas Marner's Eppie had the advantage of having it both ways since she was legally legitimate but, for the purposes of the story, a bastard; the legal legit-imacy was enough to satisfy the academic censor. Let it not be thought that I exaggerate; I speak from experience, and although there is no time or place here for a complete documentation of my conclusions, I submit that the crite-

Reprinted from *Dickens Studies Annual* 1 (1970): 225–37 by permission. Copyright © AMS Press, Inc.

rion for high school reading is usually—or at any rate used to be—one of superficial absence of any "immoral" element. Yet it is ironically noteworthy that *A Tale of Two Cities,* on a less superficial level, is the product of a great sexual crisis in the author's life, an upheaval in his psychosexual pattern which has been but dimly comprehended. Perhaps it would be as well to recount once again the facts as they have been clarified by recent scholarship.

On 10 February, in 1851, Dickens wrote to Wills, his long-suffering editorial assistant on *Household Words,* asking Wills to play the part of a servant in the comedy *Not So Bad as We Seem,* a typical nineteenth-century play written by the prolific Bulwer Lytton for production by Dickens' semi-permanent company of amateur actors. Dickens hastened to assure Wills that he would be in good company—among talented literary amateur actors. He playfully assumed the character of Sairey Gamp:

> "Mrs. Harris," I says to her, "be not alarmed; not reg'lar play-actors, hammertoors."
> "Thank 'Evens," says Mrs. Harris, and bustiges into a flood of tears![1]

The over-burdened Wills found it impossible to add participation in his principal's theatrical ventures to his other duties, and he politely declined the offer. A little while later, Dickens wrote to his friend Augustus Egg, scenic designer of many of the productions, asking him if he could induce Wilkie Collins to accept the role. Collins did accept and thus began the friendship with Dickens which was to last until the latter's death. There was nearly fifteen years' difference in age between the two; their temperaments were fundamentally dissimilar; yet the influence of Collins on every phase of the latter years of Dickens' life and work is most marked, and there was ample indication that he tended, as time went on, to usurp the confidential position formerly held exclusively by John Forster, to the no small annoyance of that worthy gentleman.

In Collins, Dickens found an admirable traveling companion, one who introduced him to phases of life at home and abroad with which he had formerly been familiar by hearsay only, one who was reasonably free from Victorian prejudices so dear to the heart of John Forster. In Collins he found an equally enthusiastic devotee of the theatre, a competent and thorough deviser of complex plots (frequently of a most melodramatic character). It was Collins who put together the melodrama *The Lighthouse,* with a highly emotional leading role which Dickens delighted to play. It was he who was entrusted with the task of dramatizing the very worst of the Dickens Christmas numbers, *No Thoroughfare,* for professional production; and it was he who concocted *The Frozen Deep,* that queer melodrama in which Dickens played his last performance on the amateur stage. This play opened at Tavistock House on the twentieth birthday of Dickens' oldest son. It was a most elaborate affair, with one set designed to represent a scene near the North Pole, "where the slightest and greatest things the eye beheld were equally taken from the books of the polar voyagers." It was repeated several times, one outstanding series of performances being given in Manchester. Dickens writes of it in his preface to *A Tale of Two Cities:*

> When I was acting, with my children and friends, in Mr. Wilkie Collins's drama of "The Frozen Deep," I first conceived the main idea of this story. A strong desire was upon me then, to embody it in my own person; and I traced out in my fancy, the state of mind of which it would necessitate the presentation to an observant spectator, with particular care and interest.
>
> As the idea became familiar to me, it gradually shaped itself into its present form. Throughout its execution, it has had complete possession of me; I have so far verified what is done and suffered in these pages, as that I have certainly done and suffered it all myself.[2]

Much of the idea of *The Frozen Deep* seems to have originated with Dickens himself rather than with Collins. It was Dickens who inserted the "comedy relief," Dickens who wrote the verse prologue which Forster spoke from behind the curtain before the opening, closing with these words:

> But, that the secrets of the vast Profound
> Within us, an exploring hand may sound,
> Testing the region of the ice-bound soul,
> Seeking the passage at its northern pole,
> Soft'ning the horrors of its wintry sleep,
> Melting the surface of that "Frozen Deep."[3]

The plot of the play whose hero Dickens so greatly longed to "embody in his own person" is worthy of being examined closely, when we consider how much it meant to him during his composition of *A Tale of Two Cities* and how clearly it constituted a turning point in his life.

The first act makes us acquainted with four young ladies living in Devon, each of whom has a lover serving with a Polar expedition. Clara Burnham not only has her betrothed out in the icy regions, but the rejected lover who was sworn to kill him wherever and whenever they meet, though he does not even know the name of his rival. Clara, haunted by the fear that some mysterious influence may reveal them to each other, tells her story to Lucy Crayford. As she does so, a crimson sunset dies away to grey and Nurse Esther goes about the house murmuring of scenes that come to her from "the land o' ice and snaw." She stands, as night falls, by the misty blue of the window, describing to the young ladies her bloody vision from the Northern seas. Lucy Crayford shudders and calls for lights: Clara Burnham swoons.

The second act is set in the arctic regions. The stranded men are in a hut deciding who is to go and seek relief. Frank Aldersley is chosen by lot, and when somebody else falls out, Richard Wardour has to accompany him. Just before they start Wardour discovers that Aldersley is his hated rival.

The third act takes place in a cavern in Newfoundland. The girls, smartly dressed in crinolines, their Scotch nurse, and some members of the expedition are present, but neither Wardour nor Aldersley. Presently a ragged maniac rushes in and is given food and drink. He has escaped from an ice-floe but is not too demented to recognise and be recognised by Clara Burnham, who suspects him of having murdered her Frank. As soon as he understands this he goes off, returning a few minutes later with Aldersley in his arms to lay at Clara's feet. "Often," he gasps, "in supporting Aldersley through snow-drifts and on ice-floes have I been tempted to leave him sleeping!" He has not done so and is now exhausted to death.[4]

Dickens played Wardour; and Collins, Aldersley. Purposely for the "part," each of them grew a substantial beard which he kept in later life. During the early private showings and at the special performance for the Queen, the women's roles were played by lady amateurs. However, when it was decided to repeat the play at Manchester for the benefit of the late Douglass Jerrold's family, it became apparent that the size of the house (it held three thousand spectators at one performance) would require the engagement of professionals for the women's roles. It was on the recommendation of a friendly theatrical manager that Mrs. Ternan and her two daughters, Maria and Ellen, were engaged for the production. Mrs. Ternan played the Scottish nurse; Maria Ternan played the leading role of Clara Burnham; and Ellen played one of the other girls, probably Lucy. Now it must become at once apparent that the tale which pictures Ellen in tears in the wings of the theatre, in agony over the scanty costume she was to wear in *The Frozen Deep* (!) must be apocryphal. As a matter of fact, Dickens had known Ellen at least since the spring of 1857 when he had met her, really in tears in her dressing room because she was to play the role of Hippomenes in Talfourd's *Atalanta,* a part in which she might well be alarmed at having "to show too much leg." However, it was during the brief period of rehearsals at Tavistock House, with Maria and Ellen rushing in and out of his study, Ellen perching on the arm of his chair and turning soulful eyes upon him as he instructed her in the interpretation of her role, that young love began to spring anew in the breast of the forty-five-year-old author. Collins was enthralled by Dickens' brilliance during the Manchester performances. "Dickens," he wrote, "surpassed himself. He literally electrified the audience."[5] And well he might, for the clock had turned back. He was once again the eighteen-year-old who was going to make his fortune as an actor in Covent Garden.

Aghast for a moment after the first emotional shock and passed, Dickens tried to run away from himself again, this time with Collins. The trip is the one described in their joint literary effort known as *The Lazy Tour of Two Idle Apprentices.* When it was over, the problem was solved and Dickens had cast Victorian morality to the winds and was an ardent suitor for the favors of the young lady. A word as to the choice between the two sisters. It was Maria whose acting ability had most impressed the critical director, and he wrote of her performance in the glowing emotional orgy of a letter to Miss Burdett-Coutts. Yet it was to Ellen that he was sexually attracted. After all, there are limits to the extensions of a real-life *Maria*. Two of them (Maria Beadnell and Mary Hogarth) had passed into agonizing oblivion. The Mary-figure, the virgin-mother, was still the dominant image, but a little disguise, a little displacement of the emotional tone was clearly needed—and the choice fell upon the sister-image, Ellen. After all, the Superego in the irrational Unconscious might be lulled into a sense of security by the pretense that it was to *Mary's sister* that he was still being "true"!

It was in such troubled days that *A Tale of Two Cities* was conceived and, for the most part, written. It was the work used to launch the new publication *All the Year Round,* which succeeded *Household Words* after Dickens' break with his former publishers, occasioned by his frantic desire to suppress the Ternan scandal. The whole work is impregnated with the spirit of the theatre. Its structure is dramatic and Dickens is reported to have sent proof sheets to Henri Regnier with a view toward immediate dramatization for the French theatre. The work has a complicated plot-structure which yet stands up better under analysis than any novel since *Barnaby Rudge,* with which it at once compels comparison. Like that former work, it is markedly deficient in humor. There seems to be no room in it for both the old comedy and also the new Collins-inspired melodrama. There is not even as much comedy in the new work as in *Barnaby Rudge,* the former novel of revolutionary days, for Miss Pross and Jerry Cruncher cannot bear even so much of the burden as was formerly shared by Miss Miggs and Sim Tappertit.

The compulsive quality of the writing of *A Tale of Two Cities* is revealed in the preface quoted as moment ago. Whenever we find an author stressing such compulsions, we can safely conclude that we are dealing with "repressed" inspiration from unconscious sources. The most striking effect upon the novel of the emotionally disturbed period which produced it lies in the Dr. Jekyll-Mr. Hyde aspect of its leading male character. The word "character" is used in the singular intentionally, for in *A Tale of Two Cities* Dickens developed even more fully than was usual for him the tendency to embody his own ideal of himself, his own Fantasy-Hero in two or more characters (*multiple projection*). Charles Darnay and Sydney Carton are two plainly delineated faces of the same coin. Their names are extensions of a familiar pattern. The fortunate-unfortunate French nobleman bears his author's Christian name with a surname which uses the first initial of *Dickens* to bear out the fantasy of noble birth in disguise, since Charles is said to have assumed the name Darnay upon dropping the hated appellation Evrémonde, adapting his new surname from his mother's noble name of D'Aulnay, eliding the aristocratic *de* in deference to British taste. In the name Sydney Carton the trend is more hidden; yet it too is a simple cipher, easily susceptible of solution—as it is meant to be. The *Charles* element is transferred to the *Car-* syllable of the last name; in the first syllable of *Sydney,* we have the same softening of *Dick-* which may be noticed in the name *Jarndyce* (pronounced Jahn-diss) in *Bleak House,* here reversed (another reversal) to form *Syd.* The implication is apparent. Both Carton and Darnay are Dickens (not literally, of course, but in fantasy); the point is further stressed by the fortuitous fact that they look alike.

Consider this last point for a moment. Carton, during Darnay's English trial for treason, points out the resemblance between himself and Darnay to his senior counsel, Mr. Stryver, who uses it (so it is said) to discredit the testimony of a witness, a witness who had testified that he had seen the defendant Darnay descend by stealth from the Dover mail in order to spy upon a garrison and dockyard, admitting that he had never seen the accused upon any other occasion.

"You say again you are quite sure that it *was* the prisoner?" The witness was quite sure.

"Did you ever see anybody very like the prisoner?" Not so like (the witness said), as that he could be mistaken.

"Look well upon that gentleman, my learned friend there," pointing to him who had tossed the paper over, "and then look well upon the prisoner. How say you? Are they very like each other?"

Allowing for my learned friend's appearance being careless and slovenly, if not debauched, they were sufficiently like each other to surprise, not only the witness, but everybody present, when they were thus brought into comparison. My Lord being prayed to bid my learned friend lay aside his wig, and giving no very gracious consent, the likeness became much more remarkable. My Lord inquired of Mr. Stryver, (the prisoner's counsel), whether they were next to try Mr. Carton (name of my learned friend) for treason? But Mr. Stryver replied to my Lord, no; but he would ask the witness to tell him whether what happened once, might happen twice; whether he would have been so confident, having seen it; and more. The upshot of which was, to smash this witness like a crockery vessel, and shiver his part of the case to useless lumber. (II, iii)

Now any competent trial lawyer will recognize that this is very bad cross-examination. The fact that Mr. Darnay resembled Mr. Carton does not really impeach the credibility of the witness' testimony, unless, as the presiding judge suggested, it had been counsel's intention to show that Mr. Carton was also in the neighborhood at the time. An identification by a witness may be impeached far better by his inability to pick the prisoner out of a group of people (a "line-up," for example) who do *not* in any way resemble one another. Yet for Dickens it fits into a set pattern. Darnay is first accused of treason in England (treachery, betrayal of his country, let it be remembered—parallel in fantasy-life to a man's "betrayal" of his wife). He is saved by his *alter ego,* Carton. Seventeen years later the accusation of betrayal is renewed before another, "foreign" tribunal—foreign both geographically and in the standard of loyalty which it imposes. Now Carton is impotent. He cannot plead in the new court. He cannot answer the fatal and misguided denunciation of the destructive father-image, the Law. But he can assume the place of his double and die in his stead, making a propitiatory sacrifice of himself by which he clears and saves the innocent person of the favored hero. Never was there a more felicitously contrived scapegoat pattern.

All of the virtue which would make the favored lover worthy of his virgin is embodied in Jekyll-Darnay. All of the vice— gloomy, Byronic, objectively unmotivated and unexplained—is concentrated in Hyde-Carton (who, of course, never gets the girl), for whom it is purged away by his "full, perfect, and sufficient sacrifice," not for the sins of the whole world, to be sure, but for the sinful love of one Charles Dickens for one Ellen Ternan. Even the self-satisfying sense of resurrection, an "undying" after death, is accomplished by the final picture of Sydney's mind just before the guillotine falls, envisaging the rosy future which is to follow for all concerned, even his own rebirth in his child-namesake. How can Ellen hesitate now? Her middle-aged lover is not only the most fascinating of men; he is also (by a vicarious propitiatory sacrifice) the most guiltless, and she will share that pristine state of innocence with him forever!

Lucie is basically only one more in the line of Dickensian virgin-heroines whom the critic Edwin Pugh felicitously called "femininities."[6] Yet, as Professor Edgar Johnson clearly saw, there was a subtle distinction.

> Lucie . . . is given hardly any individual traits at all, although her appearance, as Dickens describes it, is like that of Ellen, "a short, slight, pretty figure, a quantity of golden hair, a pair of blue eyes," and it may be that her one unique physical characteristic was drawn from Ellen too: "a forehead with a singular capacity (remembering how young and smooth it was), of lifting and knitting itself into an expression that was not quite one of perplexity, or wonder, or alarm, though it included all the four expressions." . . . The fact that Lucie and Dr. Manette at the time of his release from the Bastille are of almost the same age as Ellen and Dickens does not mean that the Doctor's feeling for his daughter is the emotion Dickens felt for the pretty, blue-eyed actress, although the two merge perhaps in his fervent declaration [in his letter protesting the scandal, a letter which he "never meant to be published"] that he knows Ellen to be as "innocent and pure, and as good as my own dear daughter."[7]

But Lucie fails to fit into the pattern of the unattainable dream-virgin of the earlier novels in at least one other respect. Most of Dickens' earlier heroine-ideals do not marry until the last-chapter summation of the "lived-happily-ever-after" pattern. Lucie is married, happily married, through much of the book. She maintains a household for her husband and her father, and she finds room for compassion, if not love, for the erring Carton. What is more, she has children, two of them. Yet she seems never to grow older. She was seventeen in 1775; she is, to all intents and purposes, seventeen in 1792. In the interim she has allegedly given birth to two Dickens-ideal infants, two of the most sickening little poppets we could possibly expect from one who, despite his experience as the father of ten children, still sought desperately to re-create infancy and childhood in an image which would affirm his own concept of unworldly innocence. Let the reader take a firm grip on himself and read the dying words of the little son of Charles and Lucie Darnay, who died in early childhood for no other reason, it must seem, than to give the author another opportunity to wallow in bathos.

> "Dear papa and mamma, I am very sorry to leave you both, and to leave my pretty sister; but I am called, and I must go!"
> "Poor Carton! Kiss him for me!" (II, xxi)

Poor Carton, indeed! Poor Dickens! Little Lucie is not much better, for in Paris, after her father's condemnation, when her mother is mercifully unconscious and unaware of Carton's presence, she cries out in sweet childish innocence to friend Sydney:

> "Oh, Carton, Carton, dear Carton! . . Now that you have come, I think you will do something to help mamma, something to save papa! Oh, look at her, dear Carton! Can you, of all the people who love her bear to see her so?" (III, xi)

Out of the mouths of babes! At this point there is obviously nothing for Sydney to do but head straight for the nearest guillotine.

But Sydney is not to be left wholly without his own dream girl. Just as the purified Darnay is permitted to live out his life with the "attained" (and untainted) Lucie, so the dying Carton is accompanied to his execution by the virgin-victim, the innocent seamstress whom he solaces and strengthens until the final moments of their love-death, although her first glance had revealed that he was not the man Darnay whom she had previously admired.

Since the pattern of attainability is characteristic of the primary "virgin" in this novel, the figure of the *decayed virgin*, the older freak and enemy, is markedly absent from it. A few novels back, Dickens had had such characters in the immortal Sairey Gamp (*Martin Chuzzlewit*) and Mrs. Pipchin (*Dombey and Son*); he was to have the most horrifying of them all in his very next novel (*Great Expectations*) in the person of Miss Havisham. Here Miss Pross, although she has many of the elements of the "freak" in the best Dickensian tradition, is all benevolence, with her red-headed queerness overshadowed by her devoted love and affectionate care of the virgin-queen to whom she is a substitute mother, with no flaw except her unconquerable belief in the virtue and nobility of her erring brother Solomon. Just as she, the benevolent mother-protectress, is herself merely an aged virgin, so her counterpart and rival is the childless wife (also a devoted, albeit vindictive, sister), Thérèse Defarge. The word *rival* is used advisedly, for while there is no sign of overt rivalry between the two during nine-tenths of the novel, Dickens goes out of his way to bring them face to face at the end. He strains all of his plot structure to bring Mme. Defarge to the Manette dwelling on the day of the execution to have Miss Pross left there alone to face her. Then a melodramatic physical encounter ensues between the two women, neither of whom can, in any sense of the words, speak the other's language. Lucie's bad angel falls dead (accidentally, of course, by her own hand), but the good angel is not unscathed, and if, in her later life, her "queerness" is augmented by the ear-trumpet which she will no doubt use, yet all will know that she came by this crowning, though no doubt humorous affliction in a good cause.

Although the category of mother-figure is limited, there is no lack of father-counterparts, for the law-as-father has become blended with the fear of condemnation by society, which thereby also becomes a symbolic father-figure. Society and its moral sanctions constitute the only fly in the ointment of adolescent happiness in a sinful love. We have noted that, as a propitiatory gesture, Charles's wicked father-enemy is not his father (as he well might have been) but his thoroughly aristocratic twin-uncle, who, being French, is more villainous than any British father-enemy might have been. Mr. Stryver, in his vampirish relationship with Carton, is another figure of the worthless "father" who sucks the blood of his talented "son." And since Dickens almost always maintains a balance between evil and virtuous figures in all categories, we have, on the benevolent side, Mr. Lorry, another unmarried "father," the only living figure in the gallery of scarecrows who inhabit Tellson's Bank. Midway between the two classes is the hagridden Ernest Defarge, whose every attempt at benevolence is thwarted by his vengeful wife and her abettors, the allegorically named *Vengeance* and the members of the society of Jacques. This last-named group produces one brilliantly sketched psychopath, the sadistic, finger-chewing Jacques Three.

The one remaining father-figure is the most interesting, complex, and well-developed character in the whole novel, Dr. Manette. Since he could not have been much more than twenty-five years old when he was torn from his newly-wedded English wife to be imprisoned in the Bastille for nearly eighteen years, he must have been less than forty-five when we first met him in Defarge's garret. And Dickens, let it be remembered, was forty-five when he wrote of him. Here is his portrait:

> A broad ray of light fell into the garret, and showed the workman, with an unfinished shoe upon his lap, pausing in his labour. His few common tools and various scraps of leather were at his feet and on his bench. He had a white beard, raggedly cut, but not very long, a hollow face, and exceedingly bright eyes. The hollowness and thinness of his face would have caused them to look

large, under his yet dark eyebrows and his confused white hair, though they had been really otherwise; but they were naturally large, and looked unnaturally so. His yellow rags of shirt lay open at the throat, and showed his body to be withered and worn. (I, vi)

Of course the appearance of great age in a middle-age man is rationally explained by the suffering entailed by his long, unjust imprisonment. Yet, nearly eighteen years later (the repetition of the number is meaningful), when he has become the unwitting agent of his son-in-law's destruction and has been unable to use his special influence to procure Charles' release, he is pictured as a decayed mass of senility.

"Who goes here? Whom have we within? Papers!"
The papers are handed out and read.
"Alexandre Manette. Physician. French. Which is he?"
This is he; this helpless, inarticulately murmuring, wandering old man pointed out.
"Apparently the Citizen-Doctor is not in his right mind? The Revolution-fever will have been too much for him?"
Greatly too much for him. (III, xiii)

Carton envisions his complete recovery, but we have some difficulty in believing it.

In the interim, however, he is pictured as a stalwart, middle-aged medical practitioner. His sufferings have caused a period of amnesia, with occasional flashes of painful recollection, as in the scene in which he hears of the discovery of a stone marked D I G in a cell in the Tower of London. We never know, by the way, whether his recollection at this moment is complete and whether he has, even furtively, any recall of the existence of the document of denunciation found by M. Defarge. The aspects of conscious and repressed memory are here handled with great skill by Dickens. Generally, his amnesia is reciprocal; he cannot recall his normal life during the period of relapse, or vice versa, especially when his relapses are triggered by events and disclosures which bring up memories of his old wrongs. His reversion to shoemaking for a short time after Charles proposes marriage to Lucie and again for a longer time following Lucie's marriage and Charles's final revelation of his long-suspected identity foreshadow the great disclosure which is to make him the unwitting aggressor against the happiness of his loving and beloved daughter.

When we consider Dr. Manette's conduct, however, we find that, whether Dickens consciously intended it to be or not, the doctor of Beauvais is a good psychiatrist, at least in the handling of his own illness. His shoemaking is superficially pictured as a symptom of mental regression and decay, but in its inception it must have been a sign of rebellion against madness rather than a symptom thereof. He relates that he begged for permission to make shoes as a means of diverting his mind from its unendurable suffering.

Shoemaking, truly an example of vocational therapy, was the only contact with reality that his distracted mind, otherwise cut off from reality, possessed. It was, therefore, a means of bringing about his recovery. Lucie fears the shoe-making, but she realizes that her loving presence, coupled with the availabil-ity, if needed, of the vocational contact with reality, will serve to draw him back to normal adjustment. It would seem, then, that the act of Mr. Lorry and Miss Pross, carried on furtively and guiltily, of destroying his shoemaker's bench and tools after his spontaneous recovery from the attack following Lu-cie's wedding, was a great error, an error against which the doctor, giving an opinion in the anonymous presentation of his own case by Mr. Lorry, strongly advises. For when he once again falls into a state of amnesia and confusion, af-ter the realization of the damage he has done to Charles and his impotence to remedy that damage, he calls for his bench and tools, but they are no longer to be had, and he huddles in a corner of the coach leaving Paris, a pitiful pic-ture of mental decay from which we can see no hope of recovery despite the optimistic vision of Carton's last moments.

The basic aim of this paper has been, of course, psychological interpreta-tion; but the psychological critic has sometimes been accused of neglecting the critical function of evaluation, and possibly a few concluding words might be added on that score.

In a lecture on criticism given at Harvard in 1947, E. M. Forster distin-guished beautifully between the function and method of creation and the function and method of criticism.

> What about the creative state? In it a man is taken out of himself. He lets down, as it were, a bucket into the unconscious and draws up something which is normally beyond his reach. He mixes this thing with his normal experience and out of the mixture he makes a work of art. . . . After this glance at the cre-ative state, let us look at the critical. The critical state has many merits, and employs some of the highest and subtlest faculties of man. But it is grotesquely remote from the state responsible for the works it affects to expound. It does not let buckets down into the unconscious. It does not conceive in sleep or know what it has said after it has said it. Think before you speak, is criticism's motto; speak before you think is creation's. Not is criticism disconcerted by people arriving from Porlock; in fact it sometimes comes from Porlock itself.[8]

What Mr. Forster has set forth can best be understood in the light of the road which has been taken by psychological, particularly psychoanalytic, criticism in the more than twenty years which have elapsed since the delivery of that lecture in 1947. The psychoanalytic critic of today would like to think that he comes from Xanadu rather than Porlock. He cannot claim that he consis-tently writes before he thinks, but his thinking is to some extent based on material which the bucket lowered into the depths has brought up for him.

What can he say about the permanent literary value of the work which he is discussing? He cannot of course undertake to give any absolute final judgment; it will hardly be suitable for him to do what so many academic critics do, that is, to report the state of critical opinion in the "in-group" that usually passes critical judgment in academic circles. I have suggested elsewhere that the function of the psychoanalytic critic in evaluation is to prognosticate rather than to judge. I can do no better than to quote here my preferred authority, Norman Holland:

> Saying a literary work is "good," then, from the point of view of our model, is predicting that it will pass the test of time; that it "can please many and please long"; that it is a widely satisfying form of play; or, more formally, that it embodies a fantasy with a power to disturb many readers over a long period of time and, built in, a defensive maneuver that will enable those readers to master the poem's disturbance.[9]

A Tale of Two Cities does, it seems to me, give every indication, even apart from its past history, that it "can please many and please long." Its use of the dynamic scapegoat pattern with the employment of the pattern of multiple projection, which it has been my aim to point out in this essay, does indeed embody a fantasy, a fantasy which was disturbing to Dickens and is still undoubtedly disturbing to many readers, and has used that device of multiple projection as the defensive maneuver that enables readers to master that disturbance. In that sense, there seems to be little doubt about the continuance of the perennial popularity of this often maligned but still frequently read novel of Dickens' later period.

But all of that is really by the way. Criticism of the kind which I have attempted is designed to furnish information rather than critical judgment, even of a prognostic nature; it is the kind of criticism which was described by Arthur Symons in his introduction to the *Biographia Literaria* of Coleridge:

> The aim of criticism is to distinguish what is essential in the work of a writer. It is the delight of the critic to praise; but praise is scarcely part of his duty. . . . What we ask of him is that he should find out for us more than we can find out for ourselves.

Notes

1. See Laurance Hutton, ed., *The Dickens-Collins Letters* (New York 1892), p. 6.
2. Preface to the First Edition (November 1859), reproduced in Walter Allen's Perennial Classic Edition of *A Tale of Two Cities* (New York, 1965), p. xvi. His text is taken from the Charles Dickens Edition of 1868–70.
3. Quoted in Dame Una Pope-Henneary, *Charles Dickens* (London, 1945), pp. 361–62.
4. Ibid., pp. 362–63.
5. *Dickens-Collins* Letters, pp. 78–80 (2 August 1857).
6. *The Charles Dickens Originals* (London, 1925), p. 68.

7.   *Charles Dickens: His Tragedy and Triumph* (New York, 1952), II, 973.

8.   V. S. Pritchett, article on E. M. Forster, *New York Times Book Review,* 29 December 1968, VII, p. 1.

9.   Norman N. Holland, *The Dynamics of Literary Response* (New York, 1968), p. 203: originally published in *Literature and Psychology,* XIV, No. 2 (1964). 48–55.

Charles Dickens: *A Tale of Two Cities* (1859)

NICHOLAS RANCE

For a period so near to us as that of the great French Revolution of seventeen hundred and eighty-nine—upon which a few octogenarians can even now, as it were, lay their hand—it is surprising what a dim veil of mystery, horror, and romance seems to overhang the most awful convulsion of modern times. While barely passing away, it had of a sudden risen to those awful and majestic dimensions which it takes less imposing events centuries to acquire, and towered over those within its shadow as an awful pyramid of fire, blinding those who look. It requires no lying by, or waiting on, posterity for its proper comprehension. It may be read by its own light, and by those who run; and is as about intelligible at this hour as it is ever likely to be. It is felt instinctively: and those whose sense is slow, may have it quickened by Mr Carlyle's flaming torch—flaring terribly through the night. He might have been looking on in the crowd during that wild night march to Versailles, or standing at the inn door in the little French posting town, as the sun went down, waiting wearily for the heavy berline to come up. Marvellous lurid torch that of his. Pen dipped in red and fire, glowing like phosphoric writing. His history of the French Revolution, the most extraordinary book, to our thinking, in its wonderful force, picturesqueness, and condensation, ever written by mere man. There is other subsidiary light, too, for such as look back—light from tens of thousands of pamphlets, broadsides, handbills—all honest, racy of the time, writ by furious hearts, by hands trembling with frensy and excitement—hands streaked with blood and dust of the guillotine: read by mad wolfish eyes at street corners on the step of the scaffold by lamplight. Hawked about, too, by hoarse-mouthed men and women, to such horrible tune as *Le Pere Duchesne est terriblement enragé aujourd'hur.* An awful, repulsive cloud, darkening the air for such as look back at it. Vast shower of ribaldry, insane songs, diatribe, declamation—all shot up from that glowing crater. An inexhaustible study!

The long quotation is from a *Household Words* article. "The Eve of Revolution," which appeared in June 1858. Dickens was a selective editor, and it may be assumed that the attitudes expressed in the article, one of a series on the French Revolution in *Household Words* in the late 1850s, coincided with his own view. Those who run may read the Revolution—or the slow may read it in Mr. Carlyle's book. Dickens felt that to challenge Carlyle's evaluation

Reprinted by premission of Barnes and Noble Books.

would be less than modest: "It has been one of my hopes to add something to the popular and picturesque means of understanding that terrible time, though no one can hope to add anything to the philosophy of Mr. Carlyle's wonderful book." And yet, according to *Household Words,* the Revolution remained "an inexhaustible study." In England, despite John Wilson Croker's research, the awful dimensions of the Revolution discouraged scholarly investigation. Carlyle, in 1837, remarked of his countrymen's revolutionary studies that "he who wishes to know how a solid *Custos rotulorum,* speculating over his port after dinner, interprets the phenomena of contemporary universal history, may look in these books: he who does not wish that, need not look"; and Carlyle himself never found time to visit Paris. Still, his version of the Revolution was sufficient unto the age. To look minutely into the phenomenon still haunting Europe was to go blind in the awful pyramid of fire.

Written in the years 1857–59. *A Tale of Two Cities* was as much a tract for the times as Carlyle's history, published twenty years before. The revolutions of 1848, and subsequent events, particularly in France, aroused insatiable interest in the circumstances of the first French Revolution. G. H. Lewes seized the opportunity to publish in 1849 a popular biography of Robespierre, since the February revolution had once more brought his "name and doctrines into alarming prominence." In September 1851, the historian Croker described revolution as

> the one great subject that now occupies and agitates throughout Europe—but especially in France and England—the pens of all who write—the passions of all who feel, and the earnest and anxious thoughts of all who concern themselves about either the political or social systems under which we live or *are to live.* To advocate or to deprecate—to forward or to retard—to applaud for imitation or to expose *in terrorem* the progress of Revolution—such, wherever and to whatever extent a political press exists, is now its almost exclusive occupation.

The Revolution was painfully contemporary history for Dickens: "I have so far verified what is done and suffered in these pages, as that I have certainly done and suffered it all myself." Carlyle's work, and that of the French historian Michelet, were also composed in emotional turmoil. To Carlyle, the history was "a wild savage book, itself a kind of French Revolution," while Michelet interrupted his labours to inform a correspondent,

> I am accomplishing here the extremely tough task of reliving, reconstituting and suffering the Revolution. I have just gone through *September* and all the terrors of death; massacred at the Abbaye, I am on the way to the revolutionary tribunal, that is to say, to the guillotine.

Still, the received version of the Revolution—that "awful, repulsive cloud," detached from the world—allowed English historians and historical novelists an escape from suffering. On the one hand, the Revolution was vital prehistory, and Dickens must write a novel warning his generation not to provoke the English sansculottes. On the other, it was an historical monstrosity, incapable of breeding. *A Tale of Two Cities* wavers between the two positions and gradually settles for the more comfortable. In April 1855, Dickens had written:

> I believe the discontent to be so much the worse for smouldering instead of blazing openly, that it is extremely like the general mind of France before the breaking out of the first Revolution, and is in danger of being turned by any one of a thousand accidents . . . into such a devil of a conflagration as never has been beheld since.

In 1857, he thought "the political signs of the times to be just about as bad as the spirit of the people will admit of their being," and expected the next dose of cholera to make "such a shake in this country as never was seen on Earth since Samson pulled the temple down upon his head." Dickens' subject was all too relevant to the age, and could not be treated as an "inexhaustible study." Revolutionary militancy, once described, is abstracted from its antecedents: England has nothing to learn from a freakish occurrence, and the novel's admonitory thesis is nullified. The opening pages argue not only that late eighteenth-century England was in many ways very like pre-revolutionary France, but also that England has not changed much since. On the final page, the prophetic Sydney Carton sees France "making expiation for itself," and the Manettes "peaceful, useful, prosperous and happy" in England.

Dickens takes refuge in the dogma of national characteristics. The English need not worry about revolutions in France because the French are the sort of people who are always having revolutions. A main reason for the warmth with which Tocqueville's *L'Ancien Régime et la Révolution* was greeted in England in 1856 was that he made such evasion respectable. Tocqueville's book was influenced by the experience of the June Days of 1848. The heroic People of Michelet's *Histoire de la Révolution Française* (1847) had materialised as the turbulent proletariats of the great cities of Europe. Tocqueville had seen the first essay at social revolution repressed with a savagery that made the Paris Terror seem a mild affair, and Louis Bonaparte elevated to the presidency on a tide of popular enthusiasm in the plebiscite of December 1848. While Tocqueville did insist that the march of democracy could not be stopped, and that the Revolution was still operative, its continuity, stressed in the title, with the past of the Ancien Régime was strangely qualified:

> but for the antecedent circumstances described in this book, the French would never have embarked on it; yet we must recognise that although their effect was cumulative and overwhelming, they would not have sufficed to lead to such a drastic revolution elsewhere than in France.

The conceding of significance to national character gratified reviewers eager to take the concession as the book's moral, and the *Westminster* blithely concluded "with the author, that no people but the French could have made such a Revolution, so sudden, so violent, so full of contradictions." *Household Words* had not waited for Tocqueville to justify English complacency, and the article "Liberty, Equality, Fraternity, and Musketry" of 1851 relates to the final escape from revolutionary France in *A Tale of Two Cities*. The author crosses the channel on a sight-seeing tour, and is glad to return in one piece.

> As I saw the last cocked hat of the last gendarme disappear with the receding pier at Havre, a pleasant vision of the blue-coats, oilskin hats, and lettered collars of the land I was going to, swam before my eyes; and, I must say that, descending the companion-ladder, I thanked Heaven I was an Englishman.

In the 1853 article "Perfidious Patmos," it is claimed that England cures exiles of rancour: "the very climate seems to have a soothing and mollifying influence on the most savage foreign natures." But the tone of the article is not quite that permeating the conclusion of *A Tale of Two Cities*. *Household Words* in the early 1850s is John Bullish, but by the time of the novel, theories of national character are respectable intellectual currency, and the authenticity of that character can be quietly assumed.

Despite Tocqueville, the press in the late 1850s still wrote of the first French Revolution in cautionary terms, though the precise nature of the warning was debatable: either there would be revolution if parliamentary reform were conceded, or there would be if it were not. The English historians of the Revolution upheld the first position, and for Croker, Alison and Smyth, the men of 1789 were as guilty as those of 1793. The Reign of Terror was the natural and inevitable consequence of the opening of the floodgates. In January 1859, the *Quarterly* thought Bright's plan for the revision of the franchise a revolutionary project, which would turn the whole order of things upside down. Drily, Whitwell Elwin remarked that "the scheme was tried in France, and all the world knows with what result." In 1858. *The Times* was invoking "the dreadful glare of '89, the horrors of '93," making the usual point that if reform in the late 1850s seemed plain sailing, so had it in France in 1789. The opponents of reform were fond of pointing to the despotism of Louis Bonaparte as the necessary culmination of popular rule. According to W. E. Aytoun, writing in *Blackwoods* in 1859, the Emperor was what the French had earned by "practically carrying into effect those very doctrines which Mr. Bright and his followers advocate": breaking down ancient landmarks, abolishing aristocracy, elevating democracy. The reformers, for their part, were capable of paying the guardians of the floodgates the same revolutionary compliment. *The Times* was opportunist as always, and while one month it might preen itself and the country generally on the striking absence of masses with fiery eyes in the tradition of 1831, the least agitation converted the paper to reform and the sluggards were menaced in their own coin. Only six weeks after the ironical reference to the plain sailing of '89, that argument was turned on its head and, in February 1859, readers reminded that the greatest things were done in a day: "the institutions of old France were overthrown, like the Bastile, in a moment of delirium." The moral here is to reform while times are quiet.

The invocation of the French Revolution by radicals and conservatives alike was more than a debating ploy, and denials of its relevance to England betrayed nervousness. The *Westminster* reviewer of Tocqueville is petulant: "if any man at that time had known what the French were as well as we know now, he would not have been surprised at anything that happened." The shying away from the threat of revolution in England, detectable here, is responsible for certain attitudes to the past recurrent in the literature of the period, and which have been noticed in the Introduction. In Froude's *History of England* and its reviews, the estrangement which is a feature of life in the class-divided modern city is identified with the human condition; and those cut off from their contemporaries come to feel the still greater difficulty of relating to the past as inevitable. Dickens was acutely aware of isolation and fear in the great city, and was capable of taking a detached view. It is the main force of *Little Dorrit* (1855–57) to depict the slow and tentative coming-together of humans within the city, and to deny that isolation is an inescapable condition. But Dickens' position was ambivalent: he was within the situation he described. John Forster cites a memorandum, the idea of "representing London—or Paris, or any other great place—in the new light of being actually unknown to all the people in the story, and only taking the colour of their fears and fancies and opinions." Here Dickens feels the imprisoning subjectivism bred by urban life as new and strange, but there is little indication that he will adopt a perspective; and that is because he, too, is a prisoner.

Dickens was alert not only to the divisive social forces, but also to the opposing energy of those striving to connect; and connection triumphs in the contemporary *Little Dorrit* (contemporary in that it deals with the England of his own lifetime). In *A Tale of Two Cities,* Dickens is removed from his characters, and a sense of their capacity to survive a harsh environment; and tends to accept inter-personal estrangement as the great reality.

> A wonderful fact to reflect upon, that every human creature is constituted to be that profound secret and mystery to every other. A solemn consideration, when I enter a great city by night, that every one of those darkly clustered houses encloses its own secret. . . .

This dogmatic pessimism, unchallenged within the historical novel, leads to the final sinking of history in vapid moralising, all the more incongruous since earlier Dickens has shown some precision in the delineation of a past whose main feature, admittedly, is a striking resemblance to the present. Still, the resemblance is defined and guarantees the past an exemplary status, lost later when the fog of the nineteenth century settles more densely over its pre-history.

To the Enlightenment historian who thought human nature unchanging, the past was totally familiar, and urgently relevant to the present, not as prehistory but as a casebook of examples. Such attitudes were still current in England in the 1850s, and for W. Frederick Pollock, writing in the *Quarterly* in 1858, the historian's business was to record "the great virtues and the great crimes" of distinguished men. The course of *A Tale of Two Cities* represents a progressive falling away from the Enlightenment tradition. Like the Enlightenment historians—like the English historians on the French Revolution, Croker, Smyth, Alison and Buckle—Dickens begins by taking the Revolution as exemplary. He ends by making it a special case, not because history never repeats itself, but because the revolutionaries were exceptionally wicked and moreover French.

Under pressure in the 1830s, historians had blurred their moral by portraying the revolutionaries as evil men, and Archibald Alison, in his *History of Europe* (1833–42), was sometimes inclined to attribute the Revolution to guilt, treachery and delusion. But with an awareness that the judgment negated the warning to his contemporaries, he could remark that historians conveying the Jacobins as "mere bloodthirsty wretches, vultures insatiate in their passion for destruction, are well-meaning and amiable, but weak and ignorant men," calculated to mislead rather than instruct future ages on the avoidance of revolution. Croker's esteem for Robespierre kept pace with his research. He had dealt scathingly with Robespierre in the *Quarterly* for September 1835, but in 1857, among his *Essays on the Early Period of the French Revolution,* treated the subject more thoroughly. Here he pointed out that the impartial praise of the pre-revolutionary sources to which he now referred was a positive indication of Robespierre's underrated abilities; and condemned previous historians who, instead of trying to clarify the obscurities of Robespierre's career, took "the easier course of finding nothing to doubt about."

Like the historians, the novelists dealing with the French Revolution were divided between its ascription to excessive wickedness and a broader historical view. Bulwer's *Zanoni* appeared in 1842, and Trollope's *La Vendée* in 1850. Bulwer weakens his polemical point against revolution in general by making a devil out of Robespierre in the way that the historians were learning to avoid, but Trollope is more sophisticated. Like *A Tale of Two Cities. La Vendée* is intended as a warning to the author's contemporaries: the Revolution is highly exemplary and shows the 1850s what not to do. Consistently with his main purpose, Trollope is at pains to emphasise that Robespierre was "not a thoughtless, wild fanatic." His career is a terrible instance of what happens when the populace gains political power.

In 1847, Michelet's *Histoire de la Révolution Française* appeared and, with the histories of Lamartine and Louis Blanc, was widely read in England.

Michelet was influenced by the revolutionary aspirations manifested the following year, and his history exemplified the French use of a justifying determinism in the democratic cause which alarmed English historians, and helped to provoke them to the opposite extreme, an insistence on their characters' absolute moral responsibility. Michelet's method was to coin abstractions—"Le Peuple," "La Révolution"—which acquired a motive force of their own, so that many acts hitherto considered crimes could be excused in terms of these figments working out their own inexorable destiny. What Michelet unequivocally condemns in the Revolution—he does not admire the Jacobins—does not reflect on the purity of "La Révolution," or France. The abstractions of Michelet's idealism are paralleled by those which class fears imposed on Carlyle and Dickens, and William Smyth pointed out that the determinism of the French historians could be used for conservative as well as radical purposes. Still, there appeared in 1849 in the *British Quarterly Review* a percipient analysis by E. Edwards of "Historians of the First French Revolution," which exposed the basis of English hostility to the French histories. Michelet's determinism was only the overflowing of his conviction that "whatever the immediate and apparent issues of the events narrated, a grand result was being slowly but ceaselessly evolved." It was the grand result which the English historians were fearful of acknowledging; and Edwards went on to remark that Carlyle, despite stylistic resemblances to Michelet, was actually a very different case. His history was detached, ironical, disjointed, unsympathetic. "He sees in the Revolution no development of a law of progress. For him it begins with an 'Age of paper,' and ends with a 'Whiff of grape-shot'."

Aware of the London slums, Carlyle acquired early the disenchantment with democracy that struck French historians after 1848, pervading Tocqueville and notably absent in Michelet. In "Signs of the Times" (1829), he wrote of a

> deep-lying struggle in the whole fabric of society; a boundless grinding collision of the New with the Old. The French Revolution, as is now visible enough, was not the parent of this mighty movement, but its offspring. . . . The final issue was not unfolded in that country: nay it is not yet anywhere unfolded.

Carlyle understands that the Revolution is no isolated calamity, product of the guilt, treachery and delusion of individuals; still, it is less firmly anchored in history than its causes, and already significance is attributed to popular movements only in so far as they are symptomatic of something else, the deep-rooted craving of the masses for paternal guidance. Ten years later, in *Chartism,* Carlyle wrote that it was no answer to call agitation "mad, incendiary, nefarious." Chartism had profound economic causes, and was provoked by the system of *laissez-faire* (what Tellson's Bank stands for in *A Tale of Two Cities*). But by 1839, Carlyle was less willing consistently to relate agitation to the social context. He generalises about "all popular commotions and maddest bellowings, from Peterloo to the Place-de-Grève itself," and his gathering retreat from the challenge of democracy is witnessed by contradictions within the essay. It is no answer to call popular commotions "mad"; and yet they may be equated with "maddest bellowings."

Carlyle's historical theory and practice were shaped by his growing conservation. In the 1830 essay, "On History," he protested against Enlightenment historiography and wished to substitute, for the easy assumption of a constant human nature, research into the driving forces of particular epochs. He insisted that men, as well as their environment, were always changing, and commented, "when the oak-tree is felled, the whole forest echoes with it; but a hundred acorns are planted silently by some unnoticed breeze." This meant that the most important part of our history was irrecoverably lost, and put the onus on the historian to recover what he could, while he could. Progressively, Carlyle forgot the acorns and concentrated on the more accessible oak-tree.

Scott's influence was generously acknowledged. After *Waverley,* history's "faint hearsays of 'philosophy teaching by experience' will have to exchange themselves everywhere for direct inspection and embodiment. . . ." But the curiosity of the essay on "Sir Walter Scott" (1838) is that his triumphant demonstration that the past was filled by living men does not satisfy Carlyle. These living men are reified by the claim that Scott's main appeal is nostalgic: "Consider, brethren, shall we not too one day be antiques, and grow to have as quaint a costume as the rest?" Carlyle objects that the novels offer no heroic cure for the ailing modern heart; not a criticism to be levelled at his own *Past and Present* in 1843. Despite his pleas for research, it is taken for granted that the maimed records of the past will be interpreted in the light of the historian's emotions and prejudices. In the essay, he is writing on this assumption, even while praising Scott for inaugurating another kind of history; and the Waverley novels fail as great literature because they are not sufficiently encouraging.

Scott communicated the spirit of an age through analysis of popular movements, and inspired historians to do the same. Too conscious of the past's opaqueness, Carlyle could react to Scott's example only by vulgarisation. The spirit of the age was dissociated from popular life and transformed into a much more abstract *zeitgeist,* there to guide the historian when his evidence failed him. The conception of the *zeitgeist* did not evolve from research, it substituted for research; or rather, since the *zeitgeist* engendered all things, a few facts might be assumed to reveal the essence of great events. In *The French Revolution* (1837), Carlyle responds to the fall of the universally-detested Bastille by lamenting that men have died in the process, and his moral indignation becomes an index of the event. Reviewing the book, Mazzini wrote truly that Carlyle did "not recognise in a people any collective life or collective aim. He recognises only individuals. For him, therefore, there is not and cannot be any intelligible chain of connection between cause and effect." Carlyle's quest after direct inspection and embodiment was a limited success. His characterisation of individuals was frequently acute, but of the collective movement he could embody only his own prejudices.

Writing *The French Revolution,* Carlyle was less sceptical about the accessibility of historical evidence than convinced that some data was not worth the gathering. Like Michelet, he treats summarily the events preceding the outbreak of revolution, when the daemonic suddenly erupts against the spurious, as, in Michelet, good erupts against the evil of the Ancient Regime. In "On History," Carlyle insisted that history was composed of innumerable biographies. The Ancient Regime treats the people as "masses," and Carlyle pleads for historical empathy: "masses indeed: and yet, singular to say, if, with an effort of imagination, thou follow them, over broad France, into their garrets and hutches, the masses consist of all units." What Carlyle asks of the reader is the ideal which he cannot realise as an historian. Having described the storming of the Bastille, he forgets that the Revolution is made by individuals, and lapses into empty abstraction, denouncing the fever-frenzies of Anarchy enveloping the world. He deals with units only in isolation, and the units are always the "great men," great because emancipated from a mediocre environment. Like the Revolution, the great man rises up to announce that shams shall be no more, and between shams and reality can be no interaction. Lacking antecedents, the Revolution's course is credited to "necessity." That of the French historians (especially Michelet) made the revolutionaries the puppets of moral abstractions; Carlyle's, typically English, makes them the puppets of human nature, degraded to the brutish once the floodgates are opened.

Carlyle's views on the Revolution cannot be systematised. He was proud of his reputation as its most impartial historian, but there is more contradiction than impartiality. He criticises his predecessors for recording the Reign of Terror in hysterics, and then explains the Terror by commenting that in History as in Nature, certain periods are covered over by "Darkness and the mystery of horrid cruelty." The autonomy that the forces of madness come to exercise suggests Carlyle's awareness that the Revolution was generating its own momentum; and significantly, his loathing for the Radicals grew as he wrote the book. Hedva Ben-Israel remarks of the historian, William Smyth, that "if contemporary conditions drove him to the study of the Revolution, it is even more obvious how much this study helped to formulate his political opinions and to intensify the process of his growing conservatism." The same is true of Carlyle, and also of Dickens in *A Tale of Two Cities.* For both, the experience of writing on the Revolution showed that their liberalism was not proof against the description of class war.

A Tale of Two Cities was published in 1859, twenty-two years after Carlyle's history. Dickens' letters show an urgency in their forebodings of civil conflict lacking in Carlyle's essays, and cannot be suspected of indulging in revolutionary prophecy to speed reform. Apprehension of the London sansculottes was one reason why his account was remoter than Carlyle's from the historical actuality of the French Revolution. Defensively, and more than his mentor, he too missed the collective life or aim and saw only individuals. Though Carlyle diverts attention immediately afterwards, during the storming, his eye is on the Bastille:

> At every street-barricade, there whirls simmering a minor whirlpool,— strengthening the barricade, since God knows what is coming; and all minor whirlpools play distractedly into that grand Fire-Mahlstrom which is lashing round the Bastille.

Whole sentences in *A Tale of Two Cities* are very close to Carlyle, except for Dickens' more profound inclination to subordinate the historical event to the illumination of private character. His narrative of the storming concentrates not on the Bastille, but Defarge:

> As a whirlpool of boiling waters has a centre point, so, all this raging circled round Defarge's wine-shop, and every human drop in the caldron had a tendency to be sucked towards the vortex where Defarge himself, already begrimed with gunpowder and sweat, issued orders. . . .

Dickens the novelist might seem to be realising the Revolution through its impact on the individual, but he rather implies that Defarge is the guiding force of the Revolution. The conversion of Carlyle's vibrant metaphor to a laboured simile suggests the difficulty with which Dickens dramatised his dubious version of events. The revolutionary crowd which is active in Carlyle ("whirls simmering," "play distractedly," "lashing") is acted upon in Dickens. Consistently, Carlyle's irony is subdued to the hysteria of the individual as victim, the novelist's response to his projection into the past. Madame Defarge's Bacchantes substitute for the "one woman (with her sweetheart), and one Turk" who, according to Carlyle, joined the sansculottes in storming the Bastille. The dialogue is bizarre throughout the novel, but Madame Defarge says some extraordinary things because she is a mad puppet talking to herself; she enjoys the splendid isolation which is Darnay's, when he crosses to Paris during the Terror in the hope of restraining the revolutionary fury. Amongst the crowd, Defarge is as helpless "as if he had been struggling in the surf at the South Sea": even the arch-instigator is estranged from the struggle at hand. The idea of the crowd as a natural force is narrowed down until emphasis falls only on the cruelty of nature, and the history becomes increasingly deterministic, helping Dickens to draw his generalised moral about revolutions.

In the opening pages of *A Tale of Two Cities,* Dickens sees little to choose between the condition of pre-revolutionary France and that of England in the late eighteenth century; or of England in the 1850s. Fitzjames Stephen's review missed the point by implying that the automatic sneer at the past was characteristic of the novel, despite the odd hint of Victorian complacence. Commonly derived from the French Revolution was the lesson of what happened when a country's aristocracy abjured its responsibilities and ceased to govern, and reviewing Tocqueville's account in the *Edinburgh*, W. R. Greg found a picture "of that destruction of all *class cohesion*—that dissolution of the entire nation into a mere crowd of unconnected units—which made the convulsion, when it did come, utterly unopposed and irresistible. . . ." Dickens' England in the 1780s is precisely a "crowd of unconnected units," with no one playing a defined social role. "The highwayman in the dark was a City tradesman in the light," and the ease of the transition suggests a resemblance between the two occupations. The social fabric, so far from being settled for ever, is ripe for violent change.

At this point, Dickens is not merely attacking harsh rulers who ought to be more charitable. For Carlyle in *Chartism*, democracy was "the consummation of No-government and *Laissez-faire*." In the novel, Jerry Cruncher thinks of his occupation and tells himself, "you'd be in a Blazing bad way, if recalling to life was to come into fashion. . . ."; but as well as being a body-snatcher, Jerry is also a messenger for Tellson's Bank, which equally would be in a bad way. The society trusting its wealth to Tellson's vaults provides dead bodies in plenty for Jerry to dig up again. The great keys of the underground strong-rooms at Tellson's correspond to those of the Bastille; and as the Bastille is the symbol of oppression in France, so is Tellson's in England. Its broad social tendency is reflected in the depersonalisation of its employees: Lorry's life is spent "turning an immense pecuniary mangle." Dickens hints that if oppression continues, there will be a storming of Tellson's, whose great keys will open the vaults for good.

Dickens' assault on the system of *laissez-faire* does not, however, survive his descriptions of revolution in France. He is induced to settle for any society that is non-revolutionary, forgetting that the old regime in England had seemed patently to invite revolution. Gradually, Lorry becomes an unequivocally positive figure; at first because, despite his disclaimers, he unites "friendship," "interest," and "sentiment" with banking. Later, Lorry's virtue is inseparable from his attachment to Tellson's. During the Revolution, he occupies rooms in the Parisian branch of the bank, "in his fidelity to the House of which he had grown to be a part, like a strong root-ivy." The root-ivy simile looks sinister, but the undertones conflict with Dickens' intended meaning, and are a confused remembrance of the days when Tellson's itself seemed a decidedly sinister institution. What Tellson's stands for in England is made plain after the outbreak of revolution, when the aristocratic emigrées flee there as to a natural haven. It is nevertheless at this stage that Dickens begins to approve of the bank. He has stressed that England has been brought close to revolution by political and economic reaction; yet when (for Dickens) a roughly similar state of affairs has provoked revolution in France, Tellson's can somehow be portrayed as a source of social stability.

Though the doctor has been victimised by the old regime in France, the Manettes' safety is linked with that of the money in Tellson's vaults, which is safe enough under Lorry's guardianship. They have not always enjoyed such security. The house in Soho had been "a very harbour from the raging streets," but Dickens associates the wreaths of dust in Soho with those raised by the Parisian sansculottes. Gradually, he identifies with that British orthodoxy regarding the Revolution as "the one only harvest ever known under the skies that had not been sown," a random occurrence bearing no warning for England. He continues to state that the revolution is the product of intolerable oppression, but the tale moves in another direction. The career of Miss Pross is significant. Her chauvinism begins as a joke, more John Bullish than the articles on France in *Household Words*. When she asks why providence should have cast her lot in an island if she was intended to cross the sea, Dickens is being gently satirical; less gently, he satirises those claiming their social rank from providence. But at the end of the novel, in the woman-to-woman struggle with Madame Defarge, Miss Pross's chauvinism is justified: her courage is specifically English, "a courage that Madame Defarge so little comprehended as to mistake for weakness." Miss Pross becomes an agent of the derided providence, and writing to Bulwer in 1860, Dickens gravely defended her enemy's "accidental" death.

> Where the accident is inseparable from the passion and action of the character; where it is strictly consistent with the whole design, and arises out of some culminating proceeding on the part of the character which the whole story has led up to, it seems to me to become, as it were, an act of divine justice.

Miss Pross literally harbours Lucie Manette from the raging streets. Embodied in Madame Defarge, the Revolution derives less from oppression than French depravity, which is no match for English virtue.

At the beginning of the novel, Dickens sees the Revolution as a rebuff to middle-class ideology. His scorn for the mentality (Lorry's) vindicating business as "a very good thing, and a very respectable thing," is reminiscent of Carlyle's strictures on the limitations of the Girondins. But Dickens cannot sympathise with the actual revolutionaries whom he portrays, and tells us why in his account of Madame Defarge:

> . . . the troubled time would have heaved her up, under any circumstances. But, imbued from her childhood with a brooding sense of wrong, and an inveterate hatred of a class, opportunity had developed her into a tigress.

Madame Defarge can be excused for being revolutionary in a general kind of way, but not for her class ideology, whose violence provokes a corresponding violence in Dickens. The blood-smeared eyes of the sansculottes sharpening their weapons in Tellson's yard are "eyes which any unbrutalised beholder would have given twenty years of life, to petrify with a well-directed gun." "Unbrutalised" reads ironically, and there is more irony if we remember the petrified Monseigneur. Dickens now prefers the stony hearts of the aristocracy to the revolutionary crowd, and would play the Gorgon with history as the French aristocrats tried to do.

Early in the novel, since the ruling class has reneged on its responsibilities, virtue is not a connotation of fine dress. Dickens' later tendency, to assume that clothes make the man, derives from the persuasion that nations must be composed of unconnected units, each one a "profound secret and mystery to every other." Dickens becomes indignant with revolutionary innovations. From the look of the tribunal, he comments, it would seem that "the felons were trying the honest men." The moral order turned upside down will be that wherein "honest" justice is meted out to felons; presumably the judicial norm in non-revolutionary society. Darnay has contrary experience of the English bench. Oddly, though, he recoils from the aristocrats in La Force through an "instinctive association of prisoners with shameful crime and disgrace." Sympathy with the victims of revolution leads Dickens to share with Darnay the conventional prejudice which has been invalidated.

Sydney Carton's career is problematic: he is clearly a failure, but Dickens sometimes seems to be asking whether in such a society as Carton finds himself, it is not a virtue to be a failure. While he may be simply weak, "the man of good abilities and good emotions, incapable of their directed exercise," the kind of strength leading to success is exemplified in Stryver:

> anybody who had seen him projecting himself into Soho while he was yet on the Saint Dunstan's side of Temple Bar, bursting into his full-blown way along the pavement, to the jostlement of all weaker people, might have seen how safe and strong he was.

Tellson's strongrooms are also "safe, and strong, and sound, and still"; and the stillness here is an emblem of the ultimate stultification of Stryver's bustling activity. Stryver's success as a lawyer is based on the exploitation of the weak Carton, while his own contribution to the partnership is to be "glib," "unscrupulous," "ready" and "bold." These business virtues combine with a resentment of democratic movements threatening to jeopardise his opulent living, and at Tellson's, he broaches to the emigrées his plans for "blowing the people up and exterminating them from the face of the earth. . . ." Stryver's disposition towards the French revolutionaries is shared by Carton as he ceases to be the mere jackal. While Madame Defarge points him to the National Palace, Carton reflects that "it might be a good deed to seize that arm, lift it, and strike under it sharp and deep." In the face of revolution, Carton is as willing to resort to repressive brutality as any *homme sensible,* and his progressive ennoblement in the novel cannot be dissociated from his acquisition of bourgeois traits. Yet once, Carton had been seen not only as weak (that is one explanation), but also as among the numerous victims of a ruthlessly competitive society. "And whose fault was that?" asks Stryver, when Carton complains of his failure. Carton feels that it was Stryver's, whose "driving and riving and shouldering and pressing" forced his partner to a self-preserving "rust and repose."

Carton also competes, unsuccessfully, with Charles Darnay for the love of Lucie Manette, and his pining for the middle-class doll undercuts his subversive potential from early on. It is implied that his failure in love is inevitable, but the pining over Lucie is not convincing: there are qualities in the Carton who talks back to Stryver which suggest more backbone. Perhaps, and without slighting Lucie, Dickens was hinting that domestic content depended on worldly fortune; and that in the society he was treating, this was not for everybody. Lucie rejects Stryver, too, while Darnay is the happy medium: undoubtedly successful, but earning his modest income conscientiously as a private tutor. What is important in Carton's case is that the rebel should die at the hands of the revolutionaries on behalf of Lucie and the middle-class family, and if the situation seems contrived, that is all to the point. Anyway, the enigmas of Carton's career—the strained progress from rebel to revolutionary victim, and the dubious values which accompany his ennoblement—are shelved at his death, along with other problems which the historical novel has raised, not always intentionally. If Carton has been corrupted within history (as Dickens may have sensed), his death is a comprehensive retreat from the world's stain. As the guillotine falls,

> the murmuring of many voices, the upturning of many faces, the pressing on of many footsteps in the outskirts of the crowd, so that it swells forward in a mass, like one great heave of water, all flashes away.

At the end, Carton prophesies a secure and happy England without relation to the England presented earlier; nor, one would have thought, did the France of 1859 merit his optimism.

It is the passivity of the future state which is insisted upon, and Carton's death is the logical consummation of a novel increasingly stressing the blessings of inertia as the Revolution proceeds. Activity (movement in history) is associated with corruption, passivity with preserved innocence. Lorry, praised as the best possible man "to hold fast by what Tellson's had in its keeping, and to hold his peace," is beyond criticism because he refuses to enter the historical argument. History begins with the Fall, the collapse of timeless innocence, and the Carmagnole is "emphatically a fallen sport" but as the dance passes, leaving Lucie frightened and bewildered, "the feathery snow fell as quietly and lay as white and soft, as if it had never been." Quietly, the snow obliterates the marks of history, and returns the world to a uniform white.

This, rather than the fallen historical world of Madame Defarge, is Lucie's habitat. Before becoming respectable, Carton called her a doll; accurately since, although Lucie marries and has several children, she never acquires a character. Throughout, she enjoys the immunity to time which England offers her at the close.

To state mechanically what is mechanically executed, the theme of resurrection pervades the novel. Dr Manette is saved from burial alive in the Bastille, but has gone mad, and needs Lucie's loving care to revive his senses. Darnay is twice rescued by Sydney Carton from what seems certain death, in London and Paris, and Jerry Cruncher is a "Resurrection-man", or body-snatcher. There are two mock funerals, those of Cly, the Old Bailey spy, and Foulon, who causes a servant to be buried in his stead and is "recalled to life" only to be slaughtered by the Parisian crowd. Resurrection suggests a possible moral resurgence, and early in the novel, the idea of that resurgence is inseparable from social change. Dickens is curiously honest about Dr. Manette's second resurrection, the restoration to mental health. "In a mysterious and guilty manner," Lorry hacks to pieces the shoemaker's bench, while Miss Pross holds the candle "as if she were assisting at a murder": their secret destruction seems like "a horrible crime," but the patient cannot be cured otherwise. Lorry's and Miss Pross's demolition of the momentoes of the Bastille precedes its razing by the revolutionaries.

Later in *A Tale of Two Cities,* destruction and secrecy are simply wicked. Resurrection assumes exclusively Christian connotations, and as Carton prepares to die to save Darnay, the words of the Anglican burial service recur to his mind. The Christian position is the same as Carlyle's in "Signs of the Times": "to reform a world, to reform a nation, no wise man will undertake; and all but foolish men know, that the only solid, though a far slower reformation, is what each begins and perfects on *himself.*" Dickens is forced to such modest wisdom through his fear of revolution in England, and yet in a way he is still being honest. Carton yearns less for resurrection than the "far, far better rest." Finally, the escape from history is enough.

Nation and Generation in *A Tale of Two Cities*

Albert Hutter

It is the interplay of the personal and the social, of the individual psychic development and the general political and economic evolution—with each "causing" and influencing the other . . .—that makes for the powerful social change
that we call history.

Bruce Mazlish, James and John Stuart Mill

Two revolutions, one generational and the other political, determine the
structure of *A Tale of Two Cities*. We require a combination of critical methods—literary, psychoanalytic, historical—to illuminate the novel's complex
structure and its impact on different readers. Lee Sterrenburg writes that
Dickens' vision of the French Revolution may be influenced by "a personal
daydream only he can fully fathom. But he is able to communicate with his
readers because he has rendered his daydream in terms of a publicly meaningful iconography."[1] Since *A Tale of Two Cities* is also a tale of two generations,
the iconography of father-son conflict carries a particularly powerful social
resonance.[2]

Dickens' novel was published in 1859, a year that Asa Briggs calls a
"turning point" in the "late Victorian revolt against authority." This revolt
originated "in mid-Victorian society. What happened inside families then influenced what happened in many areas of public life later."[3] The major publications of 1859, from *The Origin of Species* and Marx's *Critique of Political Economy* to Samuel Smiles's *Self-Help,* stand poised between the anticipation of a
later ideological revolt and the still-powerful memory of the French Revolution. That revolution and subsequent English social reform inevitably
changed Victorian father-son relations. But the changing Victorian family, in
turn, reshaped society.[4] As much as any other work of 1859, *A Tale of Two
Cities* demonstrates the correlation between family and nation, and it uses the
language of psychological conflict and psychological identification to portray
social upheaval and the restoration of social order.

Reprinted by permission of the Modern Language Association of America from *PMLA* 93 (1978):
448–62.

Nation and generation converge in the earliest chronological event of *A Tale of Two Cities,* Doctor Manette's story of the Evrémondes' brutality (III, x, 303–15).[5] The Evrémondes rape a young peasant girl, wound her brother, then summon Manette to treat their victims. When Manette tries to report these crimes, he is incarcerated in the Bastille. He writes a full account of his experience—damning the Evrémondes to the last of their race—and hides this personal history in his cell. Defarge finds the document and uses it as evidence against Charles Darnay, né Evrémonde. The events Manette describes, a microcosm of the larger narrative, trigger the major actions and reversals of the double plot. The rape itself implies social exploitation, a class-wide *droit du seigneur.* Conversely, one peasant's attack on his master anticipates the nation's reply to such abuse. The Evrémonde who raped the girl and murdered her brother will later run down a small child from the Paris slums, and as a result will be "driven fast to his tomb." The retaliation denied one peasant, a generation earlier, is carried out by the revolutionary "Jacques." Even the Paris tribunal at which Manette's story is read reflects a struggle between parents and children: Manette has condemned his son-in-law to death.

Class conflict here reveals a hidden psychological conflict that recurs throughout the novel. Manette is taken at night and forced to witness the aftermath of a violent sexual assault. His abductors have absolute power, and any knowledge of their activities carries grave risk: "The things that you see here," the Marquis warns young Manette, "are things to be seen, and not spoken of" (III, x, 311). Violence and sexuality, combined with a mysterious nocturnal setting and a dangerous observation, suggest a primal scene. Such scenes arouse anxiety about being caught spying, and they invariably reflect parent-child conflict.[6] The political significance of this drama intensifies its psychological meaning. Evrémonde's absolute power, for example, resembles the father's absolute power over his child. The novel's virtual obsession with spying, its comic subplot, and its descriptions of revolutionary violence all further suggest primal-scene fantasies. But if we mistake this primal-scene reading for a full explanation of the novel, we only succeed in isolating one meaning and subordinating the others. We could as easily argue that the dominant class struggle—not simply in the novel but in Victorian history—is being expressed through the powerful language of childhood trauma: the nation is symbolized by the family; a national and historical struggle is made particular, and particularly vivid, through a personal and psychological narrative. The two explanations are not mutually exclusive. But to integrate them we must first analyze the whole work and locate the reader's experience in the structure of the text itself. It can be shown that the psychological chronology of the *Tale's* plot, turning as it does on Manette's story, duplicates a psychological chronology common to the experience of most readers.[7]

Manette's story is the narrative equivalent of a trauma: it recalls an event that precedes all the other action of the novel and organizes that action, although it is not "recovered" until quite late in the novel. Modern psychoanalytic theory recognizes the retrospective quality of trauma, the way in which the individual reconstructs his past life to conform with present conflicts and thereby invests a past event with significance—some of it real, often some of it imagined.[8] Manette's document stands in a similar relationship to the larger novel: within the structure of the *Tale* it acts like a traumatic memory, reliving the significant antecedent events of the entire plot at the climax of Darnay's second trial. The document reveals the combination of public and private acts that informs the narrative; it records the "primal scene" of the text itself.

Because Dickens makes this document the hidden nexus of the plot, it must bear a considerable weight of coincidence. The abused peasants are the brother and sister of Madame Defarge; Ernest Defarge was originally Doctor Manette's servant; and Manette, before being rushed off to the Bastille, even meets his future son-in-law. Manette is sought out by the Marquise St. Evrémonde, who has "a presentiment that if no other innocent atonement is made" for the wrongdoing of her husband and brother-in-law, "it will one day be required" of little Charles (III, x, 314)—a prophecy as remarkable as any of the "spiritual revelations" satirized by Dickens in the first chapter.

Like the story of Doctor Manette, the larger action of the novel turns on seeing what was never meant to be seen, an experience symbolized by the extensive use of a "Gorgon's Head." This mythical figure, which turned those who looked at it into stone, is now itself a "stone face [which] seemed to stare amazed, and, with opened mouth and dropped under-jaw, looked awe-stricken" (II, ix, 120).[9] The novel begins by opposing things hidden and things revealed. The passengers on the Dover Mail "were wrapped to the cheek-bones and over the ears, and wore jack-boots. Not one of the three could have said, from anything he saw, what either of the other two was like; and each was hidden under almost as many wrappers from the eyes of the mind, as from the eyes of the body, of his two companions" (I, ii, 4–5). And we are repeatedly aware of eyes, hundreds of eyes, at critical moments in the text, such as Darnay's appearance at his London trial:

> Everybody present . . . stared at him. . . . Eager faces strained round pillars and corners, to get a sight of him; spectators in back rows stood up, not to miss a hair of him; people on the floor of the court, laid their hands on the shoulders of the people before them, to help themselves, at anybody's cost, to a view of him—stood a-tiptoe, got upon ledges, stood upon next to nothing, to see every inch of him. ("A Sight"—II, ii, 58)

At Darnay's second Paris trial, Dickens halts the action by a momentary frieze of staring spectators:

In a dead silence and stillness—the prisoner under trial looking lovingly at his wife, his wife only looking from him to look with solicitude at her father, Doctor Manette keeping his eyes fixed on the reader, Madame Defarge never taking hers from the prisoner, Defarge never taking his from his feasting wife, and all the other eyes there intent upon the Doctor, who saw none of them—the paper was read, as follows. (III, ix, 302)

The novel is filled with spies, from a hero twice accused of spying, to the comic spying of Jerry Cruncher, Jr., on his father, to the spy Barsad and "the great brotherhood of Spies" (II, xxii, 211) who inhabit St. Antoine. Even the dead men, their heads on Temple Bar, remind us of "the horror of being ogled" (II, i, 50). And the novel closes with an obsessive parade of violence, the revolutionaries worshiping the guillotine and previewing its victims at mass trials.

Spying, like virtually everything else in this novel, has two meanings—one public, the other private. The official spies, like Barsad, are instruments of repression and representatives of the "fathers," the men in power. But in other contexts, like the Cruncher scenes, children spy on their parents. In both cases spying expresses the *Tale's* dominant conflicts. Thus the Gorgon's Head witnesses much more than the murder of the Marquis: it sees the deadly struggle between two generations, which is climaxed by implicit filicide and patricide. Dickens anticipates the public murders of the Revolution while suggesting the private conflict of Charles Darnay through the subtle mixture of two plot lines. First, the Marquis—Charles's uncle, who is virtually indistinguishable from Charles's father ("Can I separate my father's twin-brother, joint inheritor, and next successor, from himself?" [II, ix, 117])—runs down a child (II, vii). When the Marquis returns home, the child's avenger clings to the underpart of the Marquis's carriage (II, viii). The Marquis is vaguely uneasy when he learns that someone was seen hanging from his carriage, but by the end of the chapter his thoughts have shifted to his nephew. He inquires whether Charles has arrived and is informed "not yet." Early in the next chapter (II, ix), the Marquis believes he sees a shadow outside his window as he is eating, but the servants find nothing. And again, his vague uneasiness is replaced by an uneasiness over the arrival of his renegade nephew. Dickens' description encourages us to feel one preoccupation merge with the other:

"Monseigneur, it is nothing. The trees and the night are all that are here."
. . . the Marquis went on with his supper. He was half-way through it, when he again stopped with his glass in his hand, hearing the sound of wheels. It came on briskly, and came up to the front of the château.
"Ask who is arrived."
It was the nephew of Monseigneur. He had been some few leagues behind Monseigneur, early in the afternoon. He had diminished the distance rapidly, but not so rapidly as to come up with Monseigneur on the road. (II, ix, 113)

The nephew of Monseigneur arrives and dines with his uncle. Their genteel conversation reveals a deadly turn of mind, particularly on the part of the Marquis, whose face

> . . . was cruelly, craftily, and closely compressed, while he stood looking quietly at his nephew, with his snuff-box in his hand.
> Once again he touched him on the breast, as though his finger were the fine point of a small sword, with which, in delicate finesse, he ran him through the body. . . . (II, ix, 117)

However, Charles himself alludes to his uncle's death—something the Marquis is quick to comment on:

> "This property and France are lost to me," said the nephew, sadly; "I renounce them."
> "Are they both yours to renounce? France may be, but is the property? It is scarcely worth mentioning; but, is it yet?"
> "I had no intention, in the words I used, to claim it yet. If it passed to me from you, to-morrow—"
> "Which I have the vanity to hope is not probable." (II, ix, 118)

But the Marquis, in his vanity, is mistaken. Before dawn, he will be "run through" in the very chambers where they speak, by the shadowy, gaunt figure who has moved in and out of his thoughts all day, trading places with his nephew.

The Marquis has desired the death of his nephew, and Charles, more covertly, has imagined the sudden death of his father's twin. There is the suggestion, but never the realization, of both filicide and patricide. But the exchange between the Marquis and his nephew is framed by the murder of a child and the murder of the Marquis himself. The former symbolizes the Marquis's murderous impulses toward his brother's child, as well as the cruelty of the French ruling classes toward their dependents, like the abuse witnessed by Doctor Manette eighteen years earlier. At the same time, the revenge that follows is both an actualization of Charles's revenge against his father's surrogate and a gesture that shows the French peasantry rising up to murder its rulers, as they will ultimately murder the father of their country in the revolutionary act of regicide. Dickens clarifies these connections when he describes the rumors that follow the capture of the Marquis's assassin:

> ". . . he is brought down into our country to be executed on the spot, and . . . he will very certainly be executed. They even whisper that because he has slain Monseigneur, and because Monseigneur was the father of his tenants—serfs— what you will—he will be executed as a parricide. . . . his right hand, armed with the knife, will be burnt off before his face . . . into wounds which will be made in his arms, his breast, and his legs, there will be poured boiling oil,

melted lead, hot resin, wax, and sulphur; finally . . . he will be torn limb from limb by four strong horses." (II, xv, 162)

That Darnay should flee such a country is hardly surprising, but the political reasons for flight are intensified by his personal desire to avoid the retribution prophesied by his mother for the sins of his fathers. And the futility of that flight becomes apparent with his return to France after the Revolution. Darnay's fate is to be forced, against his conscious desire, into a deadly struggle with his fathers: his own father, his father's identical twin, his father-in-law. Although Darnay and Manette learn to respect and love each other, their goodwill is repeatedly subverted by events. Charles's marriage to Lucie nearly kills Manette, and Manette's document in turn condemns Darnay to the guillotine. The characters seem to be moved by something larger than their individual desires, by the sins of a nation, which inevitably lead only to more sin, to an orgy of murder and retribution. The political meaning of these acts is intensified by a deep and persistent psychological theme, at times so perfectly merged with the political that one and the same act may be construed as personal revenge, patricide, and regicide.

If the murderer of Evrémonde symbolically enacts Darnay's violence and vengeance, then Sydney Carton enacts another side of Darnay's character and pays for the hero's aggression. Carton's sacrifice is a convenient, if implausible, device to free Charles from the Bastille; it is also an attempt to solve an insoluble political dilemma. The revolutionaries justifiably overthrow their rulers, but their hatred leads to excesses that turn despised oppressor into sympathetic victim. The sins of the fathers are endlessly repeated, from generation to generation, and Dickens' unrealistic solution creates a character who, Christlike, will sacrifice himself for the sins of all mankind. But Carton's transformation from guilty scoundrel to hero also indicates a deeper, psychological transformation. This paragon of irreverence, having mocked and antagonized Mr. Lorry, now achieves a sudden closeness to the old banker. He notices Lorry crying over Charles's plight:

"You are a good man and a true friend," said Carton, in an altered voice. "Forgive me if I notice that you are affected. I could not see my father weep, and sit by, careless. And I could not respect your sorrow more, if you were my father. You are free from that misfortune, however." (III, ix, 293)

For the first time in his knowledge of Carton, Lorry sees a "true feeling and respect"; once he decides to sacrifice himself, Carton becomes something like an ideal son and rediscovers his father in Lorry. Sydney then thinks back to his youth, and his dead father:

Long ago, when he had been famous among his earliest competitors as a youth of great promise, he had followed his father to the grave. His mother had died, years before. These solemn words, which had been read at his father's grave, arose in his mind as he went down the dark streets, among the heavy shadows, with the moon and the clouds sailing on high above him. "I am the resurrection and the life, saith the Lord: he that believeth in me, though he were dead, yet shall he live: and whosoever liveth and believeth in me, shall never die." (III, ix, 297–98)

These words dominate Carton's subsequent feelings. He transforms his life by internalizing his father's image, using Lorry as a surrogate: his earlier aimlessness dissolves and a new mission identifies him with the most famous—and self-sacrificing—of sons. Carton begins to achieve a sense of historical and personal identity, and the novel ends with Carton reborn through his namesakes, Lucie's son and grandson. And with Carton's newfound strength and purpose, Darnay becomes "like a young child in [Carton's] hands." Unconscious, Darnay is delivered to old Manette and Lucie and carried out of France like a sleeping baby (III, xiii). This sequence suggests that, as the hero's double internalizes paternal authority and willingly sacrifices himself to it, the innocent hero may be reborn.

The British world of business offers a different, more pragmatic solution to father-son struggles. Samuel Smiles, a widely read apostle for the self-made man, speaks for a common British chauvinism when he contrasts England and France:

> . . . [the English system] best forms the social being, and builds up the life of the individual, whilst at the same time it perpetuates the traditional life of the nation . . . thus we come to exhibit what has so long been the marvel of foreigners—a healthy activity of individual freedom, and yet a collective obedience to established authority—the unfettered energetic action of persons, together with the uniform subjection of all to the national code of Duty.[10]

This description integrates independent action and submission to authority. Because Dickens' France prevents such integration, unrestrained selfishness and anarchy tear the country apart. Although England has both unruly mobs and abundant selfishness, the British control the central conflict between sons and fathers, independence and authority.[11] In a land of opportunity the individual submits himself to a generalized authority, which he then internalizes—at least according to Smiles and most other Victorians.[12] The virtues of "promptitude," "energy," "tact," "integrity," "perseverance"—the whole list of ingredients in Smiles's recipe for success in business—involve the same psychological dynamic: turn external tyranny into internal censorship and control. Self-Help opposes external help. Patronage, money, support in any form inhibit imitating one's business "fathers" and, by struggle and hard work, repeating their success. Government itself is internalized: "It may be of comparatively little consequence how a man is governed from without, whilst everything depends upon how he governs himself from within. The greatest slave is not he who is ruled by a despot . . . but he who is the thrall of his own moral ignorance, selfishness, and vice" (Smiles, p. 3). The description fits Carton perfectly, at least until his conversion. Carton demonstrates his moral degeneration by willingly playing jackal to Stryver's pompous lion. Their relationship in turn demonstrates the Victorian businessman's divided personality: he hopes to rise in the world but he must never become a "striver," particularly in a field like law, where one must appear unruffled, cool, above all a gentleman. Dickens' social insight is conveyed by caricature and specifically by a psychological division that embodies an enforced social separation, not unlike the two sides to Wemmick in *Great Expectations.*

Smiles's ideal is to rise gracefully, working hard but never seeming to toil or manipulate. He tells the story of an architect who, in spite of extensive education and training abroad, was forced to start humbly: "He determined to begin anywhere, provided he could be employed. . . . he had the good sense not to be above his trade, and he had the resolution to work his way upward. . . . he persevered until he advanced by degrees to more remunerative branches of employment" (pp. 208–09). Charles Darnay does the same:

> . . . with great perseverance and untiring industry, he prospered.
>
> In London, he had expected neither to walk on pavements of gold, nor to lie on beds of roses: if he had had any such exalted expectation, he would not have prospered. He had expected labour, and he found it, and did it, and made the best of it. In this, his prosperity consisted. (II, x, 123)

For Carton, however, such qualities are only "a mirage of honourable ambition, self-denial, and perseverance" (II, v, 85). He denies his own ambition and projects it onto the gross reality of Stryver.[13]

The two cities of Dickens' *Tale* embody two very different public expressions of father-son conflict. In England, particularly in the world of business, repression is internalized: it becomes a psychological act rather than a political one. As public repression is diminished, internal aggression is brought under control, and the generation in power transmits its own authority—its own image—to those who follow. In France, political repression is much stronger, as is the political retaliation of the oppressed. Dickens distorted the reality of the French Revolution to fit precisely into this liberal vision of the causes of revolution (and the need for a prophylactic reform), exaggerating the brutality and repression of the ancien régime and reducing the uprising itself to a nightmare of populist, radical reaction.[14] Dickens' historical distortion clearly states the prevailing British liberal attitudes toward political repression and reform, toward the value of business and free enterprise, and, implicitly, toward the frequent, and frequently unconscious, struggle between fathers and sons throughout the century.

Jarvis Lorry is the ideal businessman. Business may be Lorry's defense against feeling, as he hints in his warning to Lucie that "all the relations I hold with my fellow-creatures are mere business relations" (I, iv, 21); but his thorough identification with his employer, Tellson's, endows him with a mercantile nobility. Fearing that Tellson's customers would be compromised by the seizure or destruction of documents—"for who can say that Paris is not set afire to-day, or sacked to-morrow"—he decides that he alone can protect their interests. His age and personal safety are not at issue: ". . . shall I hang back, when Tellson's knows this and says this—Tellson's, whose bread I have eaten these sixty years—because I am a little stiff about the joints? Why, I am a boy, sir, to half a dozen old codgers here!" (II, xxiv, 225). Lorry's language demonstrates not only his chivalry but also his clear filial relation toward his "House," which feeds him; his identification with Tellson's also gives him strength and, significantly, youth. At several points in this scene Darnay repeats his admiration for Lorry's "gallantry and youthfulness."

Elsewhere in the novel, Dickens describes the peculiar business education provided by Tellson's:

> When they took a young man into Tellson's London house, they hid him somewhere till he was old. They kept him in a dark place, like a cheese, until he had the full Tellson flavour and blue-mould upon him. Then only was he permitted to be seen, spectacularly poring over large books, and casting his breeches and gaiters into the general weight of the establishment. (II, i, 51)

Although the obvious satire here may temper Lorry's heroism, it is, for Dickens, comparatively gentle, and its humor softens the antagonism between the old and the young. Dickens is certainly not flattering in his appraisal of Tellson's—"very small, very dark, very ugly, very incommodious" (II, i, 49)—but his criticism of this dangerously antiquated operation is checked by a humorous acceptance, a feeling that, old-fashioned as it is, it produces good men, trust, honor. Smiles, too, stresses the heroism of banking:

> Trade tries character perhaps more severely than any other pursuit in life. It puts to the severest tests honesty, self-denial, justice, and truthfulness; and men of business who pass through such trials unstained are perhaps worthy of as great honour as soldiers who prove their courage amidst the fire and perils of battle. . . . reflect but for a moment on the vast amount of wealth daily entrusted even to subordinate persons . . . and note how comparatively few are the breaches of trust which occur amidst all this temptation. . . . the system of Credit, which is mainly based upon the principle of honour, would be surprising if it were not so much a matter of ordinary practice in business transactions. . . . the implicit trust with which merchants are accustomed to confide in distant agents . . . often consigning vast wealth to persons, recommended only by their character . . . is probably the finest act of homage which men can render to one another. (pp. 224–25)

Through a characteristic reference to parents and children, Dickens equates Tellson's with England: "Any one of [the] partners would have disinherited his son on the question of rebuilding Tellson's. In this respect the House was much on a par with the Country" (II, i, 49). Compare this mild satire with the savagery of Dickens' attack on other bureaucratic strongholds, like the Circumlocution Office of *Little Dorrit*. The very name "Tell son" enjoins the paternalistic institution to reveal to its dependents the secrets of the House, although it takes a ridiculously long time to do so. Imparting secrets to a son resolves not only generational conflict but also the problem of spying. Wait long enough, the "sons" are implicitly advised, make the interests of the House *your* interests, internalize the father's authority, and all things will become known.

A Tale of Two Cities has been consistently criticized for what Dickens himself called its "want of humour."[15] John Gross writes:

> Above all, the book is notoriously deficient in humour. One falls—or flops—back hopefully on the Crunchers, but to small avail. True, the comic element parodies the serious action: Jerry, like his master, is a "Resurrection-Man," but on the only occasion that we see him rifling a grave it turns out to be empty, while his son's panic-stricken flight with an imaginary coffin in full pursuit is nightmarish rather than funny.[16]

Young Jerry's experience occurs in the chapter entitled "The Honest Tradesman" (II, xiv), and its comedy, which is indeed closer to nightmare, extends the "serious action" of the novel more thoroughly than Gross allows: "The Honest Tradesman" combines national, commercial, and generational conflict.

Above all else, Young Jerry is "impelled by a laudable ambition to study the art and mystery of his father's honest calling" (II, xiv, 153). We see this particular scene through the boy's own close-set, staring eyes, and the landscape reflects Jerry's spying, his desire to see into the mystery of his father's nocturnal expeditions: lamps "wink," while the gravestones and the church tower spy in turn on the prying men and the peeping child. Jerry witnesses a peculiar form of "fishing":

> They fished with a spade, at first. Presently the honoured parent appeared to be adjusting some instrument like a great corkscrew. Whatever tools they worked with, they worked hard, until the awful striking of the church clock so terrified Young Jerry, that he made off, with his hair as stiff as his father's. (II, xiv, 154)

The language amuses us in part because it is sexually suggestive, with its "great corkscrew" and the hair that stands up and stiffens. But such language also comically expresses Young Jerry's ambition to grow up and become his father. His desire to find out what his father does and to emulate him inverts the novel's dominant struggle: the identical appearance of the Crunchers defines their essential unity. Resemblance—sinister in the Evrémonde twins and dramatic and theatrical between Carton and Darnay—is here the comic assertion of a common identity. Jerry, Jr., is a perfect replica of his parent, and a perfect parody of the conservative ideal. At first annoyed by his child's curiosity, Jerry, Sr., finally responds with favor because he realizes that this family succession offers no threat at all; the son will forfeit his own identity to take on his father's: "There's hopes wot that boy will yet be a blessing to you," Jerry, Sr., says to himself, "and a recompense to you for his mother!" (II, xiv, 156).

The father's pursuit of an "honest trade" has more than a mercantile meaning for his son, as Dickens' ambiguous language suggests throughout this chapter:

> There was a screwing and complaining sound down below, and their bent figures were strained, as if by a weight. By slow degrees the weight broke away the earth upon it, and came to the surface. Young Jerry very well knew what it would be; but, when he saw it, and saw his honoured parent about to wrench it open, he was so frightened, being new to the sight, that he made off again, and never stopped until he had run a mile or more. (II, xiv, 154)

The following morning, Jerry wakes up to see his father beating his mother on their bed for something that had gone wrong during the night, something attributed to her praying or "flopping tricks"—a term, like "Resurrection-Man," that parodies both religion and sex. Jerry's surname indicates his feeling for his wife, his desire to crunch her, and that mixed demonstration of sexuality and violence characterizes his language. "You have no more nat'ral sense of duty," he tells her, "than the bed of this here Thames river has of a pile, and similarly it must be knocked into you" (II, xiv, 155).

Jerry's language, like his mysterious nocturnal affairs, parodies the sexual violence of the Evrémondes' rape described by Doctor Manette. In one sense the comic episode may be read as another primal scene: a boy spies on his father's mysterious doings at night and later witnesses his father beating his mother on their bed; throughout, the language is both violent and implicitly sexual. At the same time, the comedy reproduces the combination of father-son conflict and social struggle present in Manette's story and traced throughout the novel. Yet because it approximates a primal scene so closely, the characteristic merging of violence and sexuality becomes here more grotesque than funny. Such language, like Jerry's generally ambiguous behavior, strains the text and limits its comic effectiveness.[17] John Gross observes that the resurrection theme cannot justify what Jerry does; however, the resurrection theme is itself subordinate to the larger thematic struggle between sons and fathers.[18] The structure of "The Honest Tradesman" reflects the structure of the *Tale:* it is at once psychological and social, suggesting both a child's vision of his parents' sexuality and the historical nightmare of the French Revolution. The comedy revises the novel's central conflicts and offers its own resolution. But that resolution cannot be sustained, and both the language and the setting of the comedy too strongly reveal the nightmare that informs it.

Dickens' familial and political revolutions are expressed by his varied use of splitting throughout the novel, so that the theme of the work becomes as well its characteristic mode of expression. From the title through the rhetorically balanced opening paragraphs, Dickens establishes the "twoness" of everything to follow: characters are twinned and doubled and paired; the setting is doubled; the women, as we shall see, are split; the historical perspective is divided between an eighteenth-century event and its nineteenth-century apprehension. "Splitting" thus describes a variety of stylistic devices, particularly related to character development and plot. But "splitting" also has two important psychoanalytic meanings: a splitting of the individual (specifically, the ego) and a splitting of the object. That is, an individual may deal with a specific problem, relationship, or trauma either by dividing himself or by dividing the problematic "other" (parent, loved one). Splitting is a fundamental mode of psychological defense and a key concept in the development of psychoanalytic theory. It originated in a description of schizophrenia and is now recognized as a central mechanism of multiple personality; but it may also be part of a normal adaptive strategy for coping with any intense relationship.[19]

Dickens manipulates both emotional conflict and its solution by "splitting" in the technical, psychoanalytic sense: his characters distance their emotions from an immediate, and disturbing, reality (thus Lorry's remark to Lucie about his lack of feeling or Carton's apparent ability to separate himself from everything except the "higher" emotions at the close); he divides a single ego into two (Carton/Darnay); and he splits the "object," allowing one person (Charles's uncle) to bear the brunt of the hero's hatred or aggression toward Charles's father. Conversely, Dickens' use of doubles may suggest, not splitting, but reunifying something once divided or divisible: the comic identification of Jerry, Jr., with his father or the larger movement between London and Paris, which connects seemingly disparate incidents and persons and ultimately unites the two plots. Even in the famous rhetoric of the opening, the balanced opposites suggest their own ultimate fusion. The use of splitting in a work this long is too varied and extensive to justify simple praise or blame—splitting is primarily a descriptive term—but it should clarify the understandably divided critical assessment of the novel.[20]

Fitzjames Stephen had originally called the book's tone "thoroughly contemptible," while Dickens thought it could be the best story he had written.[21] Sylvère Monod makes a more balanced appraisal, noting the special intensity of the revolutionary passages but finding the origins of that intensity in a "personal interest" that breaks down the proper distance between author and subject. Monod at times seems to withdraw his approval, but he is simply reflecting the work's contradictory quality: "Few would refuse to admit that the *Tale* is very much a contrived product," he has recently written, "[or] that the contrivance is usually superb."[22] In addition to citing the lack of sustained comedy in the novel, critics have complained about the contrivance and sentimentality of Carton's role and about Dickens' oversimplification of a complex historical event.[23] I have suggested that the failed comedy of the Crunchers derives, in part, from a failure to control, or sufficiently disguise, the primal-scene material implicit throughout the text. Dickens' historical oversimplification reflects, as we have seen, a merging of family and class struggles that was both characteristic and particularly problematic in the nineteenth century. Carton's role, both as a "double" to the hero and as a melodramatic scapegoat at the close, develops the dual conflicts of the novel; indeed, much of the sentimentality of Carton-as-Christ is derived from his conversion, via Lorry, into the good son and the good conservative. Carton's solution is that of any son—or class—that willingly accepts the pain or injustice inflicted upon it by parents or rulers, and such a solution is not particularly satisfying to most readers. In his peculiarly calm and heroic way, Carton stands for the ideals of conservative belief, in the family and the nation, but he finally assumes too many meanings and is required to connect too many threads of the novel. He suffers chronically from meaning too much in relation to too many other characters and themes and, like Manette's document, unites too many incidents; he becomes more strained as he becomes more important.

Other kinds of splitting in *A Tale of Two Cities* far more successfully project the text's central conflicts, precisely because they require no resolution. Dickens' caricature of the lion and the jackal, for example, exploits an inherent, unresolvable tension in his social subject. The division of labor between Carton and Stryver powerfully suggests not only Carton's divided self but the divided goals and morals of Victorian business. Divided imagery, like split objects, also contributes to the intense passages describing the Terror:

> False eyebrows and false moustaches were stuck upon them, and their hideous countenances were all bloody and sweaty, and all awry with howling, and all staring and glaring with beastly excitement and want of sleep. . . . men stripped to the waist, with the stain all over their limbs and bodies; men in all sorts of rags, with the stain upon those rags; men devilishly set off with spoils of women's lace and silk and ribbon, with the stain dyeing those trifles through and through. Hatchets, knives, bayonets, swords, all brought to be sharpened, were all red with it. (III, ii, 248–49)

The passage effectively combines images and emotions that the Victorians normally separated. In the revolutionary scenes the women are characteristically stronger and more savage than the men. Dickens further confuses sexual roles by connecting delicate and deadly images: "lace and silk and ribbon. . . . Hatchets, knives, bayonets, swords." And these images in turn anticipate the hellish dance of the revolutionaries:

> They advanced, retreated, struck at one another's hands, clutched at one another's heads, spun round alone, caught one another and spun round in pairs, until many of them dropped. While those were down, the rest linked hand in hand, and all spun round together: then the ring broke, and in separate rings of two and four they turned and turned until they all stopped at once, began again, struck, clutched, and tore, and then reversed the spin, and all spun round another way. . . . No fight could have been half so terrible as this dance. It was so emphatically a fallen sport—a something, once innocent, delivered over to all devilry—a healthy pastime changed into a means of angering the blood, bewildering the senses, and steeling their heart. Such grace as was visible in it, made it the uglier, showing how warped and perverted all things good by nature were become. The maidenly bosom bared to this, the pretty almost-child's head thus distracted, the delicate foot mincing in this slough of blood and dirt, were types of the disjointed time.
> This was the Carmagnole. (III, v, 264–65)

Both passages sharply juxtapose opposites: murder and celebration, ritual and anarchy, violence and delicacy. The dance itself is vividly sexual, orgiastic in fact; and witnessing a perverse "sport" more awful than any fight, an innocence now delivered into hell, intensifies the terror of this scene.

A Tale of Two Cities reflects the Victorian repudiation of sexual or powerful women by contrasting the dull but idealized heroine and her more dangerous, sexual counterpart.[24] Madame Defarge is an almost mythically frightening woman with male strength, but she has as well an animal-like beauty:[25]

> . . . [a] beauty which . . . impart[s] to its possessor firmness and animosity. . . . a tigress. . . .
> Such a heart Madame Defarge carried under her rough robe. Carelessly worn, it was a becoming robe enough, in a certain weird way, and her dark hair looked rich under her coarse red cap. Lying hidden in her bosom, was a loaded pistol. Lying hidden at her waist, was a sharpened dagger. Thus accoutred, and walking with the confident tread of such a character, and with the supple freedom of a woman who had habitually walked in her girlhood, barefoot and bare-legged, on the brown sea-sand, Madame Defarge took her way along the streets. (III, xiv, 344–45)

Many subsequent versions of Madame Defarge, in film and in illustration, have made her a witch. The Harper and Row cover to *A Tale of Two Cities,* for example, shows a cadaverous old crone, gray-haired, hunched over her knitting, with wrinkles stitched across a tightened face. The original "Phiz" illustration, however, brings out Madame Defarge's beauty, her dark hair and her "supple freedom"; if we compare this with two later illustrations of Lucie, we realize that

Madame Defarge is a strong, dark-haired version of the heroine.[26] Characteristically, Dickens gives the Frenchwomen vitality, conveyed negatively as animality ("tigress"), and denies his heroine these qualities. The Frenchwomen infuse their vitality into the "fallen sport" of the Carmagnole, until they appear like "fallen women," inhabiting a world of violence and overt sexuality. For Madame Defarge's sister, aristocratic brutality extends even to violation. The clearest antecedent of Madame Defarge herself is her compatriot, Mademoiselle Hortense, from *Bleak House*. Hortense "would be handsome," laments Dickens, "but for a certain feline mouth. . . . she seems to go about like a very neat She-Wolf imperfectly tamed" (p. 158). She is both attractive and frightening, and her violence is expressed by sexuality. When Bucket tells Hortense that Mrs. Bucket has helped to trap her, Hortense replies, "tigress-like":

> "I would like to kiss her!". . .
> "You'd bite her, I suspect," says Mr. Bucket.
> "I would!" making her eyes very large. "I would love to tear her, limb from limb." (p. 742)

Hortense virtually becomes Madame Defarge when she applies to Esther for service, and Esther finds that the "lowering energy" of the woman "seemed to bring visibly before me some woman from the streets of Paris in the reign of terror" (p. 320).[27]

Lucie, by contrast, is the perfect Victorian female, the ideal home companion, a loving stereotype. She achieves blandness by playing *both* child and mother (and largely skipping anything in between), so that she is all things to all generations. Darnay acknowledges that Lucie's love for her father is "an affection so unusual, so touching . . . that it can have few parallels":

> "when she is clinging to you, the hands of baby, girl, and woman, all in one, are round your neck. . . . in loving you she sees and loves her mother at her own age, sees and loves you at my age, loves her mother brokenhearted, loves you through your dreadful trial and in your blessed restoration. I have known this, night and day, since I have known you in your home."
> Her father sat silent, with his face bent down. (II, x, 126)

Most readers, unfortunately, do the same.

Dickens' violent and passionate Frenchwomen characterize not only the Carmagnole but virtually every set scene of the Revolution: "The men were terrible, in the bloody-minded anger with which they looked from windows, caught up what arms they had, and came pouring down into the streets; but, the women were a sight to chill the boldest" (II, xxii, 212). While the rape of Madame Defarge's sister dramatizes the exploitation of personal "wealth," Madame Defarge turns beauty into power and violence, finally into terror. Her revenge is all the more awful because it reverses the sister's helplessness—or, more generally, the assumed passivity of Victorian women and of the lower classes. Madame Defarge is more implacable than her husband; her closest ally is a woman who personifies revenge; and the most murderous and frightening figure of all is "the figure of the sharp female called La Guillotine" (III, iv, 259). The Frenchwomen embody Dickens' political moral: the more violently you exploit and distort in one direction, the more violent and distorted will be the reaction. And Dickens frames his moral with the language of procreation and violation: "Sow the same seed of rapacious license and oppression over again, and it will surely yield the same fruit according to its kind" (III, xv, 353).

Throughout his career, Dickens split both his hero and the hero's loved ones, particularly in a setting of generational conflict. Monks, the villainous half-brother of Oliver Twist, and Uriah Heep and Steerforth in *David Copperfield* establish a pattern of the hero's guilt and expiation that would later define the essential relationship between Carton and Darnay.[28] In *Oliver Twist* there is also a simple parental choice—Brownlow or Fagin—that becomes far more complex in *David Copperfield,* when David, in his first marriage, seems to behave like his hated stepfather, Murdstone.[29] Dickens makes a more complex use of split egos and split objects in *A Tale of Two Cities,* although he handles splitting most successfully in the novel that immediately follows: *Great Expectations* extensively uses alter egos, and its action is built around Pip's developing relationship to his various fathers—Joe, Jaggers, Magwitch. By returning to the first-person narrative of *David Copperfield,* Dickens united—internalized—the conflicts that were externalized in *A Tale of Two Cities* and never satisfactorily reunited at its close. Pip is both Darnay and Carton, he is both heroic and guilty, and he even experiences the complex conflicts of the Victorian world of business, as described here in *A Tale of Two Cities.*[30]

Edgar Johnson has written that "*A Tale of Two Cities* has been hailed as the best of Dickens's books and damned as the worst. It is neither, but it is certainly in some ways the least characteristic. . . ."[31] This essay tries to show, on the contrary, that in *A Tale of Two Cities* Dickens is concerned with two connected themes that preoccupied him throughout his career: the generational and political conflicts he repeatedly expressed through the technique of splitting. However, because that technique is used so pervasively in *A Tale of Two Cities,* it makes the novel seem uncharacteristically concentrated in style and, at times, uncharacteristically strained or humorless. The novel's particular combination of individual psychology and broad social concerns thus accounts for its unique qualities, its intensity, and its failures. *A Tale of Two Cities* dramatizes two dominant conflicts of the Victorian age—and of our own.

Notes

1.   "Psychoanalysis and the Iconography of Revolution," *Victorian Studies,* 19 (1975), 247.

2. Dickens considered "Two Generations" as a possible title for the novel. See Philip Collins, quoting from Forster's *Life*, in "A Tale of Two Novels," *Dickens Studies Annual*, 2 (1972), 342.

3. *Victorian People* (Chicago: Univ. of Chicago Press, 1970), p. 298. Fred Weinstein and Gerald M. Platt (*The Wish to Be Free* [Berkeley: Univ. of California Press, 1969]) combine psychological and sociological theories to discuss changing family and political patterns from the Enlightenment to the twentieth century. In *Psychoanalytic Sociology* (Baltimore: Johns Hopkins Univ. Press, 1973), Weinstein and Platt stress a "fundamental articulation between personality and society as action systems which stems from the 'unconscious' commitment in both systems to the same set of generalized symbolic codes" (p. 89). Neil Smelser's studies of revolutionary groups and patterns avoid "reductionistic or simplistic causal statements" while fully acknowledging the issues raised by competing methodological structures ("Social and Psychological Dimensions of Collective Behavior," *Essays in Sociological Explanation* [Englewood Cliffs, N.J.: Prentice-Hall, 1968], pp. 92–121, esp. p. 110). See also Smelser, *Social Change in the Industrial Revolution* (London: Routledge and Kegan Paul, 1959); John R. Gillis, *Youth and History* (New York: Academic Press, 1974); and William J. Goode, "The 'Fit' between Conjugal Family and the Modern Industrial System," *World Revolution and Family Patterns* (London: Collier-Macmillan, 1963), pp. 10–26.

4. In *James and John Stuart Mill: Father and Son in the Nineteenth Century* (New York: Basic Books 1975), pp. 7–8, Bruce Mazlish writes:

> Industrial and scientific revolutions, along with political ones, posed a problem of cultural transmission that was new in its intensity and placed an enormous strain on parent-child relations. In the nineteenth century the most dramatic form this took was in a heightened sense of father-son, i.e., generational, conflict. Much attention has been given, and rightly so, to class conflict at this time as a mechanism of social change. I am suggesting that generational conflict is at least of equal importance.

5. All quotations from Dickens' works are from the *New Oxford Illustrated Dickens* (London: Oxford Univ. Press, 1947–59). All citations to *A Tale of Two Cities* are given parenthetically by book, chapter, and page.

6. Freud wrote that, if very young children witness parental intercourse, "they inevitably regard the sexual act as a sort of ill-treatment or act of subjugation: they view it, that is, in a sadistic sense." He first used the term "primal scene" in the Wolf-Man case (1918), affirming that the child equates intercourse with parental aggression; the scene arouses the child's sexual excitement and leads to anxiety and guilt (*The Standard Edition of the Complete Psychological Works of Sigmund Freud*, 24 vols., trans. and ed. James Strachey et al. [London: Hogarth, 1953–64], V, 585; VII, 196; XVII, 7–122; abbreviated hereafter as *SE*). An excellent modern discussion of the concept of the primal scene and varied definitions is provided by Aaron H. Esman, "The Primal Scene: A Review and a Reconsideration," *Psychoanalytic Study of the Child*, 28 (1973), 49–81.

7. Norman N. Holland's recent work, particularly *Poems in Persons* (New York: Norton, 1973) and *5 Readers Reading* (New Haven: Yale Univ. Press, 1975), demonstrates the personal base in all critical acts and the need for a more sensitive appreciation of reader response. Murray M. Schwartz argues convincingly that any interpretation describes something neither entirely within us nor "out there" in the apparently objective text, but in an intermediate space, the "transitional" space defined by the British psychoanalyst D. W. Winnicott ("Where Is Literature?" *College English*, 36 [1975], 756–65). I am not persuaded, however, that each critic need describe in detail his psychological interaction with the text. In this essay, to locate the reader's experience "elsewhere" (in the text itself) does not constitute a "fallacy of mis-

placed concreteness" (Schwartz, p. 760). It is, rather, an attempt to generalize not only from my personal reading of the novel but from my understanding of a larger psychoanalytic and historical dynamic. I try to locate within the text a structure that seems to provoke a common response in many readers through different historical periods.

8. See particularly Ernst Kris, "The Recovery of Childhood Memories in Psychoanalysis," *Psychoanalytic Study of the Child,* 11 (1956), 54–88; see also Joseph Sandler, "Trauma, Strain, and Development," *Psychic Trauma,* ed. Sidney S. Furst (New York: Basic Books, 1967), pp. 154–74. The Hampstead Research Group explains the term "retrospective trauma" in this way: "By this we mean that the perception of some particular situation evokes the *memory* of an earlier experience, which under the present conditions becomes traumatic. . . . The ego's sudden perception of . . . a link between present fantasy and the past memory may be a traumatic experience. Here the memory functions as a present perception" (Sandler, p. 164). Freud uses the terms "retrospective fantasies" (*Zurückphantasien*) and "deferred action" (*Nachträglichkeit*). For a full discussion of these terms and their history, see J. Laplanche and J. B. Pontalis, *The Language of PsychoAnalysis,* trans. Donald Nicholson-Smith (New York: Norton, 1973). Kris argues that "the further course of life seems to determine which [early] experience may gain significance as a traumatic one" (p. 73). Furst stresses the importance of this concept because "in some instances trauma can be diagnosed only in retrospect" ("Psychic Trauma: A Survey," *Psychic Trauma,* p. 32).

9. In an article on the "Medusa's Head," Freud writes that the horror of seeing a Gorgon's head is associated with the "horror" of sexual discovery (specifically a child's first view of female genitalia); Freud's interpretations here are readily connected with the primal-scene experience. At times he seems almost to be describing the particular horror experienced by young Jerry Cruncher, as I show later. "The sight of Medusa's head," writes Freud, "makes the spectator stiff with terror, turns him to stone" (*SE,* XVIII, 273–74).

10. *Self-Help; with Illustrations of Character and Conduct* (1859; rpt. London: John Murray, 1862), p. 7.

11. The mob is "a monster much dreaded" (II, xiv, 149) in England as well as in France. But the English version is softened by narrative point of view and by relatively mild defining images. We observe the English mob at the mock burial of Cly or the bloodthirsty crowd at Darnay's London trial through the disarming comic vision of Jerry Cruncher. But our impression of the French crowd is either unmediated or mediated in a more frightening way, as when Lorry, appalled by the awful scenes at the grindstone and desperate to prevent Lucie from witnessing them, intensifies the reader's own emotion (III, ii). The British crowd at Darnay's trial is "ogreish" (II, ii, 59), and on Darnay's acquittal its members are "baffled blue-flies . . . dispersing in search of other carrion" (II, iii, 73). However ugly and disturbing, the metaphor suggests a diminutive and controlled menace, in contrast to the descriptions of the French mobs ("wolfish," "insatiable"). The French are more terrifying in their celebration of Darnay's initial release than are the English in hoping for a conviction; and when Darnay is finally convicted in France, the crowd raises "a sound of craving and eagerness that had nothing articulate in it but blood" (III, x, 315).

12. Weinstein and Platt argue that a critical change between the eighteenth and twentieth centuries turns on a "capacity for emotional withdrawal" manifested through the world of business: "business generally became the special province of men. . . . The relationship of father to son . . . became more conscious; centered in the ego, it was therefore capable of a higher degree of control. This control permitted critical examination of the father's position, and on this basis the first steps were taken toward the inclusion of the sons in the family structure" (*Wish to Be Free,* pp. 13–14). French society before the Revolution could not appropriately resolve the inevitable tensions of generational change: the choice was sharply drawn between passive acceptance of authority and active rebellion. (As we have seen, Darnay creates a false, third solution in attempting to flee his country and his fathers.) The postrevolutionary world of business could, however, resolve both national and family conflict within the psyche of the in-

dividual. Dickens' contrasting images of France and England, however crudely drawn, accurately reflect, respectively, the historical and social conditions for revolution and stability suggested by Weinstein and Platt. See also "On Social Stability and Social Change," in *Psychoanalytic Sociology*, pp. 91–122.

13. Dickens himself confirmed the connection between generational struggle and the Carton-Stryver episode of *A Tale of Two Cities*. Before 1856 Dickens had conceived of a story to be "centered on 'Memory Carton,' jackal to a legal lion, the action to span 'Two Generations' " (Collins, "A Tale of Two Novels," p. 342).

14. Hedva Ben-Israel, *English Historians on the French Revolution* (Cambridge: Cambridge Univ. Press, 1968), p. 98; William Oddie, *Dickens and Carlyle: The Question of Influence* (London: Centenary, 1972), pp. 63–71; Michael Goldberg, *Carlyle and Dickens* (Athens: Univ. of Georgia Press, 1972), p. 103. Most recently, Gordon Spence has argued that "Dickens appears to have been out of sympathy with the French people, except when they were oppressed victims: he was not stirred by their revolt, but his imagination was stimulated by his loathing when they committed atrocities" ("Dickens as a Historical Novelist," *Dickensian*, 72 [1976], 21). Dickens' sympathy, or lack of it, is best explained here on psychological rather than political grounds. When the French people are oppressed, they merit Dickens' lavish sympathy for all the oppressed children of his novels. But when the French justifiably revolt, their aggression implies the ultimate atrocity—patricide—and must be repudiated.

The source material for *A Tale of Two Cities* reveals Dickens' unstated, and probably unconscious, conservative view of the family. Both Oddie and Goldberg show Carlyle's influence on Dickens and the influence of a shared culture, and a common iconography, on both men. Dickens had read one of Carlyle's sources, Mercier's *Tableau de Paris*, which describes the sacrifice of General Loiseroilles, who assumes his son's place at the guillotine and dies for him. If Dickens conceived Carton's substitution for Darnay from this story, he has transformed the disguised iconography of revolution into a conservative parable. In Mercier's account, and in Carlyle's repetition of it, the father is sacrificed so that the son may live and grow; this supposedly real event lends itself to an imaginative splitting and identification on the part of the audience, who can attribute aggression to the "filial" revolutionaries while identifying themselves with the guiltless son. In Dickens' novel Carton assumes the position of the son—in relation to Lorry, in identification with Christ—and dies for a universal sin as well as for the particular sin that makes Darnay an Evrémonde and a representative of the ancien régime. In addition to Goldberg and Oddie, see Collins, "A Tale of Two Novels," and J. A. Falconer, "The Sources of *A Tale of Two Cities*," *Modern Language Notes*, 36 (1921), 1–10.

15. Quoted in John Forster, *The Life of Charles Dickens* (London: Chapman and Hall, 1872–74), III, 329.

16. "*A Tale of Two Cities*," *Twentieth Century Interpretations of* A Tale of Two Cities, ed. Charles E. Beckwith (Englewood Cliffs, N.J.: Prentice-Hall, 1972), p. 26.

17. "*A Tale of Two Cities* is admittedly one of the most strained of Dickens' works, and [Fitzjames] Stephen has little trouble in exposing the mechanism of its grotesqueness which he does with sadistic relish" (George H. Ford, *Dickens and His Readers* [1955; rpt. New York: Norton, 1965], p. 104).

18. In *Charles Dickens: The World of His Novels* (Cambridge: Harvard Univ. Press, 1958), J. Hillis Miller sees another, larger meaning in the resurrection theme. He argues that it suggests a "direct contact with the transhuman." On this basis Miller is able to connect the revolutionary and love stories of the novel, noting the limitations of plot but noting, as well, Dickens' success "in seeing the act of self-sacrifice from the inside" (p. 248).

19. Schizophrenia is itself derived from the Greek term for a "splitting of the mind"; the term was first introduced into psychiatry by Eugen Bleuler in 1911. Freud was concerned primarily with the splitting of the ego, and he applied "splitting" (*Spaltung*) in a far more specific way than Bleuler. See particularly "Fetishism" (*SE*, XXI, 152–57); "An Outline of Psychoanalysis" (*SE*, XXIII, 144–207); "Splitting of the Ego in the Process of Defense" (*SE*, XXIII,

275–78). See also Laplanche and Pontalis under "Schizophrenia" and "Splitting of the Ego." According to the theory of object relations, splitting is an essential reaction of the infant to ambivalence and anxiety. The infant splits its own emotions and projects them onto another person (or "object") and then internalizes the now split object. These theories were developed from Freud primarily by Melanie Klein; see particularly *Contributions to PsychoAnalysis* (London: Hogarth, 1948) and *Developments in Psycho-Analysis,* ed. M. Klein et al. (London: Hogarth, 1952). Robert J. Stoller's *Splitting* (New York: Dell, 1973) relies on Freud's definition: Stoller describes splitting as "a process in which the ego is altered as it attempts to defend itself" (p. xvi). However, Stoller's subtle and comprehensive case history of a multiple-personality patient also draws significantly on modern object-relational theory.

    20.   The use of one aspect of splitting—the "double"—has been noted extensively in literary criticism, and it is an important concept in the French school of psychoanalytic structuralism. Perhaps the best-known example is Jacques Lacan's study of "The Purloined Letter," in which Dupin and the Ministre D. are described as mirror images (see "Seminar on 'The Purloined Letter,' " *Yale French Studies,* 48 [1972], 38–72). Robert Rogers' *A Psychoanalytic Study of the Double in Literature* (Detroit: Wayne State Univ. Press, 1970) describes a variety of literary doubles, particularly in contemporary literature. Rogers, however, uses the term "splitting" either with specific reference to narcissism (pp. 18–30) or in a general sense as interchangeable with "doubling," "fragmentation," and "decomposition" (p. 4). Leonard Manheim applies the term "multiple projection" to *A Tale of Two Cities* in "A Tale of Two Characters: A Study in Multiple Projection," *Dickens Studies Annual,* 1 (1970), 225–37. Manheim effectively demonstrates the connection between what he calls the "novel's leading male character" (Carton-Darnay) and the Jekyll-Hyde feelings of the author, particularly over the affair with Ellen Ternan. His combination of psychoanalysis and biography has different explanatory assumptions and goals from my own, but his evidence and conclusions support the textual analyses of split objects here. Harry Stone traces the relations between psychological biography and one specific fictional pattern throughout Dickens' career in "The Love Pattern in Dickens' Novels," in *Dickens the Craftsman: Strategies of Presentation,* ed. Robert B. Partlow, Jr. (Carbondale: Southern Illinois Univ. Press, 1970), pp. 1–20. Other critics have analyzed doubling and splitting on broader social and moral grounds. Joseph Gold, for example, writes that in *A Tale of Two Cities* "the desire to analyze and integrate the damned and the redeemed in metaphor is the cause of the doubleness which is at the centre of this novel." See *Charles Dickens: Radical Moralist* (Minneapolis: Univ. of Minnesota Press, 1972), p. 232. Georg Lukács sees a profound split—a total dissociation, in fact—between the moral-political and the personal-psychological dimensions of this novel. By using psychoanalytic concepts of splitting to discuss both personal and political aspects of the *Tale,* I am offering an alternative to Lukács's negative judgment; I am also attempting to explain more fully the successes and weaknesses—derived from a common source—that have prompted Lukács to claim that "Dickens . . . weakens the connection between the problems of the characters' lives and the events of the French Revolution" (*The Historical Novel,* trans. Hannah Mitchell and Stanley Mitchell from 2nd German ed. [Boston: Beacon, 1963], p. 243).

    21.   Sir James Fitzjames Stephen, "*A Tale of Two Cities,*" rpt. in *The Dickens Critics,* ed. George H. Ford and Lauriat Lane, Jr. (Ithaca, N.Y.: Cornell Univ. Press, 1961), p. 45; letter from Dickens to F. J. Régnier (15 Oct. 1859), in *The Letters of Charles Dickens,* ed. Walter Dexter (Bloomsbury: Nonesuch, 1938), III, 125–26. Dickens wrote to Régnier, however, on first completing the book, commenting, "I hope it is the best story I have written." Philip Collins wonders whether Dickens meant to stress the word "story," because, notes Collins, it may have been "his best effort, as a story, but no one then, and surely no one since, has regarded it as his best novel" ("A Tale of Two Novels," p. 336).

    22.   "Some Stylistic Devices in *A Tale of Two Cities,*" in *Dickens the Craftsman,* p. 185.

    23.   In spite of Fitzjames Stephen's obvious bias, he did identify the novel's major problems. Shaw simply dismissed the book as "pure sentimental melodrama from beginning to

end" (Introd., *Great Expectations* [Edinburgh: R. & R. Clark, 1937], p. vi), while Chesterton, who liked the *Tale,* echoed a common complaint that both Dickens and Carlyle represent the French Revolution "as a mere elemental outbreak of hunger or vengeance" (*Charles Dickens* [1906; rpt. New York: Schocken, 1965], p. 231). George Gissing was one of the first to call the book uncharacteristic in order to apologize for the sense of "restraint throughout." Dickens "aimed . . . at writing a story for the story's sake. . . . Among other presumed superfluities, humour is dismissed" (*Charles Dickens* [London: Blackie and Son 1898], pp. 54–55). Gissing anticipated a now common failure to connect the larger thematic implications of the story line to the psychological and political meanings of the text.

24. The classic description of this splitting of women is in Freud's "On the Universal Tendency to Debasement in the Sphere of Love," *SE,* XI, 179–90.

25. As both Goldberg and Oddie demonstrate, Dickens drew on Carlyle's *French Revolution* for many of his most vivid incidents and images, including the terrifying figure of Madame Defarge, who was based on the real-life Demoiselle Théroigne described by Carlyle. See Thomas Carlyle, *The French Revolution,* Vols. II–IV of the Centenary Ed. of *The Works of Thomas Carlyle,* ed. H. D. Traill (London: Chapman and Hall, 1896), esp. II, 254–55; III, 288, 293; and IV, 154. Carlyle characteristically combines sexual and violent images in some of his most intense portrayals of revolutionary emotion: "Will Guards named National thrust their bayonets into the bosoms of women? Such a thought, or rather such dim unshaped raw material of a thought, ferments universally under the female nightcap; and, by earliest daybreak, on slight hint, will explode" (II, 250). See, generally, Bk. vii, "The Insurrection of Women," esp. II, 251–54, 278.

26. Madame Defarge in "The Wine-Shop" (facing p. 160) resembles Lucie "After the Sentence" (facing p. 318) and during "The Knock at the Door" (facing p. 266); Lucie's expressions are naturally quite different, but the features of the two women are similar—both women are young and attractive. What appear to be mirror images of the two women are placed opposite each other on the wrapper of the original edition. Carlyle describes Demoiselle Théroigne as "brown-locked, light-behaved, fire-hearted" and as a "Brown eloquent Beauty . . . with the figure of a Heathen Goddess" (II, 135, 264).

Madame Defarge begins to age soon after Dickens' death. The "Household Edition" (New York: Harper, 1878), for example, shows a square-jawed, muscular Madame Defarge, looking very much like a man, on the title page. She looks older, heavier, and uglier by the end of the novel (p. 154), but is at her worst on p. 79, where she bears a remarkable resemblance to the aging Queen Victoria.

27. This last passage is noted by Michael Steig and F. A. C. Wilson ("Hortense vs. Bucket: The Ambiguity of Order in *Bleak House,*" *Modern Language Quarterly,* 33 [1972], 296), and they indicate that the image "points forward to Mme. Defarge." Hortense herself appears to have been modeled on Maria Manning, a murderer whose beauty and splendid mode of dress brought thirty thousand people to her execution. See Philip Collins, *Dickens and Crime,* 2nd ed. (London: Macmillan, 1965), pp. 235–40.

28. On *Copperfield* see Leonard Manheim, "The Personal History of David Copperfield," *American Imago,* 9 (1952), 21–43.

29. For David's behavior see particularly Gwendolyn B. Needham, "The Undisciplined Heart of David Copperfield," *Nineteenth-Century Fiction,* 9 (1954), 81–107. Some of Needham's conclusions are questioned by William H. Marshall in "The Image of Steerforth and the Structure of *David Copperfield,*" *Tennessee Studies in Literature,* 5 (1960), 57–65.

30. Julian Moynahan and Harry Stone were the first critics to point out in detail the role of Orlick as heroic alter ego. See Moynahan, "The Hero's Guilt: The Case of *Great Expectations,*" *Essays in Criticism,* 10 (1960), 60–79, and Stone, "Fire, Hand, and Gate: Dickens' Great Expectations," *Kenyon Review,* 24 (1962), 662–91. In my "Crime and Fantasy in *Great Expectations,*" *Psychoanalysis and Literary Process,* ed. Frederick Crews (Cambridge, Mass.: Winthrop, 1970), pp. 25–65, I attempt to extend this view of the hero's guilt while analyzing the father-

son conflicts (and resolutions) that characterize the novel and determine its structure. One temporary resolution of generational struggle in *Great Expectations* is achieved through the comedy of Wemmick and his "Aged P.," which is in turn based on the psychological conflicts implicit in the world of Victorian business.

31. *Charles Dickens: His Tragedy and Triumph* (New York: Simon, 1952), II, 979.

Dickens' *A Tale of Two Cities:*
The Poetics of Impasse

Lawrence Frank

A Tale of Two Cities has, for too long, been Sydney Carton's novel. The sheer melodramatic force of his last, unspoken words continues to obscure the significance of Charles Darnay's moral and psychological dilemma. Of course, Darnay is all too often a prig, a bourgeois pilgrim en route, like David Copperfield, to a secular celestial city. But he is, however ambiguously, the novel's hero. It is Carton, not Darnay, who is the foil. In the popular imagination, their rôles are commonly reversed. For who can resist either the novel's insistence in that cadenced conclusion, " 'It is a far, far better thing that I do, than I have ever done; it is a far, far better rest that I go to than I have ever known' "; or memories of Ronald Coleman as Sydney Carton? Dickens himself had been fascinated by Carton's precursor, Richard Wardour, a character in Wilkie Collins' *The Frozen Deep*. He helped to fashion the part of Wardour and then portrayed it in private, and finally, public performances of the play in 1857: Richard Wardour, like Sydney Carton, is a man who dies saving his rival's life. *A Tale of Two Cities* does not specifically emerge out of Dickens' suspicious identification with Wardour, but *The Frozen Deep* undeniably works its subversive way through a novel whose subject seems to be the French Revolution.[1]

Its ostensible subject, revolution and social change, suggests at once that *A Tale of Two Cities* is serious in ways *The Frozen Deep* is not. But its true seriousness is not that of the historical action it proclaims itself to be. There is a profoundly ahistorical thrust to the novel. George Lukács approaches the truth when he claims, in *The Historical Novel,* that the French Revolution serves as a "romantic background" to the fates of Lucie, Doctor Manette, Carton and Darnay.[2] Dickens is not primarily concerned with the forces of historical determinism. He may, in the prophetic first chapter of the novel, seek to invoke a revitalized historical imagination alert to the meaning of the past and committed to social change in the present. But the incantatory phrases of the opening pages finally give way to the nightmare vision of social chaos and

Lawrence Frank, "Dickens's *A Tale of Two Cities:* The Poetics of Impasse." *American Imago* 36 (1979): 215–44. © 1979. Reprinted by permission of The Johns Hopkins University Press.

personal impasse with which the novel ends. The French Revolution *becomes* the Carmagnole, a frenzied dance in which dehumanized revellers, their individual and even sexual identities obscured by their depravity, belie the original promise of the Revolution itself. The Carmagnole speaks of timeless, dionysian forces beyond history.

A Tale of Two Cities is not, then, one of Lukács' realist fictions in which "man is *zoon politikon*," in which the "individual existence . . . cannot be distinguished from [its] social and historical environment."[3] It is precisely the sundering of the characters' "specific individuality" from the "context in which they [are] created" which occurs in the novel. Charles Darnay's individuality is not rooted in the social reality into which he is born. He becomes one of Lukács' modernist heroes, because the decadence of the French aristocracy in the eighteenth century merges with a more permanent reality, enduring irrevocably throughout the whole of human history.

Certain unchanging facts of human existence begin to emerge tentatively in the second chapter of the novel.[4] The Dover Mail appears, immersed in a "steaming mist . . . dense enough to shut out everything from the light of the coach-lamps but these its own workings, and a few yards of road. . . ."[5] The coach suggests the self-contained nature of the little world it is, and the irremedial solitude of the three passengers, each "hidden under almost as many wrappers from the eyes of the mind, as from the eyes of the body, of his two companions." The passengers' isolation is beyond the transforming influence of peaceful, or violent, social change. It is a given of the human condition: "Man thus conceived is an ahistorical being. . . . Man is now what he has always been and always will be. The narrator, the examining subject, is in motion; the examined reality is static."[6]

Lukács, the subtle Marxist critic, perceives the ahistorical tendency in Dickens' imagination. He accounts for it by calling Dickens hopelessly bourgeois: for Lukács, the emphasis on the irremedial isolation of the individual, rather than on social alienation, involves a distortion of man's true being. But if Dickens is bourgeois, which he certainly is, it is not finally a self-serving class blindness to which he falls prey. He believes in the isolation he depicts. And Dickens' bourgeois vision shapes the characteristic manner in which he imagines change and renders the origins of the French Revolution. Dickens, the subtle bourgeois novelist, inevitably imagines historical situations in domestic, familial, terms. Most readers of *A Tale of Two Cities,* and I include myself, tend to forget that the novel, literally and figuratively, originates in a rape. The dying woman whom the St. Evrémonde twins summon Doctor Manette to attend, on a December night in 1757, will prove to be the ravished sister of Thérèse Defarge. The episode is charged with social and historical implications: the rape points to the ruthless exploitation of one class by another, and to the consequences which must follow. But the rape has other, more volatile implications which come to dominate the novel. In their patriarchal relationship to their tenants, the St. Evrémonde twins prey upon those who stand, figuratively, in the place of sons and daughters to them. Unwittingly, Doctor Manette, himself a potentially rebellious son, finds himself in the midst of a primal scene in which the father is engaged in dark and unspeakable acts. He is confronted, in the starkest terms, by the power of the father.

Dickens has initiated a family drama in which generations impinge upon each other's fate. The national struggle Dickens sets out to depict becomes a generational one in which ideology and class cease to be central. The conflict between generations presents itself as recurring and inescapable, not subject to amelioration as social conditions are, at least hypothetically, subject to change. Generation is forever pitted against generation; sons, and daughters, writhe forever in the grasp of unyielding fathers. And it is Charles Darnay, not Sydney Carton, whose career reveals the son's complex, perhaps doomed, struggle to free himself from the father's tyranny.

The unyielding nature of the father, and the past for which he stands, is embodied in the St. Evrémonde château: "It was a heavy mass of building, that château of Monsieur the Marquis, with a large stone court-yard before it, and two stone sweeps of staircase meeting in a stone terrace before the principal door. A stony business altogether . . . [as] if the Gorgon's head had surveyed it, when it was finished, two centuries ago" (II, ix). The inertia of the French aristocracy, its stony indifference to the needs of the poor, its arrogant effort to deny time and to perpetuate itself forever are *there* in Ruskinian terms. The present Marquis is no more than an extension of the house, at best a living version of one of the "stone faces of men" adorning it. He gazes at the world from behind his "fine mask" of stone, enduring a self-inflicted paralysis as he speaks for his class, and the primacy of the father and the past.[7] His charge, as he sees it, is to transmit to his nephew, Darnay, the Gorgon's spell under which *he* has lived, the St. Evrémonde legacy of social and personal repression. For the Marquis, " 'Repression is the only lasting philosophy' " (II, ix). In denying the claims of those beneath him and the fact of his own mortality, the Marquis is almost as dead as the gargoyles his own face resembles.

The Marquis St. Evrémonde is indistinguishable from his château. The pile of stones, like the dust mounds of Old John Harmon in *Our Mutual Friend*, expresses the father's determination to perpetuate himself, in defiance of time and his heirs, even through life-denying forms. In this way, *A Tale of Two Cities* is analogous to another, later, novel exploring the fate of dynastic ambitions. In William Faulkner's *Absalom, Absalom!*, as John Irwin observes, ". . . Sutpen's revenge requires that he found a dynasty, for the proof that he has succeeded in becoming the father will finally be achieved only when he bequeaths his authority and power to his son as an inheritance (a gift, not a right), thereby establishing the son's dependence on his father and thus the father's mastery."[8] The Marquis does not quite seek Sutpen's revenge upon a society which has affronted him. Perhaps his effort to achieve the "father's mastery" of the son involves a bizarre protest against his own acquiescence to his " 'natural destiny' " as others once saw it. But the Marquis, as the twin of Darnay's dead father, clearly stands in the place of the biological father as his surrogate.

Darnay's sense of the wrongs perpetrated by his family involves him in a complex relationship, both to the uncle and the dead father. His defiance of his uncle's command that he accept his destiny is an attack upon the past, the "father's time," upon the father himself: " '. . . [I am] bound to a system that is frightful to me, responsible for it, but powerless in it; seeking . . . to have mercy and to redress; and tortured by seeking assistance and power in vain' " (II, ix). Darnay speaks, far more directly than usual, for all the troubled sons, and daughters, of Dickens' later novels. They confront the father's authority, his will, his legacy, binding them to the past, to sterile repetitions of the habitual stance of the dead father. In *Our Mutual Friend,* the all-too-literal Harmon Will tempts John Harmon into an acceptance of his father's twisted values, into becoming a mere instrument, or appendage, of the father. In acquiescing, Harmon would forfeit his right to be a father on his own terms. To Darnay, the Marquis speaks of the primacy of the father's time, a chronicle of social injustice, murder and rape. In his defiance, Darnay renounces a dead, and a potentially deadening, past: he affirms his right to create a new, more viable tradition.[9]

On the night of Darnay's formal renunciation of his country, his property and his family name, Gaspard assassinates the Marquis St. Evrémonde. The two events merge in the narrative line of the novel. But this is not melodramatic coincidence. Darnay's renunciation is a form of rebellion: he has dealt a fatal blow to his uncle, his family and the repugnant values of the past. The Marquis' murder serves as a seal to Darnay's decision, made five years before, to confer upon himself a new name, and a new identity as a good bourgeois. The implications of Darnay's act, metonymically fused with Gaspard's, are all too clear. The mender of roads, who brings the news of Gaspard's execution to the Defarges, has heard the villagers whispering " '. . . that because [Gaspard] has slain Monseigneur, and because Monseigneur was the father of his tenants—serfs—what you will—he will be executed as a parricide' " (II, xv). The bankrupt feudalism of Bourbon France still tries to assert the validity of the patriarchal relationship between master and tenant that it has itself subverted. The dead Marquis has failed in every way as the "father" of his peasants, even as the surrogate father of his nephew. But the inviolable person of the father remains a cornerstone of the philosophy of repression by which the Marquis lives, and dies. Assassins like Gaspard have been traditionally dealt with as parricides. Their punishment is a warning to every restive son:

> "One old man says at the fountain, that his right hand, armed with the knife, will be burnt off before his face; that, into wounds which will be made in his arms, his breast, and his legs, there will be poured boiling oil, melted lead, hot

resin, wax, and sulphur; finally, that he will be torn limb from limb by four strong horses." (II, xv)

The assassin's right hand, " 'armed' " with the knife, is mutilated so that no other hand or arm will be raised against the father. The assassin's body is so completely violated that no one at the execution may think even of his body as his own; it belongs to the father. The body, the self, is subject to mutilation at the father's whim. To threaten the father, even as Darnay does, is to commit the ultimate sin against the society and the past for which the patriarchal figure stands.

Gaspard's execution is less barbaric than those in earlier reigns: he is merely hanged. But vestiges of the old ritual persist: " 'On the top of the gallows is fixed the knife, blade upwards, with its point in the air' " (II, xv). The knife is symbolic by design, standing for the hand and arm that wielded it, while conjuring up the old terror of the father's revenge upon the sons who challenge him. By bringing Darnay and Gaspard together upon the night of the Marquis' assassination, Dickens effectively unites them. Darnay, in his act of renunciation, has incurred the guilt of the parricide.

The trial in the Old Bailey is chronologically prior to the Marquis' death, but it serves, in spite of its mockery of justice, to raise the complex issue of Darnay's guilt. Darnay's perception of the crowd in the courtroom anticipates the description of the executions of Gaspard and those parricides who were his predecessors: "The accused, who was (and who knew he was) being mentally hanged, beheaded, and quartered, by everybody there, neither flinched from the situation, nor assumed any theatrical air in it" (II, ii). "Treason" and parricide are one, the punishment for either crime the same. Darnay is figuratively on trial for his continuing rebellion against France (not England) and the father. But, surely, evil fathers, like corrupt regimes, *must* be defied. The son is not obligated to acquiesce to a tyrannical father or to the past he embodies. But if the son's defiance, regardless of its form, is perceived by father and son as parricide, the son's own sense of his necessary act becomes shrouded in guilt. If the need to create new personal and social forms leads to the original sin against the father, it becomes a task from which most men shrink. Self-assertion, viewed always as parricide, becomes impossible.

Darnay's muted heroism lies in his effort to change and to become free of the father through the creation, ex nihilo, of a new identity. He incurs the parricide's guilt. Nonetheless, his remains a flawed renunciation, a suspect rebellion. His dying mother, in imploring him " 'to have mercy and to redress,' " has committed him to a Sisyphean labor. Darnay falters before his all-too-accurate perception of the " 'misery and ruin' " about him. He speaks of a " 'curse' " on the land, and thinks only of placing the St. Evrémonde property " 'into some hands better qualified to free it slowly (if such a thing is possible) from the weight that drags it down . . .' " (II, ix). But there are no hands better qualified than his own. He may not delegate his responsibilities to others, to minor functionaries like the befuddled Gabelle. In his renunciation Darnay reveals a tendency to self-deception. He wants to obliterate the past, to elude the responsibility he has acknowledged as his alone.

The authenticity of Darnay's revolt is undermined by other factors. Through his spies the Marquis has learned of his nephew's relationship to Doctor Manette and Lucie. The Marquis is a cynic, revelling in ironies of which Darnay cannot be aware. But cynics more than occasionally touch the raw nerve of truth: " 'A Doctor with a daughter. Yes. So commences the new philosophy!' " (II, ix). For the Marquis Darnay is fulfilling his destiny, repeating a version of that act to which Doctor Manette became an unwilling witness. The Marquis also senses that Darnay is a little *too* eager to accept the idea of a curse upon the St. Evrémondes. Darnay calls England his refuge. But it is not England as much as the Manette household in Soho which lures Darnay away from his native France. The "new philosophy" of which the Marquis speaks with such disdain may, after all, be founded primarily on Darnay's selfish desire for Lucie and the tranquility over which she presides. The son's rebellion, with all its inherent risks, has been almost emptied of meaning. Darnay faces a new risk, akin to that described by V. E. von Gebsattel in "The World of the Compulsive":

> We see that an action can be completely executed, in the sense that it has served to implement a purpose, without being completed—or indeed, having occurred at all—in terms of its life-historical meaning. Although it is done, it is as if it had not been done. The person, as a living being moving ahead in time, does not enter into the objective performance of his action, and therefrom arises—after the completion of the action—doubt as to the reality of its occurrence.[10]

"Although it is done, it is as if it had not been done." Darnay is a "parricide" who has not accepted the implications and consequences of his act. He has defied the primal taboo, and has achieved nothing.

In fleeing the social and personal paralysis embodied in the St. Evrémonde château, Darnay unwittingly embraces it. He moves from an unyielding past towards a tentative future with Lucie which is, itself, but another encounter with everything he has denied. He is Oedipus fleeing Corinth, only to find himself on the road to Thebes. The trial in the Old Bailey, quite apart from its chronological place in the novel, introduces Darnay to the fate with which he dimly struggles throughout *A Tale of Two Cities*. His guilt is multiple and paradoxical: he is the would-be parricide and the man for whom the act has had no "life-historical meaning." He is fixed in an untenable situation, aware of a sense of guilt which is finally existential in nature: he is in a treasonous relationship, to himself and others.

Over Darnay's head "there [is] a mirror, to throw the light down upon him":

Crowds of the wicked and the wretched had been reflected in it, and had passed from its surface and this earth's together. Haunted in a most ghastly manner that abominable place would have been, if the glass could ever have rendered back its reflections, as the ocean is one day to give up its dead. Some passing thought of the infamy and disgrace for which it had been reserved, may have struck the prisoner's mind. . . . he looked up; and when he saw the glass his face flushed. . . . (II, ii)

This is a uniquely Dickensian moment. Darnay's reflection mingles, if only in his own imagination, with the reflections of "the wicked and the wretched" who once stood where he now stands. The experience defines Darnay's unconscious relationship to himself and to others. Momentarily, Darnay has looked into the hidden currents of himself, those currents suggested in Dickens' brooding meditation in the third chapter of the novel: "No more can I look into the depths of this unfathomable water, wherein, as momentary lights glanced into it, I have had glimpses of buried treasures and *other things* submerged" (I, iii, italics mine). The face floating beneath the mirror's surface cannot be effaced because it exists at some level within Darnay's own consciousness, and potentially within the consciousness of others.[11] In ways he does not yet acknowledge, he shares in the guilt of all those who have stood in the prisoner's dock and who have been condemned, rather than exonerated. The Marquis St. Evrémonde has failed to turn Darnay into another stone figure like himself. But, the ambiguities of Darnay's flawed rebellion have, ironically, fixed Darnay's guilt-ridden image of himself. During his trial Darnay pulls back from his moment of intuitive self-knowledge. But this vision of himself lurks within Darnay, waiting to return from the depths, "as the ocean is one day to give up its dead."

Dickens has suggested forms of culpability, and their consequences, unacknowledged by any court of law, but present in the court of one's own consciousness. Yet, for much of *A Tale of Two Cities,* Dickens avoids a direct exploration of the impact of Darnay's bad faith upon his life. Rather, he explores Darnay's condition indirectly. Even Sydney Carton, as the "Double of coarse deportment," only cryptically signals that beneath the façade of Darnay's conventional self there is a deep-seated dislocation of the spirit. As the jury deliberates, Darnay and Carton stand "side by side, both reflected in the glass above them" (II, iii). A process of displacement occurs, as it does later in the novel in the metonymic relationship of Darnay and Gaspard. The mirror fleetingly contains two identical reflections. But only fleetingly, for Carton's reflection usurps Darnay's, at least that reflection Darnay has glimpsed buried in the mirror, and in the self. Detached from its origin, it gains an autonomous existence of its own.[12] Carton suggests Darnay's passive and guilty self, the self which can tell Lucie, " 'I am like one who died young. All my life might have been' " (II, xiii). He attests to the state of paralysis in which the respectable Darnay will, in fact, be living until the outbreak of the Revolution.

This relationship between counterparts underlies all that happens when Darnay and Carton are left alone together in the darkness outside the Old Bailey. Darnay is still " 'frightfully confused regarding time and place' "; he feels " '. . . hardly . . . to belong to this world again' " (II, iv). Under such circumstances, before the reprieved conventional self has managed to re-establish its primacy, the shadow self asserts its existence. Carton, only now, and perhaps never again, speaks freely of his own self-abhorrence and warns his Double of the dangers facing him. Carton, an artist of despair, knows the subtle ways in which the will may be subverted. His own sense of "the blight on him," to which he has resigned himself, has attuned him to the same blight secretly at work in others. He tries to pierce the complacency of Darnay, who may eventually misuse his own talents, but he fails. The episode ends with Carton in earnest discourse with *his* image, reflected in a glass upon the tavern wall. He has perceived a version of himself from which he is irrevocably cut off: he is as alienated from conventional potentialities within himself as Darnay seems to be from those darker potentialities he has implicitly denied.

Curiously, this meeting never leads to an evolving, complex relationship. Dickens knowingly exploits Doppelgänger relationships in his most successful psychological fiction. But in *A Tale of Two Cities* none of the dramatic intensity of David Copperfield's friendship with Steerforth or of Eugene Wrayburn's obsession with Bradley Headstone emerges from the interview between Darnay and Carton. Darnay dismisses the evening with Carton from his consciousness, repressing any understanding of the man who has saved his life. He can speak of Carton only "as a problem of carelessness and recklessness"; he chooses to see no more. Dickens has decided to make Carton's life as shadowy as possible, in part a consequence of his similarity to the character of Richard Wardour in *The Frozen Deep*.[13] Carton, unlike Darnay, seems to lack a significant past. There are vague references to a "youth of great promise," to student days in Paris, and to his father's death. But Carton remains in the shadows, a literary blank cheque to be called upon at the novel's end to resolve the apparently irresolvable.

However, Darnay and Carton are linked by a shared experience, the common fate of every son. Their lives are significantly shaped by dead fathers and the father surrogates they encounter. Darnay defies his uncle, the Marquis; Carton contends with Stryver, "a man of little more than thirty, but looking twenty years older . . ." (II, iv). Old enough, in appearance, to be Carton's father. Stryver even bullies Carton in a parental way: " 'You summon no energy and purpose. Look at me' " (II, v). Carton's response implicitly condemns Stryver: " '. . . you were always somewhere, and I was always—nowhere' " (II, v). This is the son's eternal complaint against the father who refuses to give him space in which to exist.[14] It is the only challenge to

Stryver that seems potentially telling. In his self-destructive manner, Carton defies Stryver's summons to a conventionally energetic life of " 'driving and riving and shouldering and pressing' " which denies the integrity of others. Stryver, the pale English version of the Marquis St. Evrémonde, asks Carton to model himself upon *him,* to shoulder his way through the world: but Carton prefers not to.

Fathers and forms of parricide remain at the center of *A Tale of Two Cities.* Dickens chooses to dwell occasionally upon Darnay's experience in England as a bourgeois hero. But Darnay's economic strivings are really only of secondary importance. His relationship to Lucie, and especially to her father, is far more significant. Darnay has come to England to fulfill his destiny through his encounter with the Manettes. Lucie and the Doctor have taken lodgings near Soho-square. The courtyard of the house in which they live brandishes "a golden arm starting out of the wall of [a] front hall," the emblem of "some mysterious giant," an invisible worker in precious metals who shares the building with the Manettes by day (II, vi). The detail seems hardly worth noting. Yet it points to the true nature of Darnay's evolving relationship to Manette. The presence of the seemingly anomalous golden arm is related to Dickens' conscious pun upon Manette's name, "la main," French for hand, and becomes a part of the parricidal matrix in the novel. The golden arm has a specific, and telling, antecedent in *David Copperfield.* When he first meets Mr. Spenlow in Doctors' Commons, David notices Spenlow's gold watch-chain: "[it] was so massive, that a fancy came across me, that he ought to have a sinewy golden arm, to draw it out with, like those which are put up over the gold-beaters' shops."[15] The similarities between David Copperfield's and Charles Darnay's situation are clear enough: the play with Dickens' own initials simply emphasize them. Like David and Mr. Spenlow, Darnay and Manette are fated to become rivals, not only for Lucie's love, but for supremacy in their own relationship. Lucie only appears to be the center of the "tranquil bark" anchored in the quiet corner in Soho. The golden arm of the "mysterious giant" does not proclaim Lucie's maternal dove, but Manette's potency, the father's potency of arm and hand. In his new life, Manette has become "a very energetic man indeed, with great firmness of purpose, strength of resolution, and vigour of action" (II, x).

Darnay has fled his " 'natural destiny' " in France, only to encounter it in England. He has denied one father in the form of the Marquis; now he meets in Manette the father he might have chosen for himself. Quite apart from the issue of the St. Evrémonde legacy and Manette's imprisonment, there occurs the mythical meeting of the son seeking to become a parent in his own right and the father who may thwart his efforts. And, as in *David Copperfield,* the fate of the father becomes problematic: must Manette, too, die, as Mr. Spenlow does, to make way for the son?

Manette is a far more complex, and powerful, father surrogate than the others abounding in Dickens' novels: the golden arm, the emblem of force and potency, attests to that. The virtual sterility of characters like Mr. Jarndyce in *Bleak House,* Daniel Doyce in *Little Dorrit* and Noddy Boffin in *Our Mutual Friend* makes them attractive to those who seek them out. Their goodness, and their childlessness, is reassuring: they pose no threats to Esther Summerson, Arthur Clennam or John Harmon, whose real parents, living or dead, are formidable, and destructive, figures. But Manette has experienced real suffering and managed a precarious recovery. He is neither ineffectual nor childless. His love for Lucie competes with Darnay's, as Darnay himself vaguely recognizes: " 'I know,' said Darnay, respectfully, '. . . that between you and Miss Manette there is an affection so unusual, so touching, so belonging to the circumstances in which it has been nurtured, that it can have few parallels . . .' " (II, x). Darnay's language suggests Cordelia and Lear, Dickens' own little Nell and her grandfather. It also hints at the ambiguity of Manette's love for his daughter, who has entered his life not as an asexual child, but as a young woman. Darnay's persistent, and unnerving, scrupulosity takes him closer and closer to the truth: " 'I know that when [Lucie] is clinging to you, the hands of baby, girl, and woman, all in one, are round your neck' " (II, x). Darnay thinks he understands the sanctity of Manette's and Lucie's love for each other. He has, however, defined Manette's relationship to Lucie as a marriage to the idealized Victorian bride.[16] Inevitably, he and Manette are rivals. But Darnay vows not to displace the father, not to lay hands upon him: " '. . . I look . . . [not] to divide with Lucie her privilege as your child, companion, and friend; but to come in aid of it, and bind her closer to you, if such a thing can be' " (II, x). But " 'such a thing' " cannot be. Poor Manette can answer only with silence, and a "look which [has] a tendency in it to dark doubt and dread." He suspects Darnay is a St. Evrémonde and recognizes the various threats his future son-in-law must pose to himself.

Darnay continues upon an increasingly labyrinthine process of self-deception. He cannot fulfill his vow to Lucie's father. If Manette were Jarndyce, Doyce or Noddy Boffin, things would be different. But the golden arm of the mysterious giant retains its emblematic force. Darnay has promised that loyalty to the father which, if he is to become both husband and father himself, he cannot honor. Eventually, he must raise his own hand and arm against Manette, if only figuratively. He must, in time, assert himself and his own rights and deny those of Manette. Once again, Darnay is flirting with fixation and arrest. Even the benign father must finally give way before the legitimate claims of the young. Perhaps, for once, the transfer of power from father to son will not necessitate either the father's death or the son's defeat.

The dead-end into which Darnay is moving is complicated by other factors which are directly connected to his decision to leave France. He tries earnestly to identify himself with Manette as a " 'voluntary exile from France; like [him], driven from it by its distractions, oppressions and miseries' ": " '. . . I look only to sharing your fortunes, sharing your life and home, and being faithful to you to the death' " (II, x). This speech can be accepted at face value only if we ignore the ominous ambiguity of the word, " 'death,' " and if we abandon our capacity to make important moral distinctions. Darnay's experience has not been Manette's. He has been victimized by his own class in the sense that he feels repugnance for the moral and political heritage he is expected to uphold. But Darnay has not been persecuted as Manette, Thérèse Defarge, Gaspard and countless others have. The only legitimate basis for Darnay's identification with Manette lies in his renunciation of his title: he has refused to perpetuate the crimes of the past. But he has also abdicated his responsibilities to his own class and to the peasants who continue, as he knows, to suffer. France remains unchanged in spite of Darnay's gesture of revolt.

Darnay, as son and social rebel, clings precariously to the fragile conception of himself formulated in his interview with Manette. The interview ends upon a masterstroke of rectitude designed to consolidate Darnay's identity. Darnay asks Manette to speak to Lucie neither in his favor, nor against him. The Doctor is effectively stymied. He has no real choice but to say, " '. . . [if there were] any fancies, any reasons, any apprehensions, anything whatsoever, new or old, against the man she really loved—the direct responsibility thereof not lying on his head—they should all be obliterated for her sake' " (II, x). Manette's words fail to arouse curiosity, or foreboding, in Darnay although they allude, however indirectly, to all the facts that Darnay's account of himself has skirted. But Manette has conferred that absolution Darnay has been seeking: absolution from those crimes he has not himself committed, but which his class and his family have. An absolution devoutly to be wished. But one which no man, not even a victim of the St. Evrémondes, may confer. In *A Tale of Two Cities,* there is no absolution for the father's deeds, no refuge from generational conflict.

Darnay's marriage to Lucie Manette resolves nothing. It leads only to another act of parricide on Darnay's part. His revelation of his true identity, confirming what Manette already suspects, causes the Doctor's relapse: after the ceremony ". . . Mr. Lorry observed a great change to have come over the Doctor; as if the golden arm uplifted there, had struck him a poisoned blow" (II, xviii). The golden arm no longer stands for Manette's paternal strength alone. Now it announces the son's emerging power. The phrasing in the passage recalls the murder of the Marquis and the punishment inflicted upon parricides like Gaspard, whose corpse has been left hanging from the gallows, poisoning the village well below it. Once more Darnay is the unwitting parricide, subject to the guilt and punishment which is the parricide's timeless fate. This time Manette recovers after regressing to his pathetic condition as the shoemaker of the North Tower. But he remains vulnerable to future, more final, blows from the son's arm.

A Tale of Two Cities, like so many of Dickens' novels, has led to impasse, to a sense of the impossibility of normal change and growth. Darnay seems condemned to a perpetual repetition of that parricidal act he has committed in France. It undermines all that he does. He may prosper in London. He may marry and have children. But his life remains false, based upon a denial of his guilt and his responsibility. In their nocturnal interview Carton has warned, " 'Don't let your sober face elate you, . . . you don't know what it may come to' " (II, iv). The face with which Darnay meets the world masks that *other* face he has glimpsed in the Old Bailey mirror. As usual, in Dickens' novels, the issue is defined in an indirect way. The news of Darnay's impending marriage reaches the Defarges in Saint Antoine through John Barsad, now a spy for the French monarchy: " 'And speaking of Gaspard . . . , it is a curious thing that [Manette's daughter] is going to marry the nephew of Monsieur the Marquis, for whom Gaspard was exalted to the height of so many feet; in other words, the present Marquis' " (II, xvi). Barsad's apparently casual observations connect Manette's persecution, the Marquis' murder, Gaspard's execution and Darnay's marriage. Darnay would protest that he is not " 'the present Marquis,' " that he has relinquished the title. But one "father" has been slain. The "son," his heir, lives in self-imposed exile while the peasants of the St. Evrémonde estate endure their scarecrow existence in the midst of a France that is now a wasteland. Darnay, the father, has left unchanged the lives of those to whom he is directly responsible. He lives " 'unknown in England,' " where he is " 'no Marquis' ": unknown to his tenants in France; unknown to his wife; unknown, finally, to himself.

Darnay's trial for treason has never ended. It pursues its subterranean course during the years of domestic tranquility in Soho. But the outbreak of the Revolution in 1789 brings this period of serenity to its necessary end. The failure to produce change in France, in part, Darnay's failure, leads to violent upheaval. A "living sea," an "ocean of faces," sweeps across France, engulfing the old order. In Saint Antoine its "scarecrows" raise a "forest of naked arms," struggling "in the air like shrivelled branches of trees in a winter wind: all the fingers convulsively clutching at every weapon or semblance of a weapon that was thrown up from the depths below . . ." (II, xxi). Arm, hand, blade join in the final, convulsive assault upon the father. The day of judgment has come at last. This ocean of faces, "whose depths were yet unfathomed and whose forces were yet unknown," returns us to the mirror in the Old Bailey: "Haunted in a most ghastly manner that abominable place would have been, if the glass could ever have rendered back its reflections, as the ocean is one day to give up its dead." In Paris the ocean yields up its dead. In their lust for retribution, the revolutionaries incur the guilt of "the wicked and the wretched" who once stood in the prisoner's dock. The language Dickens uses indicates that they exist in that relationship to Darnay which he has so long denied, that he participates in the events of the Revolution.

Once begun, the national orgy of retribution becomes a frenzied vegetation rite, an attempt to placate the gods and to rid France of its moral pestilence. The ritualistic element in the Revolution expresses itself in the capture and execution of old Foulon, who has " 'caused himself to be represented as dead, and [has] had a grand mock-funeral' " (II, xxii). The people of Saint Antoine resurrect Foulon, whose crime has been to tell " 'the famished people that they might eat grass.' " They resurrect, and punish him: Foulon's severed head is impaled "upon a spike, with grass enough in the mouth for all Saint Antoine to dance at the sight of" (II, xxii). Old Foulon becomes a version of Frazer's corn-god effigy, standing simultaneously for the king and the father: he is mutilated and returned to the earth, so that the nation, the people and the wasted land be renewed.

In a remarkably compressed sequence of events Dickens merges the social and personal dimensions of the novel. Foulon's ruse is only one of a series of feigned deaths to which others have resorted. The most extravagant example is the mock-funeral of Roger Cly, informer and cohort of John Barsad (himself dead to his original name, Solomon Pross). But the Marquis St. Evrémonde has been dead to the suffering of the people. Even Charles Darnay has died: he has entered a limbo of complicity in which he still exists. Events sweep over Foulon, Darnay and France itself. Water transforms itself into fire, in this period of elemental chaos, and reaches out to destroy the St. Evrémonde château which has stood for both social and personal paralysis throughout the novel. The revolutionaries' naked arms, earlier compared to the "shrivelled branches of trees," cease to be atrophied and ineffectual. As a living forest of smoke and flame, they now attack the château which seems "as if it were the face of the cruel Marquis, burning at the stake. . . ."[17] We are very close to the world of *Totem and Taboo* here. The assassination of the Marquis, repeated in the ritualistic execution of Old Foulon, is performed once more, as if a single act of parricide is not enough. The château, and all it represents, disintegrates: "Molten lead and iron boiled in the marble basin of the fountain; the water ran dry; the extinguisher tops of the towers vanished like ice . . . and trickled down into four rugged wells of flame" (II, xxiii). The father's effort to perpetuate himself through a tyrannical social system, impregnable stone and subservient progeny has come to this. The Gorgon's spell is broken at last. Revolution has become the only way to alleviate social and personal impasse. The political event mirrors the individual upheaval to which figures like Darnay will soon be exposed. The Revolution inundates France with blood and flame: it is one parricidal act which seeks to run its full course.

The patriarchal forces encouraging impasse and denying change and evolution succumb to the Revolution. Sustained tyranny causes and demands retribution, which may itself be subverted by the intensity of its fervor. Even Charles Darnay, who has futilely tried to elude his responsibility through exile and marriage, finds himself resurrected into the flux of events. The identity, the self, he has so carefully shaped more than fourteen years before, when he appeared on the packet-ship, " 'in the dead of night,' " must yield, like the St. Evrémonde château, to the chaos of the times: Darnay must relinquish his present identity or become its victim.

The opportunity for change first presents itself to Darnay at Tellson's in London. With the Revolution the Bank functions as the refuge of Monseigneur "as a class," a class which has taken to its collective heels, abandoning France to her fate. Darnay inevitably finds himself talking to Mr. Lorry in the midst of the vain chatter and complaints of people to whom he is still related in ways he prefers not to understand: "And it was such vapouring all about his ears, like a troublesome confusion of blood in his own head, added to a latent uneasiness in his mind, which had already made Charles Darnay restless, and which still kept him so" (II, xxiv). The disorientation Darnay once felt on the night of his trial for treason returns. All the repressed doubts about the legitimacy of his past acts are aroused. Through Gabelle's letter, addressed to " 'Monsieur heretofore the Marquis St. Evrémonde, of France,' " Darnay's natural destiny inescapably confronts him.[18] The disparaging observations by the emigrés and Stryver about "the Marquis who was not to be found" ironically hit the mark. Each malicious comment possesses that element of truth he can't ignore: he *is* " 'a craven who [has] abandoned his post' "; there *is* " 'contamination in such a scoundrel' " (II, xxiv). However unwittingly, Darnay, like old Foulon, has in effect told his tenants to eat grass. He has struck Manette a poisoned blow by his very presence in England. Gabelle's letter, his plea to the emigrant to whom he has remained loyal in his way, almost to death itself, transforms a "latent uneasiness" into a crystallized realization.

Darnay moves out of Tellson's into the quiet of the Temple near which the heads of executed felons were once "exposed . . . with an insensate brutality and ferocity worthy of Abyssinia or Ashantee" (II, i). Temple Bar alludes to the trial in the Old Bailey and to the fates of the Marquis and old Foulon. It is the appropriate place in which Darnay's uneasiness can finally express itself: ". . . in his horror of [his uncle's murder] . . . , and in the aversion with which his conscience regarded the crumbling fabric that he was supposed to uphold, he had acted imperfectly . . . . in his love for Lucie, his renunciation of his social place . . . had been hurried and incomplete" (II, xxiv). In these reflections, Darnay confronts the common omissions and failures of men everywhere, in all ages. He has succumbed to the temptations time always offers: ". . . the events of this week annihilated the immature plans of last week, and the events of the week following made all new again; . . . to the force of these circumstances he had yielded:—not without disquiet, but still without continuous and accumulating resistance" (II, xxiv). Darnay's life in England has hardened into an imprisoning conception of himself which no longer seems valid. The cynicism of the dead Marquis has been confirmed by events. And Darnay must now live with the wreckage of an obsolete self.[19]

Such insights into one's most tenaciously held illusions are inevitably disquieting. Once again, Darnay recoils in an effort to convince himself of his innocence: ". . . he had oppressed no man, he had imprisoned no man; . . .

[he had] thrown himself on a world with no favour in it, won his own private place there, and earned his own bread" (II, xxiv). But in earning his own bread, in the best bourgeois manner, he has permitted others to starve. He has failed to unify his private and his social obligations: he remains, in spite of his protests, "the Marquis who was not to be found." The barren fields of the St. Evrémonde estate and its peasants' gaunt faces belie his right to a private place, with its negation of broader responsibilities. Darnay's "illusion" that he may "guide this raging Revolution that was running so fearfully wild" lacks a real basis. His sense of superiority to the revolutionaries, "bad instruments" working out "bad aims," his confidence that "he [is] better than they," reveal how easy, and necessary, it may be to repair the broken web of one's existence with threads of fancy. Darnay, but not Dickens, fully expects his intentions to be "gratefully acknowledged in France" as if they were achieved realities (II, xxiv). Such thoughts reveal the extent to which good, but misguided, men have shared in the making of the Revolution, and their inability to perceive clearly their guilt.

Darnay succumbs to his own half-truths and to the lure of Paris, the Loadstone Rock: "In seasons of pestilence, some of us will have a secret attraction to the disease—a terrible passing inclination to die of it. And all of us have like wonders hidden in our breasts, only needing circumstances to evoke them" (III, vi). Darnay's failure to comprehend his true situation, and how he will be seen by those in France, is *his* disease, corresponding to "the leprosy of unreality" which has struck down the ancien régime. His journey to Paris becomes a ritual shaping the endings of Dickens' mature novels. David Copperfield travels to Yarmouth through a violent storm, to find Steerforth's body washed ashore, almost at his feet. Esther Summerson pursues Lady Dedlock through the London maze, until she discovers her, dead, near Nemo's grave. Eugene Wrayburn seeks out Lizzie Hexam in the mill town on the Thames, where he is attacked and nearly drowned. In each case the physical journey is an inner, psychic one, a descent into a personal maelstrom. An unresolved dilemma comes to pose a threat to the character's existence. Darnay's renunciation of the St. Evrémonde name has not led to personal autonomy and integrity; not even to authentic fatherhood. "Unknown" even to his own family, he is a true father neither in England nor in France.

Darnay's journey to France involves a return to that moment in which he has tried to deal with the past by denying its claims upon him. At first, he claims that he has returned " 'of [his] own will.' " But, at last, he must see that he has no choice, that he responds to forces within himself not fully understood. As one revolutionary cries, " 'His cursed life is not his own!' " (III, i). The ride towards Paris through the soggy darkness is a personal nightmare. He is compelled to recognize that he " '[is] lost. . . . All here is so unprecedented, so changed, so sudden and unfair, that [he is] absolutely lost' " (III, i). The circumstances are not even primarily Dickens' comment upon the chaos and the injustice of the Reign of Terror. Through them he reveals not only universal flux and discontinuity, but the further erosion of Darnay's conventional notions of himself.

The "mire-deep roads" and the darkness lead to the prison, La Force, a place metaphorically under water. Darnay enters the watery depths of the Old Bailey mirror, of himself, to encounter an aristocratic version of "the wicked and the wretched" faces once reflected there. The prisoners, "spectral" in the "squalor and misery" of La Force, rise ceremoniously to greet him, as the imagined faces in the mirror greeted him before. Darnay's sense that the prisoners are "Ghosts all!" confirms his own deadness and culpability. He belongs with them. The "long unreal ride," like "some progress of disease," has culminated in this crisis of a will infected with paralysis. Darnay has been plunged into the depths from which he has pulled back, just as so many characters in *Our Mutual Friend,* both sons and fathers, are plunged into the baptismal waters of the Thames. His confidence in his own innocence has proved false. Now he finds himself among those who, like himself, confront the paradox of innocence and guilt. With the appearance of the gaoler, "so unwholesomely bloated, both in face and person, as to look like a man who had been drowned and filled with water," Darnay finally knows despair: " 'Now am I left, as if I were dead' " (III, i). It is never clear that Darnay perceives that there is a certain justice in a fate that he has partially forged for himself.

The root of Darnay's despair remains the falseness of his relationship to himself and others. Dickens captures this, as always, through oblique allusions to Darnay's condition. The revolutionary Tribunal addresses him as "Charles Evrémonde, called Darnay," denying that he has established in England an identity worthy of its recognition. The novel, in its sub-plots, plays repeatedly with this issue. Even Miss Pross' encounter with her long-lost brother, Solomon, echoes this central concern. The exposure of Barsad's double identity with its moral duplicity poses a real threat to his life. Jerry Cruncher's comic wonder about Pross' true "name," combined with his first-hand knowledge of Roger Cly's mock-funeral, deftly connects the issues of identity and responsibility, authenticity and bad-faith. Darnay, like Solomon Pross, could be subjected to a version of Jerry Cruncher's interrogation about *his* two names. St. Evrémonde was not his name " 'over the water' " in England: " 'which of the two goes first,' " which has priority, the family name of St. Everémonde or the self-conferred name, Charles Darnay? Darnay insists that he has ceased to be a St. Evrémonde, that he is innocent of crimes against the French people. But his first acquittal by the Tribunal is followed almost immediately by his subsequent arrest on new charges. This second arrest is true to Darnay's condition, to a state of psychic "arrest," growing out of his failure to cope with the suspect nature of his claims to innocence.

As usual, the father, in his various aspects, presides over these events. Doctor Manette arrives in Paris with Lucie, ostensibly to save Darnay's life. As a former victim of the ancien régime, he returns to Paris as one of the few sons who has raised his hand against the father and survived to become, himself, a father. Manette feeds upon the disorder of the Reign of Terror. He passes through maddened men and women, sharpening their weapons at the grindstone, and pushes "the weapons aside like water." He is a Mosaic figure, determined to lead his family safely out of France: "For the first time he felt that in that sharp fire [of captivity], he had slowly forged the iron which could break the prison door of his daughter's husband, and deliver him" (III, iv). He is once more the mysterious giant of the golden arm. Lucie and Mr. Lorry turn to a Manette "exalted by the change" and rely upon him. He has successfully displaced Darnay as the father, reasserting the claims to ascendancy he has apparently relinquished for so many years.

With this transformation, Manette exists as a formidable threat to Darnay. He secures Darnay's acquittal by the Tribunal during the first trial. And a thrill of exultation resonates in his words to Lucie: " 'You must not be weak, my darling, . . . don't tremble so. I have saved him' " (III, vi). Manette has won a victory in court—and a victory over Darnay. For Darnay will always be in debt to Manette, always owe him his very life. The father may triumph in many ways: the hostility of the Marquis St. Evrémonde may, finally, be less potent than the benevolence of Manette. Darnay may once again be effectively cut off from fatherhood and the right to father forth himself in the presence of the now truly patriarchal Manette.

Dickens' uneasiness on this very point informs the conclusion of *A Tale of Two Cities*. Manette's renewed ascendancy is fleeting. With Darnay's return to prison, Manette's "new life," set in motion after years of dormancy, ends. For even the benevolent father must be felled, preferably not by the son's hand, but by another Gaspard or the force of circumstances. Manette becomes one of Darnay's accusers. His written account of the events leading to his imprisonment is *his* legacy, *his* will: a curse upon the St. Evrémondes and " 'their descendants, to the last of their race' " (III, x). It is a son's curse upon the father and the decadent patriarchy of which Darnay, as the present Marquis, is a part; it is a father's curse upon the son-in-law who threatens the father's dominance. As son to Darnay's father, as father to Darnay's son, Manette has never fully granted the absolution Darnay has sought. Now he has reached out to point an accusing finger at his son-in-law. His word could send Darnay to La Guillotine, which the revolutionaries jestingly speak of as "the best cure for the headache[:] it infallibly [prevents] the hair from turning grey . . ." (III, iv). La Guillotine is the Gorgon's head of the Revolution; its impact reaches out to touch everyone. It cures the headache caused by time by inflicting upon its victims either the stasis of death or psychic trauma. The tormented man who denounced the St. Evrémonde race becomes not so unlike the dead. Marquis who once urged Darnay to accept the curse of his natural destiny. And he suffers a similar fate. With Darnay's second arrest, Manette is turned "into stone . . . as if he were a statue . . ." and becomes, yet again, the broken prisoner of the Bastille.

By now Darnay's destiny is clear: he is always to be the parricide. Manette wanders the streets of Paris aimlessly, only to return to Mr. Lorry's chambers, pleading in "a whimpering miserable way" for the shoemaker's bench that once sustained him. Surely the golden arm has descended once again to strike another poisoned blow. But, as in the murder of the Marquis, the significance of Manette's undoing is obscured. Manette seems the victim of poetic justice: his curse upon the Evrémondes, " 'to the last of their race,' " includes his own daughter and grandchild and justifies his own ruin. For Dickens the struggle between father and son never leads to unqualified victory for one or the other. Instead, it produces yet another impasse. Manette is overcome by his seemingly gratuitous act of vengeance. Darnay's triumph, if it occurs, will inevitably involve the near destruction of Lucie's father. There is no simple way, perhaps no way at all, to resolve the impasse. The victory of the father or the son entails a price few would willingly exact. Finally, Dickens himself chooses to circumvent the logic inherent in his own fiction. Characteristically, he seeks a resolution, one which seems to acknowledge the son's claims. He calls upon Darnay's "Double of coarse deportment" to prevent Darnay's fixation in his role as unwilling parricide, and to rescue him from death.

Sydney Carton has also responded to the pull of the Loadstone Rock, to the "secret attraction" of the pestilence raging in France. The siren call of death touches him, as it has Darnay. The two share in a single venture involving despair, "death" and the possibility of a genuine autonomy. As Doubles they may participate in a process which frees them from the father and the past. But one of them may have to die so that the other may survive. In *Beyond Psychology,* Otto Rank offers an interpretation of "twin-traditions" which may illuminate some of the dynamics at work in *A Tale of Two Cities:*

> In our modern conception of the Double, the killing of the alter-ego invariably leads to the death of the hero himself, that is, suicide; at earlier stages [in history], on the contrary, the sacrifice of one of the twins was the condition for the survival of the other. Hence, in twin-mythology the typical motif of fratricide turns out to be a symbolic gesture on the part of the immortal self by which it rids itself of the mortal ego.

The twin who dies stands for the mortal self; the surviving twin, freed from his mortal part, becomes immortal, no longer subject to time and death. But the significance of twins goes beyond a simple dualistic conception of the self:

> twins were considered self-created, not revived from the spirit of the dead, but generated through their own magic power, independent even of the mother. In the totemistic system . . . no fatherhood was acknowledged. The twins have dispensed with the mother, too, and are dependent only upon each other.

Mothers are strangely absent from *A Tale of Two Cities.* The idealized Lucie remains ineffectual other than as the guiding angel both of Darnay and Carton.

It is the masculine Miss Pross, a later Betsey Trotwood, who suffers deafness in her effort to save Lucie and the others from Thérèse Defarge, a truly sensual creature, who has forsaken her sexuality for the pleasures of retribution. If there is a potential mother in the novel, it must be the sister of Thérèse Defarge: the woman whose death sets in motion the complicated events surrounding Darnay's heroic saga. The novel, having dispensed, however violently, with the mother, moves to dispense with the father too. The hero, whom Otto Rank sees as the historical successor to the twin in those myths dealing with fratricide, possesses the unique ability to create himself. The immortality of the surviving twin leads to that "utter independence which makes the twin the prototype of the hero."[20] The hero has no need to acknowledge, or to turn against, a progenitor—male or female—who threatens his primacy and autonomy. He becomes the father, even the mother, of himself through the agency of the twin who dies for him. Dickens' use of the Double becomes his way of resolving that which is irresolvable on a realistic level: the relationship between parent and child, the dead and the living.

Sydney Carton, as Charles Darnay's mortal self, has been dragged for years "in [Stryver's] wake, like a boat [or a corpse?] towed astern" (II, xxi). He is the son who has not defied the father, but who has settled into what he calls " 'rust and repose.' " He surfaces in Paris at the moment Miss Pross and Jerry Cruncher are badgering Solomon Pross about Pross' true identity. When he strikes in to identify Barsad, Carton solves the riddle of identity for Darnay as well. His death will serve to unify the split within Darnay's consciousness and resolve his perplexing duties as son and father. In the process, Carton will both dispense with the father, by saving Darnay, and propitiate him, as Gaspard has done before him. It is clear to Miss Pross that he has undergone a transformation: ". . . there was a braced purpose in the arm and a kind of inspiration in the eyes, which not only contradicted his light manner, but changed and raised the man" (III, viii). The reference to the arm is fleeting. But it suggests, once more, the arm, the hand, the blade. In his altered state Carton is no longer dissipated, irresolute. He has become a son capable of raising his hand against the father. He is the son who has rebelled against the slain Marquis, the son who has inadvertently struck down the apparently benevolent Manette. And as Darnay's mortal twin, Carton also embodies the unacknowledged failure of Charles Evrémonde, called Darnay. Carton's death will free Darnay from the social guilt of the St. Evrémondes as a family. It will also serve to placate the dead father, the murdered uncle and the stricken Manette. For in Dickens' imagination the hero-son must be spared any of the consequences for asserting his right to exist.

As he wanders through Paris, awaiting the verdict of Darnay's last trial, Carton thinks of his own father: "These solemn words, which had been read at his father's grave, arose in his mind. . . . 'I am the resurrection and the life, saith the Lord: he that believeth in me, though he were dead, yet shall he live: and whosoever liveth and believeth in me, shall never die' " (III, ix). The

Christian implications of the passage are powerful, and moving. But they should not obscure the central preoccupations in the novel: the dilemma posed by the father's death; the yearning for absolution and rebirth through self-creation; the desire to be freed from the paradoxes of being in time. None of these complex issues is satisfyingly resolved by Carton's death or by allusions to the Crucifixion.[21] Rather, they are swept away just as everything that Carton sees before he dies "flashes away" with the fall of the blade. The "crowd . . . that . . . swells forward in a mass, like one great heave of water" (III, xv), baptizes Carton unto death, and delivers Darnay back to life.

But that life will remain as specious as the other life he has lived prior to his return to France. In prison Darnay has dreamed of being "free and happy, back in the old house in Soho. . . . A pause of forgetfulness, and then he had even suffered, and had come back to [Lucie], dead and at peace, and yet there was no difference in him" (III, xiii). The dream reveals Darnay's strong will to live. But the nature of that life he envisions is, in fact, a form of death. For only death may confer upon Darnay forgetfulness and peace. Carton's prophetic vision at the end of the novel is irrelevant. There is no life without conflict; without moral ambiguity and divided loyalties; without the unrelenting pressures of the father and the past. The whole of *A Tale of Two Cities* is a testament to this fact. But Darnay's dream denies all this: it is a return to an imaginary time prior to the father. Darnay wants to be restored, "with no change in him," to Lucie whose proper abode is the world of dreams. And, yet, the Marquis St. Evrémonde has been assassinated. Doctor Manette has been destroyed, reduced to a helpless, whimpering old man. The fires of the Revolution still burn. The peasants on the St. Evrémonde estate continue to assert their legitimate claims within the context of Dickens' own patriarchal, even feudal, imagination. With Carton's death these realities flash away as if they were, after all, only a dream. Darnay's obligations, to the living and to the dead, are severed by the ironically " 'innocent atonement' " Darnay's mother has prophesied: the literally though not figuratively innocent Carton dies so that the guilty Darnay may survive.

Within *A Tale of Two Cities* the structure of the poetics of impasse emerge in almost crystalline form. The death of Sydney Carton, the twin, makes at best only ritualistic sense, as it evades and obscures the other issues posed by the novel. Dickens imagines with remarkable clarity the recurring encounter between father and son: the impetus to become a father which requires the setting aside of the good or the bad father with the inevitable claims he makes upon the son through his very existence. Dickens, like Faulkner, simply cannot imagine a viable resolution to the encounter, the voluntary stepping aside of the father to make way for the son: "The primal affront that the son suffers at the hands of the father and for which the son seeks revenge throughout his life is the very fact of being a son. . . ."[22] There is no imaginable way, other than that of ritualistic sacrifice, to effect the transfer of authority and power from one generation to the next. Such a transfer becomes, for Dickens, inseparable from the act of parricide. This vision of the son's dilemma leads to the ahistoricism of this apparently historical novel. For parricide is both an inevitable and an intolerable crime: the father remains sacrosanct in the face of the son's most legitimate claims to be free of him. The only resolution is to die, to gain access to that " 'better land' " of which Sydney Carton speaks before his execution: " '. . . there is no Time there, and no trouble there.' " The world of *A Tale of Two Cities* remains one of intolerable impasse or unthinkable chaos. Not even Carton's sacrifice, the act which has made the novel so ineradicably *his,* can end the recurring struggle between generations, between fathers and sons.

In the closing pages of *A Tale of Two Cities,* impasse reigns. Allusions to the filial heroism of Christ's atonement, muted parallels to the mythology of twins, do not convincingly depict that passing on of authority from father to son that Dickens wishes to effect. Doctor Manette's condition at the end of the novel captures the paradox Dickens has posed. His is the defeat of a legitimately rebellious son at the hands of a St. Evrémonde who, in spite of his protests, stands in the father's place, after all, in his relationship to Manette. Yet, the defeat is also, clearly, that of the father who has sought control of the son's destiny. The broken Manette, the quintessential Double in the novel, suggests the fate of every son, of every father. It is a fate that Dickens as son, father and artist cannot imaginatively accept. In *Great Expectations* and in *Our Mutual Friend,* Dickens will once again explore the eternal encounter of fathers and sons. For if Jerry Cruncher is, at last, only a comic and ineffectual Resurrection-Man, Dickens the artist is the Resurrection-Man in earnest, striving to recall to life those thwarted sons, and fathers, whose natural destiny, like Charles Darnay's, threatens finally to overwhelm them.

Notes

1.   See Robert Louis Brannan, ed., *Under the Management of Mr. Charles Dickens: His Production of "The Frozen Deep"* (Ithaca: Cornell Univ. Press, 1966); and Philip Collins, "A Tale of Two Novels: *A Tale of Two Cities* and *Great Expectations* in Dickens' Career," *Dickens Studies Annual,* 2 (1972), 336–351.

2.   George Lukács, *The Historical Novel,* trans. Hannah and Stanley Mitchell (Boston: Beacon Press, 1963), p. 243. See, also, Michael Goldberg, *Dickens and Carlyle* (Athens: Univ. of Georgia Press, 1972), pp. 100–128.

3.   Georg Lukács, *Realism in Our Time,* trans. John and Necke Mander (New York: Harper & Row, 1971), p. 19.

4.   Lukács *Realism,* p. 20. I am paraphrasing Lukács' quotation of an observation by Thomas Wolfe.

5.   Charles Dickens, *A Tale of Two Cities,* The New Oxford Illustrated Dickens (London: Oxford Univ. Press, 1949), Bk. I, ch. ii. Subsequent quotations of this edition of *A Tale of Two Cities* will be followed by book and chapter numbers in parentheses.

6.   Lukács, *Realism,* p. 21.

7.   I would like to acknowledge my debt, at this point, to Steven Marcus' discussion of *Barnaby Rudge* in *Dickens: From Pickwick to Dombey* (New York: Basic Books, 1965), pp. 169–212; and to Taylor Stoehr's discussion of Dickens' style in general and *A Tale of Two Cities* in particular in *Dickens: The Dreamer's Stance* (Ithaca: Cornell Univ. Press, 1965), pp. 1–33 and pp. 195–203.

8.   John T. Irwin, *Doubling and Incest/Repetition and Revenge* (Baltimore: The Johns Hopkins Univ. Press, 1975), p. 105.

9.   Much of my discussion of *A Tale of Two Cities* is influenced by José Ortega y Gasset, "History as a System," in *History as a System and other Essays Toward a Philosophy of History,* trans. Helene Weyl (New York: W. W. Norton, 1961), pp. 165–233.

10.   V. E. von Gebsattel. "The World of the Compulsive," trans. Sylvia Koppel and Ernest Angel, in *Existence,* ed. Rollo May, Ernest Angel and Henri F. Ellenberger (New York: Simon and Schuster, 1958), p. 177.

11.   My discussion of the mirror has been influenced by Jacques Lacan, but especially by Maurice Merleau-Ponty. "The Child's Relations with Others," trans. William Cobb, in *The Primacy of Perception,* ed. James M. Edie (Evanston: Northwestern Univ. Press, 1964), pp. 96–155. See particularly Merleau-Ponty's discussion of the "stade du miroir," pp. 135–144.

12.   See Otto Rank, *The Double: A Psychoanalytic Study,* trans. Harry Tucker, Jr. (Chapel Hill: The Univ. of North Carolina Press, 1971), and "The Double as Immortal Self," in *Beyond Psychology* (New York: Dover Publications, 1958), pp. 62–101.

13.   For a more traditional psychoanalytic discussion of *A Tale of Two Cities* see Leonard Manheim, "A Tale of Two Characters: A Study in Multiple Projection," *Dickens Studies Annual,* 1 (1970), 225–237.

14.   See Irwin, p. 113: "Is there no virgin space in which one can be first, in which one can have authority through originality?"

15.   Charles Dickens, *David Copperfield,* The New Oxford Illustrated Dickens (London: Oxford Univ. Press, 1948), ch. xxiii.

16.   See Alexander Welsh, "The Bride From Heaven," in *The City of Dickens* (Oxford: Oxford Univ. Press, 1971), pp. 141–179.

17.   See Stoehr, pp. 21–25.

18.   See Stoehr, pp. 197–198.

19.   See Ortega, p. 215: "Man invents for himself a program of life, a static form of being, that gives a satisfactory answer to the difficulties posed for him by circumstance. He essays this form of life, attempts to realize this imaginary character he has resolved to be. . . . he comes to *believe* deeply that this character is his real being. But meanwhile the experience has made apparent the shortcomings and limitations of the said program of life."

20.   Rank, *Beyond Psychology,* p. 92, 96.

21.   See Irwin's discussion of Abraham and Isaac, God the Father and Jesus the Son, pp. 125–135.

22.   Irwin, p. 117.

The Purity of Violence: *A Tale of Two Cities*

JOHN KUCICH

After years of neglect, *A Tale of Two Cities* has probably become the most vigorously-defended of Dickens' works. Recently, we have had numerous apologies for the novel that have uncovered its psychological complexities,[1] its historical relevance,[2] and the subtleties of its style[3] with remarkable acuity. All of these critiques reveal that Dickens' novel is more sophisticated and more rewarding than has often been recognized. And yet, all of them seem to conclude that the novel ultimately fails in an important way: it adumbrates complex problems that escape the limited range of its "solution"—Sydney Carton's Christ-like martyrdom—which remains artificial, inadequate, and even embarrassing.[4] This constant dissatisfaction with the ending implies that the fundamental problem for readers of *A Tale of Two Cities* is not the novel's general framework of ideas;[5] the more serious problem is the novel's inability to provide an ethical or an analytical resolution—a useful resolution—to the social and psychological problems it announces, and its apparent willingness to submerge those problems in the stagey, emotionally-charged but intellectually vapid crescendoes of melodrama. In other words, what we have here is a problem with narrative mode: it is the form of the novel that troubles modern readers, that frustrates expectations generated by the rest of the novel.

At the risk of bringing us full circle back to the grounds of early complaints against *A Tale of Two Cities*,[6] I suggest that the serious uses of melodrama in the novel must be stressed if we are to understand its aesthetic wholeness. Spawned by Wilkie Collins' melodrama. *The Frozen Deep*, Dickens' novel has the play's emotional excessiveness at its very core, and any attempt to clarify the novel's thematic structure must therefore take up the challenge of that excessiveness. Recent studies have shown that debating melodrama's legitimacy as a literary mode is less profitable than articulating the ends that melodrama tries to achieve, if only in the interest of broadening our notions about the possible—and impossible—goals of narrative structure.[7] In the case of *A Tale of Two Cities*, Dickens' novelistic goals depend heavily upon his melodramatic plot. In my view, the non-rational impulses behind melodrama develop a crucial authorial intention: Dickens' novel consistently works to-

Reprinted from *Dickens Studies Annual* 8 (1980): 119–37 by permission. Copyright © 1980 AMS Press, Inc.

ward an escape from the realm of the analytical, the ethical, and the useable altogether. Instead, the novel investigates and defends desires for irrational extremity that it satisfies finally in Carton's chaste suicide. Dickens' attitude toward the role of emotional excess in human life, which is elaborately defined as the work unfolds, logically carries the novel away from orderly, intellectually-apprehendable resolutions toward a more dynamic goal: the staging of acceptable—as opposed to cruel—violence.[8]

A Tale of Two Cities is not a revolutionary novel, in the sense that it advocates political and social revolt, but it does dramatize a pressing, fundamental human need for liberating change of the most extreme kind. Dickens' novel is an enactment of human needs for an extreme release from many different kinds of confinement, and, in these terms, the novel's crucial development is a subtle change in the way violence can be valued as a vehicle for such release. That is to say, general needs for a victory over repression, which the novel embodies as a desire for violence, are purified as they are moved from the social context of the novel into the personal one: the revolutionaries' problematical desires for freedom are translated into acceptable terms by the good characters in their own struggles for freedom, and they are focused finally in the "pure" self-violence of Sydney Carton, which liberates him from self-hatred. In an abstract sense, what this means finally is that the novel's symbolic logic affirms Carton's initial tendencies toward an internal kind of violence—his dissipation—under the guise of his later, moral "conversion." This assertion, of course, presents numerous difficulties, not the least of which is the problematical relationship between physical self-destruction and psychological liberation. But by reexamining Dickens' attitude toward excess and violence throughout the novel, we can begin to see why Carton's fate is unavoidable.

A non-specific, primary desire for a radical release from limits dominates the very texture of Dickens' novel. The famous opening paragraphs of the novel launch this movement toward release, articulating frustrated desires for extremity by way of parodying the desire of the historical imagination to erupt beyond the limits of conventional significance. Mixing the historian's typical desire to proclaim the extremity of his own elected period with undermining hints of the fundamental "sameness" of all ages, Dickens' much-quoted, much-sentimentalized opening catalogues the extremes of 1775 in a series of superlatives that cancel each other out: "It was the best of times, it was the worst of times, it was the age of wisdom, it was the age of foolishness, it was the epoch of belief, it was the epoch of incredulity . . ." (I.1).[9] Despite themselves, these terms fail to produce a difference in meaning; instead, each term merely tends to produce its opposite, and to be bounded by it.[10] In this way, the opening catalogue of extremes comments more on the needs of the historical imagination—and on those of the novelist—than on the actual tenor of any particular age. It emphasizes desires for extremity at the same time that it frustrates them. As he levels extremes, the narrator even claims that his own chosen epoch is not actually different from the present one—

giving greater emphasis to his debunking satire—but that "in short, the period was so far like the present period, that some of its noisiest authorities insisted on its being received, for good or for evil, in the superlative degree of comparison only." Far from being extreme, the age is actually in the grip of a repetitive sameness in its very desire to be excessive, a desire which is trapped in conventional, competitive self-aggrandizements. And, on the level of political reality, the weighty repetition of desires for extremity is undisguised: "In both countries it was clearer than crystal to the lords of the State preserves of loaves and fishes, that things in general were settled for ever." Covertly, the belief that some kind of extremity has actually been reached becomes only the basis for dominance, as well as for repetition.

The pathetic desire for extremity within history introduces more successful desires for upheaval on the part of characters. In the beginning, for example, Sydney Carton's dissipation is presented as the result of a metaphysical crisis over limitations, and not as the vulgarity of the idle bum: Carton feels imprisoned by the banality of economic survival. Referring to himself as a "drudge," Carton, through his indifferently-valued but very real skills and through his ostentatious rejection of preferment, deliberately affronts the acquisitive business world of Stryver. With sardonic pride, Carton flaunts his lack of economic sense: "Bless you, *I* have no business" (II.4), he tells Lorry. In keeping with this violation of the code of self-interest, Carton had always instictively done work for others rather than for himself in school; and, professionally, he does all his work so that Stryver, and not himself, may claim the credit and prosper. Carton's utter intellectual competence to lead a successful, if ordinary, life gives point to his rejection of self-concern, and defines it as a choice, however unconscious he may be of his own motives and however much such a choice is painful, bringing along with it the anonymity of self-abandonment. And, if Stryver and Lorry are examples of what success means, then Carton's comparative genuiness—his freedom from the rigidities of both aggression and repression—depends on his refusal to value worldly success. It is interesting to note, too, that Jerry Cruncher later stresses the unreality of the business world by claiming that much normal business represses the final reality represented by death; defending his graverobbing to Lorry, Cruncher observes: "There might be medical doctors at the present hour, a picking up their guineas where a honest tradesman don't pick up his fardens. . . . Then wot with undertakers, and wot with parish clerks, and wot with sextons, and wot with private watchmen (all awaricious and all in it), a man wouldn't get much by it, even if it was so" (III.9). In the context of the novel's sense that the business world is artificial, and that it actively conceals the profounder reality of death, Carton's dissipation is a rejection of the world of petty survival on the broadest of philosophical grounds: he tells Darnay simply that he wants to leave "this terrestrial scheme" (II.4).

Despite the disapproval of other characters,[11] the reader may find Carton's carelessness and his reckless honesty refreshing. Carton's dissipation is somehow "pure" precisely because it is free of self-interest. From the very beginning, Dickens forces the reader to discriminate between the popular judgment about Carton's degeneracy and the possibility of his having hidden merits, often by putting his condemnations of Carton into the wrong mouths. After all, it is the ugly mob, feasting like flies on Darnay's trail, that finds Carton's appearance disreputable, and it is Jerry Cruncher, after his vulgarity has been established, who observes: "I'd hold half a guinea that *he* don't get no law work to do. Don't look like the sort of one to get any, do he?" (II.3). But Carton's superiority to the crowd very soon emerges through his intensified powers of perception: "Yet, this Mr. Carton took in more of the details of the scene than he appeared to take in; for now, when Miss Manette's head dropped upon her father's breast, he was the first to see it, and to say audibly: 'Officer! look to that young lady. Help the gentleman to take her out. Don't you see she will fall!' " The mark of Carton's genius is this very ability to penetrate to the most important, the most essential levels—to see beyond the limited vision of others, or to say what others dare not say. In other words, Carton appeals to us through his freedom from convention and from constraint. Thus, his success at Darnay's trial is a single, bold, imaginative stroke, one that Stryver calls "a rare point" (II.5). His facility for "extracting the essence from a heap of statements" shows to advantage against Stryver's plodding determination, and his frankness shines out against Mr. Lorry's restraint—at Lorry's expense, Carton observes: "If you knew what a conflict goes on in the business mind, when the business mind is divided between good-natured impulse and business appearances, you would be amused, Mr. Darnay" (II.4). Lorry's exasperated reply defines the difference between himself and Carton explicitly: "[B]usiness is a very good thing, and a very respectable thing. And, sir, if business imposes its restraints and its silences and impediments, Mr. Darnay as a young gentleman of generosity knows how to make allowance for that circumstance." But to confirm the imposing dimensions of Carton's position, the narrator tells us that Lorry was "[p]erhaps a little angry with himself, as well as with the barrister. . . ." In contrast, then, to the other good characters, whose lives are ruled by restraints of one kind or another, and despite our sense that we must disapprove of him, Carton stands out as the most vividly authentic character in the novel. Even in the love plot, Carton confides in Lucie more honestly than the others: Darnay conceals from Lucie his intended trip to France, and Manette tries to conceal from her his instinctual jealousy of Darnay. In the reader's eyes, Carton momentarily has a more intimate relationship with Lucie than either Darnay or Manette, for the reader sees Carton "open his heart" to her in the pivotal confession scene, the only scene in which a man expresses himself passionately to Lucie.

More importantly, perhaps, Carton's desire to release himself from constraints in dissipation, however much it is treated with repugnance by the good characters, is in fact not so far removed from their own desires. Darnay, who flees his own terrestrial scheme—France—is opposed to his uncle the

Marquis in much the same way that Carton is opposed to Stryver (Stryver and the Marquis are linked later in the novel, when the lawyer gathers among the disinherited French aristocracy at Tellson's and joins in their contempt for the French rebels and for the anonymous son of the Marquis). From the perspective of French aristocratic values, Darnay's teaching school is an unmentionable degradation, one that is essentially as demeaning as Carton's English unprofessionalism. And Darnay is eventually punished for this desertion of France, a punishment that implies allegorically—since it is difficult for us to understand how running from a French inheritance could be a crime—that there is some kind of moral transgression implicit in *any* release from normal human bonds. For Dr. Manette, too, release from prison is figured as a release from restrictive labor, which is represented by his obsessive shoe-making. His return home is emphasized imagistically as a release from the conservative claims of survival and self-interest largely because it frees him from the evasive narrowness of mind represented by his prison work-world. Though no longer functional, this work-world is an image of Dr. Manette's repression— his willingness to put on blinders and merely to endure, like all oblivious workmen. In its rigidly economic resonance, Manette's cobbling echoes Lorry's business-imposed restraint. However, the shadowy, disquieting destruction of Manette's work bench by Lorry and Miss Pross points to the guilt that inheres in the structure of such release: their destructive act is oddly congruent with the revolutionary destruction of the French mob. Darnay and Manette, like Sydney Carton, sin against an obscure moral law when they seek release from their respective imprisonments, no matter how much their freedom is approved by the reader.

Our ambivalent attitude toward Carton, then, is only an index of the generally problematic nature of almost any violated limits. By being political, generational, sexual, and vaguely misanthropic, desires for release in this novel acquire a kind of generality that transcends their local manifestations: such desires seem fundamentally human, while, at the same time, they seem ultimately threatening. The novel makes clear that while a desire for the destruction of psychological and social limitations may be profoundly human, it is always related to a desire for the destruction of restrictive personal identity in violence and in death.[12]

It is worth noting at this point, as a way to approach the complex relationship between release from restrictions and death, that the confluence of desires for violent release with the potential transgression implied by such release dominates the background action. On the one hand, in the initial stages of the revolution in France, it is difficult not to sympathize with the laboring class's pursuit of freedom through violence. Occasionally, Dickens dwells on the mob's achievement of "human fellowship" through their uprising,[13] and stresses the sympathetic unity of the oppressed people: "Not before dark night did the men and women come back to the children, wailing and breadless. Then, the miserable bakers' shops were beset by long files of them, patiently waiting to buy bad bread; and while they waited with stomachs faint and empty, they beguiled the time by embracing one another on the triumphs of the day, and achieving them again in gossip. Gradually, these strings of ragged people shortened and frayed away; and then poor lights began to shine in high windows, and slender fires were made in the streets, at which neighbours cooked in common, afterwards supping at their doors" (II.22). Then, too, the bursting wine cask scene, which mingles the sympathetic energy of a well-deserved holiday with ominous hints about the ultimate form of excessive "holiday" energy—the desire for blood, a word that someone writes into the wall in wine—also has the effect of linking the mob's exuberant expenditure of energy with Carton's drunkenness, as does the code name of the insurgents, the Jacques, link them with Carton and his sobriquet: the Jackal. And at this point early in the novel, both forms of energy—Carton's sottishness and the mob's—seem harmless and infinitely preferable to the alternative world of work. Like Carton's, too, the insurgents' drives for extremity have a metaphysical cast—though they do not consciously articulate it—in their collective willingness to risk life for something more valuable even than life: undefined, limitless freedom. The excessiveness of this risk of life, the way in which it breaks the mob loose from the repressive world of work, accounts for the ensuing eroticism[14]—the mob's discovery that outside of the limits of self-concern is an idyllic world of plenitude and union: "Fathers and mothers who had had their full share in the worst of the day, played gently with their meagre children; and lovers, with such a world around them and before them, loved and hoped" (II.22). Something of this plenitude of sexual arousal is also conveyed by the "Carmagnole," the dance of the rebels, which combines excessive violence with a polymorphous, eroticized fellow-feeling: "Men and women danced together, women danced together, men danced together, as hazard had brought them together. At first, they were a mere storm of coarse red caps and coarse woollen rags; but, as they filled the place, and stopped to dance about Lucie, some ghastly apparition of a dance-figure gone raving mad arose among them. They advanced, retreated, struck at one another's hands, clutched at one another's heads, spun round alone, caught one another and spun round in pairs, until many of them dropped" (II.5).

On the other hand, of course, the meaning of rebellion in France soon sours. Our reaction to the "Carmagnole" cannot be the same as our reaction to the crowd that dammed up flowing wine in the cobblestones. The scenes of violence are carefully built up to repel us gradually, and it is difficult to specify at what particular point we lose sympathy with the rebels. But it soon becomes clear that the mob's struggle for justice is totally outstripped by their brute satisfaction in the violence of dominance. Hence, although the mob's struggle has its roots in oppression and therefore takes our sympathy, the novel jolts us into a recognition of the form taken by the mob's desire for liberation—its inevitable tendency to congeal in cruelty, and to project what was once a "pure," disinterested violence outward against others.

The psychological dynamic here is specified by Hegel's Master-Slave dialectic: the Master is he who is most willing to give up his life for a greater, intangible good—a transcendent good not restricted by the economic taint of mere worldly survival. The Slave, then, is he who opts for survival rather than risking his life in a fight with the Master. In Hegel's dialectic, however, if the Master proves his greater willingness to face violent death and then survives because of the Slave's capitulation, this proved capacity for totalizing violence becomes the emblem and the instrument of his successful domination. The Master thus becomes trapped in petty factionalism when he seeks to make his transcendent liberation—proven through his willingness to die violently— endure in the form of the Slave's recognition of that transcendent violence. Consequently, there are two possible ways in which violence may be exercized: first, as a spontaneous release from slavishness through self-regardless violence—which, in temporal terms, is "pure" but also "meaningless" because it is not designed to be profitable; second, as a calculated retreat from self-abandonment toward the use of violence against others in an attempt to make one's transcendent liberation endure in the world.[15] In terms of Dickens' novel, any desire for extremity that stops short of self-annihilation becomes impure by being implicated in the temporal arena of rivalry: most obviously, the mob projects violence outwards to preserve itself while affirming its claim to the righteousness and the transcendence implied by its willingness to confront death.

In *A Tale of Two Cities,* Hegel's two dialectical forms of violence are personified and set at war with each other. The purity of self-violence clearly belongs at first to the lower classes, who "held life as of no account, and were demented with a passionate readiness to sacrifice it" (II.21). Thus, the concrete effects of the revolutionaries' violence as an annihilation of their humanity—and, therefore, a violation of their human limitations—are actualized before us: we witness the transformation of rational figures like the Defarge couple into maddened beasts during the storming of the Bastille. Furthermore, to emphasize the "unnatural" and "non-human" element in the revolutionaries' passion, Dickens made their spokesperson a woman, since, in Dickens' world, the supreme disruption of normal expectations about human nature is an absence of tenderness in women. In the Parisian violence, even La Guillotine is female. And to heighten this effect, Madame Defarge's knitting in service of violence is set in sharp contrast to Lucie Manette's "golden thread" of pacification and harmony, as well as to the "domestic arts" that Lucie had learned in Madame Defarge's France. Most importantly, this yearning for the pure release of self-violence is identified as the ultimate form of desire for freedom through the good characters: Darnay, on his last night in prison, becomes fascinated with the guillotine—he has "a strange besetting desire to know what to do when the time came; a desire gigantically disproportionate to the few swift moments to which it referred; a wondering that was more like the wondering of some other spirit within his, than his own" (III.3).[16] At one point, too, the narrator isolates the mob's fascination with the pure release of violent death, and makes of it a common human desire: "a species of fervour or intoxication, known, without doubt, to have led some persons to brave the guillotine unnecessarily, and to die by it, was not mere boastfulness, but a wild infection of the wildly shaken public mind. In seasons of pestilence, some of us will have a secret attraction to the disease—a terrible passing inclination to die of it. And all of us have like wonders hidden in our breasts, only needing circumstances to evoke them" (III.6). Thoughts like this lend a new resonance to the chapter title "Drawn to the Loadstone Rock," a chapter in which Darnay decides—for seemingly rational reasons, though he does refuse to discuss them with anyone who might restrain him— to go back to France, and help stress the novel's movement toward some kind of willed self-destruction.

The liberating intentions behind the lower classes violence, however, are only a response to the repressive image of non-human freedom and "represented" violence that define the power of the class of Monseigneur. Instead of being defined through overt acts of violence, life among the upper classes revolves around static representations of their non-humanity—emblems of their willingness to violate human limits. The Marquis' own non-humanity marks itself in his freedom from emotion—the narrator at one point describes his appearance as being "a fine mask" (II.9), and his face is compared to the stone faces of his gargoyles. In his conversation with Charles, he annihilates feeling through the codified formality of manners: "the uncle made a graceful gesture of protest, which was so clearly a slight form of good breeding that it was not reassuring" (II.9). Generally, the hallmark of status among the Marquis' class is this "leprosy of unreality" (II.7). The Fancy Ball, for example, is full of "Unbelieving Philosophers," who construct elaborately meaningless verbal structures, and "Unbelieving Chemists," who have their eyes on alchemy—both are in pursuit of the unnatural, through words or through metals. Good breeding itself "was at that remarkable time—and has been since—to be known by its fruits of indifference to every natural subject of human interest." Once again, too, the contrast is clearest in the image of the female; among the women of the Marquis' society, their chief distinction is their escape from maternity: it was "hard to discover among the angels of that sphere one solitary wife, who, in her manners and appearance, owned to being a Mother. . . . Peasant women kept the unfashionable babies close, and brought them up, and charming grandmammas of sixty dressed and supped as at twenty."

There is violence among the Marquis' class, of course, but it is colder, and has a clear function as a representation: that is, their violence is merely an occasional symbol of the mastery of the rich, since it proves their right to waste lives if they choose to—the lives of the lower orders.[17] When the Marquis asserts that running down children with his carriage is a right of his station, he takes no passionate satisfaction from the killing; he takes only a numbed confirmation of his status. Initially, when the rebels in *A Tale of Two Cities* kill, they kill in passion, while the rich kill as spectacle—as, for example, when the royal government executes the murderer of the Marquis and leaves him hanging forty feet in the air. The Marquis expresses this functionality of violence explicitly; when Charles complains that his family is hated in France for their cruelty, the Marquis answers: "Let us hope so. . . . Detestation of the high is the involuntary homage of the low" (II.9).

The Hegelian horror of *A Tale of Two Cities* is this: at the point when the revolutionaries stop short of their own willingness to brave death and attempt to make their release permanent and meaningful in the form of a Republic, they trap themselves in the reified form of diverted violence—the petty, mechanical, and cruel contortions of human rivalry. We lose sympathy for the rebels when they lose sight of their limitless freedom—their "pure" release—and become trapped in their own revenge, thus imitating their oppressors. The very name of Madame Defarge's companion is "The Vengeance," and Madame Defarge undercuts herself through an ironic imitation: she dedicates herself to destroying the innocent Darnay family just as her own innocent family was destroyed. More disturbingly, for Madame Defarge, as for the rest of the revolutionaries, passionate revenge gives way to the invention of spurious rivalry, the murder of innocent victims. The purely mechanical quality of this imitative violence is underscored by the ominous note of historical destiny in this novel: the continuous references to things "running their courses" and the metaphors of echoing footsteps and approaching thunderstorms. In Dickens' novel, the "pure" wish for release always becomes tainted when it is diverted away from the self, and when the limits that are violated become the limits of others. The victory over repression on the part of the revolutionaries leads only to imprisonment in violent rivalry, just as Dr. Manette's liberation from imprisonment leads him directly into a rivalry with his own son-in-law, and just as Darnay's flight from France lands him squarely in a relationship of rivalry to Manette. In fact, the social and personal histories of *A Tale of Two Cities* converge on the theme of release that is trapped in rivalry: the novel dramatizes the failure even of Dickens' heroes to escape the structure of rivalry in their efforts to achieve release.[18] In this novel, suppressing the rivalry inherent in release is not simply inadequate: it is elaborately examined as a strategy that fails.

Admittedly, against the background of class rivalry in France, it is at first a relief to find that the activity of the heroes is completely devoted to containing the potential rivalry inherent in their own relationships. Faced with the dangers latent in the relationships of Darnay to Carton and to Manette, the good characters try in every way to prevent rivalry from surfacing. Their virtue is entirely associated at first with repression, with their attempt to preserve relationships by denying the violence that is latent in them.

Lucie Manette is the primary reconciler and preserver—her "golden thread" represents an attempt to weave together factions, and to inhibit the tendency of her men to displace each other. The other characters co-operate universally with Lucie in her strategy of repression: Manette enjoins Darnay not to tell him the secret of Darnay's own parentage; Darnay makes special efforts to conciliate Dr. Manette, and to assure him that they are not competitors for Lucie's attentions; Carton vows to Lucie that he will not envy Darnay, or pursue Lucie herself in any romantic way; and Darnay promises Lucie that he will hold no grudges against Carton. The minor character Miss Pross is perhaps the most concise example of a thematics of suppression that the novel seems at first to valorize: "Mr. Lorry knew Miss Pross to be very jealous, but he also knew her by this time to be, beneath the surface of her eccentricity, one of those unselfish creatures—found only among women—who will, for pure love and admiration, bind themselves willing slaves, to youth when they have lost it, to beauty that they never had, to accomplishments that they were never fortunate enough to gain, to bright hopes that never shone upon their own sombre lives" (II.6). It is interesting to note, too, that, as a further emblem of the weight given to attempts to conserve, rather than to violate or to rival, *A Tale of Two Cities* actually features a businessman, Lorry, as one of its heroes—a rarity in Dickens. His conservative role as banker even allows Lorry to travel safely between the two cities: he is a kind of international reconciler. Moreover, his functions in the plot are always rescue missions: his two dramatic messages—"recalled to life" and "acquitted"—as well as his three separate rescue operations in France are in sharp contrast to the operations of the only other business establishment in the novel, the Defarge's wineshop, and to the aggressive business ethics expressed by Stryver.

However, while naked drives toward violence are repudiated through the mob's factionalism, and, conversely, through Carton, whose pure, non-competitive recklessness is merely ineffective, repression taints the efforts of the good characters to suppress their own violence. Their enforced restraint makes for an almost bleak, numbed atmosphere of good-will, instead of the generous flow of spirits necessary to Dickens' vision of a closely-knit good society in his other novels. The atmosphere of repression in the good characters' world is one reason for the notorious want of humor in this novel, and it also echoes the narrator's complaint, in the beginning of the novel, against the isolation of the individual within the narrow limits of personal identity: "A wonderful fact to reflect upon, that every human creature is constituted to be that profound secret and mystery to every other. . . . Something of the awfulness, even of Death itself, is referable to this" (I.3). The "golden thread" foursome, though it obviously had Dickens' sympathy, participates in this gloomy fact of secrecy and repression. However sobering violence and rivalry may be, then, Dickens is ultimately on the side of change, and on the side of excess. The tone of the novel, as well as the awkward tension created by the proliferation of lovers for Lucie, speeds the novel toward some kind of rupture.

The inevitability of that rupture is signaled by a larger problem within the good characters' strategies of repression: in both of the crucial relationships among the good characters, inherent violence is only imperfectly suppressed, and finally emerges—even against the characters' wills—as rivalry. In the first conflict, Dr. Manette's voluntary suppression of his opposition to Darnay—which is both political, on account of the novel's germinal incident in France, and sexual, because they are locked in a relationship of natural, generational rivalry—is itself dangerous. Often, it sinks him back into the corrosive oblivion of work as he tries to screen out his jealousy. Lorry wonders "whether it is good for Dr. Manette to have that suppression always shut up within him" (II.6). Even worse though, despite all his attempts to overcome it, Manette's involuntary rivalry with Darnay is mercilessly actualized by events. Manette's very attempts to save Darnay from the revolutionary tribunal are compromised by a dangerous, potential one-upsmanship in his performance: "[H]e was proud of his strength. 'You must not be weak, my darling,' he remonstrated; 'don't tremble so. I have saved him.' " (III.6). This one-upsmanship is stressed by the Doctor's dependence on the rivalrous mob, which is devoted to Darnay's death. And, more significantly, the production of the document recounting the story of the Peasant Family realizes Manette's rivalry in a deadly way. Of course, Manette is passive in the confrontation: only in a moment of weakness and desperate yearning for freedom did he curse the aristocratic family that he never supposed he would see again; and the production of the fatal document is carried out here by others, against Manette's will. Still, on a symbolic level, the events enact an inevitable resurfacing of rivalry as the temporal structure taken on by desires for liberation. Involuntarily, Manette is transformed from repressed victim to violent oppressor; he is identified with Madame Defarge and the rebels in their progress from one stage to the other.

In the second, more important rivalry, the one between Sydney Carton and Charles Darnay, the conditions of the rivalry are again involuntary: the two characters simply look alike, which stings Carton with a sense of his inferiority. Carton's metaphysical urges for violent release—like the desire of Manette for freedom, and like the desires of the lower class in this novel for liberation—is trapped in his envy of a rival, Darnay. Carton even selects his rival as the man who most completely displays a willingness to risk life, and who receives recognition for it: "Is it worth being tried for one's life," he says, "to be the object of such sympathy and compassion, Mr. Darnay?" (II.4). As a consequence, Carton's general bitterness about the limitations of his life focus themselves in this competition with Darnay for the clearest claim to violent self-expenditure and selflessness.

What makes the second relationship more interesting than the first is that Carton is finally able to satisfy his drive toward release in a morally legitimate way precisely through the structure of rivalry. Carton's "self-sacrifice," far from transcending structures of rivalry, actually operates within them. The will-to-power here is clear: Carton takes over Darnay's very handwriting and uses it to address an intimate message to Lucie, one that Darnay cannot understand or share; he refers to the unconscious Darnay as "me"; he envisions the surviving couple as "not more honoured and held sacred in each other's soul, than I was in the souls of both" (III.15); and he pictures Darnay's own son named after him, along with a grandson also named after himself, who comes back to France solely for the purpose of hearing the Carton story. The crowning irony in Carton's violation of Darnay's identity and his claim to Lucie's admiration is that Carton is the one who projects the others' future in the last paragraphs of the novel, while both Manette and Darnay are lying in a coach, impotent and unconscious.

As Hegel teaches, until violence is directed back toward others, it is "meaningless" in temporal terms because it ends the life of self; similarly, Carton's early, non-competitive dissolution is meaningless—despite, or rather, because of the "purity" of the violence directed against himself. But Carton's death at the end of the novel does have a "meaning" on this side of death, and, like all such meanings, this one only expresses itself through the vehicle of rivalry; that is, Carton's sacrifice is meant to be compelling because it is superior to Darnay's, since Darnay's death would have been involuntary, and because it seems to make him "more worthy" of Lucie. Carton achieves a transcendent "meaning" only by demonstrating a greater willingness to face death. At the same time, however, Carton does not appropriate for himself any undesirable associations with mastery because he makes his self-expenditure complete. By losing his life, Carton annihilates self-interest. Moreover, besides the totality of his loss, Carton also nullifies any appropriation of recognition that he might conceivably desire by refusing to reveal his sacrifice to anyone while it is in preparation. Unlike Dr. Manette's ostentatious rescue of Darnay, Carton's proceeds in secret. He informs no one—not even Lorry—and he tells Lucie only in a note meant to be opened later, so that she would know that his life had not been "wantonly" thrown away. The awesome thing about Carton's death is just this: that he goes through it alone—he even dies under someone else's name (though recognition does come, innocuously, from a stranger on the scaffold, which implies that the reader's role in supplying necessary recognition that cannot come from within the world of the novel is crucial). And, ultimately, the violent aspect of Carton's "suicide" is redeemed through the preservation of Darnay and his family. Radical self-violence is balanced with meaning derived from its being put to temporal, conservative use. As an action, Carton's is the only violent release in the novel that can claim the readers' unqualified assent, since even actions like Dr. Manette's liberation from prison or Darnay's liberation from his English trial immediately cause new, unavoidable problems of rivalry.

Carton's death blends perfectly, almost ritualistically, the two irreconcilable human values of ultimate release and temporal survival, realizing through narrative an impossible wish. In this way, Carton's death violates our expectations about the limits of human action. Like Miss Pross, who changes the meaning of murder by losing her own hearing (as if in penance) and by saving the rest of the good characters when she kills Madame Defarge. Sydney Carton, by choosing death, changes the meaning of self-destruction: he carries out his earlier desires for dissipation free from the abyss of meaninglessness implied by self-annihilation—his death is actually sanctioned through its ability to preserve the Darnay family. Finally, for the reader, Carton helps to elevate our own fascination with violent extremity: rather than watching his death pruriently as the vulgar mob had watched Darnay's trial, we share in the condemned woman's religious awe.

If the conclusion of *A Tale of Two Cities* seems contrived, Dickens is well aware of at least one side of the contrivance: the rivalrous aspect of Carton's act is clearly articulated. Readers offended by the "simple-mindedness" of Carton's crucifixion can take solace in Dickens' awareness of this dimension to the act. At the same time, however, Dickens clearly intended the conclusion to move his readers unequivocally, as only the magnitude of death dramatized as a human desire could move them. What makes this ending melodramatic is not simply Carton's death, but his undisguised *desire* for death. We are well-protected against this desire in our normal lives,[19] and, as Peter Brooks points out, one reason for critical embarrassment with the form of melodrama may very well be melodrama's refusal to censor itself.[20] For this reason, whether the conclusion of *A Tale of Two Cities* moves or embarrasses us, the reason is the same: Dickens has presented us with an image of an explicitly-desired violation of human limits, one that is presented as the only possible escape from the twin mechanisms of rivalry and repressed violence.[21] In some of the later novels, Dickens attempts to make the liberation of self-violence possible through an intensified consciousness of death, chiefly through a kind of doubling within consciousness—the kind of doubling that enables Esther to "die" to Jarndyce but live for Woodcourt, and that enables Pip both to forget and to live for Estella.[22] But, in *A Tale of Two Cities,* the synthesis of ultimate release and survival takes place only in the unstated relationship between Sydney Carton's death and the reader's awareness of that death's significance.

Notes

1. Leonard Manheim, "A Tale of Two Characters: A Study in Multiple Projection," *Dickens Studies Annual*, 1, ed. Robert B. Partlow, Jr. (Carbondale: Southern Illinois University Press, 1970), pp. 225–237, locates these complexities in the relationship between the novel's structure and the tensions of Dickens' own psychology; Albert D. Hutter. "Nation and Generation in *A Tale of Two Cities*," *PMLA*, 93 (1978), 448–462, discusses the novel's treatment of father-son relationships in the context of the Victorian family.

2. David D. Marcus, "The Carlylean Vision of *A Tale of Two Cities*," *Studies in the Novel*, 8 (1976), 56–68, claims that, rather than oversimplifying Carlyle's view of history in *The French Revolution*, Dickens, like Carlyle, expresses a desire that man find a humane basis for social action, at a time when human institutions seemed to deny the possibility of such action.

3.   See Taylor Stoehr, *Dickens: The Dreamer's Stance* (Ithaca: Cornell University Press, 1965), especially pp. 3–33, for an excellent study of the novel's metonymic structure. Stoehr also elaborates the interesting psychological interpretation that the original crime of transgression against class and sexual boundaries in the novel must be exorcised ritualistically through Carton's death.

4.   Thus, Hutter calls Carton's death an "unrealistic solution" (451); and Marcus complains that the ending is disappointing because it reflects an "inability to translate private virtue into public action" (66). John Gross, "*A Tale of Two Cities*," *Dickens and the Twentieth-Century*, ed. John Gross and Gabriel Pearson (Toronto University Press, 1962), p. 191, puts the matter succinctly: Carton's "sacrifice was trifling, since he had nothing to live for." This same dissatisfaction with the ending is implicit in analyses that claim that the doubles, Carton and Darnay, allow Dickens to imagine both successful love and freedom from guilt at the same time. Such analyses—like Manheim's or Stoehr's—unwittingly trivialize the nove by making it a projection of a purely personal wish or an elaborate attempt to dispel personal guilt.

5.   Manheim, p. 225, also suggests whimsically that scholars have been unkind to *A Tale of Two Cities* because it has been favored in secondary school curriculums.

6.   The focus of these attacks is clear. In 1859, Sir James Fitzjames Stephen objected to the "mechanicalness" of the death scene: "It is an old remark, that if dirt enough is thrown, some of it will stick; and Mr. Dickens's career shows that the same is true of pathos." *The Dickens Critics*, ed. George H. Ford and Lauriat Lane, Jr. (Ithaca: Cornell University Press, 1961), p. 42. More recently, John Gross, p. 196, objects that without a thick social atmosphere surrounding them, Dickens' characters stand out in stark melodramatic isolation.

7.   See Peter Brooks, *The Melodramatic Imagination* (New Haven: Yale University Press, 1976), or Robert B. Heilman, *Tragedy and Melodrama: Versions of Experience* (Seattle: University of Washington Press, 1968). Both critics give new respectability to the impulses behind melodrama: Brooks, by seeing in melodrama a desire for the numinous that may repel us in its baldest forms, but one that is intimately connected with the "serious" novelistic projects of James, Faulkner, Conrad, and others; Heilman, by claiming that melodrama enacts a desire for wholeness and plentitude—for a world not constrained by psychological limits—that is similar to the goals of tragic catharsis.

8.   Dickens' identification with the French mob has often been noted. See, for example, Humphry House, *The Dickens World* (London: Oxford University Press, 1941), p. 214: "He danced and slaughtered with the crowd." But House and others who share his perception usually qualify this view by stressing Dickens' neutralizing, middle-class Victorian ambivalence toward violence. My approach differs in showing how Carton's death dissolves this ambivalence.

9.   All quotations are taken from Charles Dickens, *A Tale of Two Cities*, ed. George Woodcock (New York: Penguin, 1970). Book and chapter numbers are given in parentheses.

10.   The echoes of Derridaean terminology here are intentional, though the effect of my reading is hardly structuralist: Dickens, I will argue, finds a way to fracture restrictive human structures—specifically, in *A Tale of Two Cities*, the behavioral structure of rivalry—in the interest of human freedom and originality, even if this disruption of structure requires death. Nevertheless, the presence of rigid linguistic and behavioral structures in the novel gives point to Dickens' attempt to exceed them. See Jacques Derrida, "Differance," *Speech and Phenomena*, trans. David B. Allison (Evanston: Northwestern University Press, 1973). For an interesting statement by Derrida on Georges Bataille's defiance of the concept of restrictive structure, see Jacques Derrida, "A Hegelianism without Reserves," trans. Allan Bass, *Semiotext(e)*, 2, No. 2 (1976), 25–56.

11.   This disapproval is often assimilated by critics, perhaps too easily. See, for example, Hutter, p. 452.

12.   The priority of human desires for release is the cornerstone of the philosophy of Georges Bataille. See *Death and Sensuality* (New York: Walker, 1962). For Bataille, man's fundamental sense of isolation—in his individual body, mind, and personality—induces a desire to

shatter these limits and to expend the self into a seemingly prior condition of limitlessness. The ultimate model, of course, for such expenditure is death—hence, the rationale for the death-wish.

13. The "human fellowship" of the mob has been noted before. See Sylvére Monod, "Dickens's Attitudes in *A Tale of Two Cities." Dickens Centennial Essays,* ed. Ada Nisbet and Blake Nevius (Berkeley: University of California Press, 1971), p. 180.

14. For the connection between the erotic and the death-drives, a connection denied by Freud, see Bataille, especially pp. 5–19. Bataille holds that both drives feature a yearning to violate personal limits in the search for a larger, transcendent, "impersonal" unity.

15. For a more compelling summary of Hegel's Master-Slave dialectic, see Alexandre Kojéve. *Introduction to the Reading of Hegel,* ed. Allan Bloom, trans. James H. Nichols, Jr. (New York: Basic Books, 1969).

16. This passage has been pointed out by Gross, p. 189.

17. Georges Bataille, in *La Part maudite* (Paris: Les Editions de Minuit, 1967), notes that class distinctions are normally perceived in terms of waste or excess; thus, he who has the highest position in society is he who most ostentatiously wastes money, which others greedily hoard, on things that have no survival value whatsoever: jewels, clothes, and other luxuries. Bataille claims that one of the most exclusive rights of the upper classes in more primitive societies is the right to "waste" the lives of the lower orders.

18. Hutter locates these rivalries in a Freudian notion of father-son relationships. I do not deny the pertinence of those relationships, but I believe that they are subsumed under the more general theme of rivalry. After all, Darnay and Carton are fraternal rivals, and the promiscuous quality of the French mob's violence dissociates it from any single pattern of relationships.

19. A good recent work on the subject is Ernest Becker, *The Denial of Death* (New York: Free Press, 1973).

20. See Brooks, pp. 1–23.

21. J. Hillis Miller, *Charles Dickens: The World of His Novels* (Bloomington: Indiana University Press, 1958), p. 248, with his usual astuteness, claims that, in *A Tale of Two Cities,* Dickens could not imagine how contact with the "transhuman" could lead anywhere but to death. I hope I have shown why this is so.

22. For a fuller discussion of this doubling, see my article "Action in the Dickens Ending: *Bleak House* and *Great Expectations," Nineteenth-Century Fiction.* 33 (1978), 88–109.

Carlyle, Dickens, and the Revolution of 1848

MICHAEL GOLDBERG

Critical discussion of Carlyle and Dickens on the subject of revolution has tended to concentrate on the revolution of 1789. This is hardly surprising given *A Tale of Two Cities* and Carlyle's *History,* yet such a focus has inevitably overshadowed and obscured the importance of the other revolution, the series of political explosions in the name of popular democracy which unsettled Europe in 1848 and whose impact on both writers of considerable interest. For one thing, the social upheavals of mid-century occurred at a time of decisive change in both their working lives, and not only stimulated that change but contributed to its direction.

Dickens, busy with the last numbers of *Dombey and Son* when the revolution broke out in France, stood at a turning point in his life and art. It is now an established orthodoxy to observe that at this time Dickens had come to regard Victorian society in a radically fresh way. The nature of the change in his outlook is best described by Bernard Shaw in his seminal 1912 preface to *Hard Times.* What began in *Dombey* and culminated in *Hard Times,* he suggests, was comparable to a religious conversion which led Dickens to a conviction of social sin. In *Bleak House,* the book that immediately preceded *Hard Times,* Dickens was "still denouncing evils and ridiculing absurdities that were mere symptoms of the anarchy that followed the industrial revolution. . . . He had not dug down to the bed rock of the imposture. . . . He saw nothing but individual delinquencies, local plague-spots, negligent authorities." But in *Hard Times* all this had changed. In that novel Dickens joins Karl Marx, Carlyle, Ruskin, and Morris "rising up against civilisation itself as against a disease." This broadly based perception was expressed in such books as Carlyle's *Latter-Day Pamphlets, Hard Times,* and later on in the Socialist movement which convinced even those dubious about socialism, "that the condition of the civilised world is deplorable, and that the remedy is far beyond the means of individual righteousness."[1] It is in *Dombey and Son,* written in part under the shadow of European revolution, that Dickens first expressed what Kathleen Tillotson calls "a pervasive uneasiness about contemporary society which takes the place of an intermittent concern with specific social wrongs."[2] In

Reprinted from *Dickens Studies Annual* 12 (1983): 223–32 by permission. Copyright © AMS Press, Inc.

short, Dickens had come to view social evil as a malignant organism for which the only logical cure might be the radical surgery of revolution.

The revolution and the urgent stream of such visitors to Cheyne Row as Louis Blanc, Mazzini, Gavan Duffy, and Leigh Hunt drew Carlyle closer to contemporary politics than ever before. His immediate interests found their way into manuscript and print. In his first excursion into the field of political journalism, he wrote a series of articles on Ireland, which he felt constrained to revisit in 1849, and he was busy with the rough drafts of what were to become *Latter-Day Pamphlets*. As his major production of the period, the *Pamphlets* were largely a response to the European uprisings and, as in the case of *Hard Times,* represent a turning point in Carlyle's career and reputation—a change which brought imputations, not always well founded, of a dramatic alteration in his political thinking. Froude and Forster, the two latter-day Boswells, remind us that both Carlyle and Dickens were extremely restless during this time, and as we now easily recognize they were about to move in new directions.

All of which is not to argue that the revolution of 1848 was the immediate or exclusive source of these shifts in their thinking and writing; but it formed the indispensable backdrop against which such changes occurred and should be measured.

We should remember that for both Carlyle and Dickens the first French revolution was something of an historical exercise. It was an event frozen in time, something they read about and about which they had the leisure to theorize, whereas the revolution of 1848 they saw in actual progress, shifting and changing direction almost daily. For Carlyle, the historian of revolutions, it was particularly strange to find himself in the unique position of contemporary witness to the revolts sweeping Europe, agitating Ireland and threatening to engulf England.

The first European rumblings occurred in January 1848 when rebellion broke out in Sicily, where the Sicilians succeeded in imposing a constitution on their king, as did the people of Piedmont. In Milan, where patriots manned the barricade, Marshall Radetzky encircled the fortifications around the city, and popular upheavals drove Metternich from Vienna. There were revolts in Germany and Poland, and revolution spread quickly to Paris which once again became the "city of insurrections." The Guizot government fell, and a disguised Louis Philippe fled to England much to the scornful glee of Carlyle and the consternation of Dickens. As if by "sympathetic subterranean" influence, all Europe "exploded, boundless, uncontrollable," and the year 1848 was, in Carlyle's view, "one of the most singular, disastrous, amazing, and, on the whole, humiliating years the European world every saw. Not since the irruption of the Northern Barbarians has there been the like."[3] Kings everywhere precipitously vacated their thrones as the populace took government into their own hands. The order of the day was anarchy; "how happy," observed Carlyle, "if it be anarchy *plus* a street-constable!"[4] This in general, as Carlyle described it in 1850, was "the history, from Baltic to Mediterranean, in Italy, France, Prussia, Austria, from end to end of Europe, in those March days of 1848."[5]

Though concerned about some implications of the European revolutions, Carlyle's initial reaction to the news from Paris was one of "almost sacred joy," as he wrote in the *Examiner* of March 4, 1848. The overthrow of the French monarch, "flung out; he and his entire pack, with a kind of exquisite ignominy,"[6] was cause for celebration. "It is long years," he wrote to Emerson four days later on February 28, "since I have felt any such deep-seated pious satisfaction at a public event."[7]

Dickens greeted the new republic with comparable enthusiasm, a sign if not of influence at least of compatability of sentiment. "Mon Ami," he wrote to Forster on February 29, 1848, "I find that I am so much in love with the Republic that I must renounce my language and write solely in the language of the French Republic,"[8] which he temporarily did, signing himself Citoyen Charles Dickens. Carlyle's response was predictably more analytical. He wrote an unsigned article on French politics for the *Examiner* on March 4. Another, meant to follow it on March 11, was suppressed by the editor John Forster "lest Carlyle's candour might damage the circulation of the paper."[9] This suppressed article is not included in the appendix of Richard Herne Shepherd's 1881 *Memoirs of the Life and Writings of Thomas Carlyle,* among the six articles which he noted "are all we have been able to trace" of "Carlyle's fugitive political contributions to journalism."[10] Nor is it to be found in the 1892 reprinting of Carlyle's articles in Percy Newberry's *Rescued Essays.* The article, entitled "Prospects of the French Republic," is, however, in the Forster collection at the Victoria and Albert Museum. In it Carlyle makes a contrast between the first and the second French republics and in so doing implicitly invites a comparison of the Romantic and Victorian responses to revolution. The two great advantages of the newly emerged republic are that it is secure from outside attack: "all nations in the presence of their own inevitable democracy know well that this Republic is not a thing to be lightly or suddenly attacked"; and also "no Frenchman now expects a millennium close in the rear of it, which in regard to the old Republic all Frenchmen did." The new republic is "not required to be miraculous, but only to be a practicable one. Enthusiastic hope is not there to issue in fierce disappointment." In short, the high millennial hopes bestowed by the Romantic era on the first French republic, only to be cruelly betrayed during the reign of terror, had given way in Victorian times to more realistic expectations. Carlyle, of course, feared that like all modern republics the French one was likely to prove to be only a "government of Talkers," that is, "a government that does not govern but merely produces parliamentary eloquence." Still the Republic was France's noblest feat, and "the world's chief heroism for two hundred years." The new provisional government had started well, and as what was to follow was "hidden in black clouds," Carlyle wrote, we can only say "may it be wise" and "from the heart of all good citizens of all countries bid it good speed." That was early in March, when Carlyle saw the third French revolution as a stage in the completion of the first, part of a revolutionary process whose accomplishment was essential, "for rest is not in the world till then."[11]

However, by the end of March and the beginning of April, Carlyle was no longer so sanguine about the political prospects in France. In a letter to Thomas Erskine on March 24, he found in "this immense explosion of democracy" cause for both celebration and despair, and he predicted long years of "weltering confusion" before "anything can be *settled* again." Hardly since the "invasion of the wild Teutons and wreck of the old Roman Empire has there been so strange a Europe, all turned topsy turvy."[12] By April, the "future for all countries" filled him "with a kind of horror."[13]

In March, Carlyle told Emerson, who was then visiting England, that he had known "European revolution was inevitable," but he had "expected the old state of things to last out his time." In the light of recent European events he revised his estimate to give "our institutions, as they are called, aristocracy, church, etc., five years. . . ."[14]

Carlyle's prediction was soon disproved by events, for the European revolutions spent their energy without accomplishing their long-term aims. It is true that before the threat of popular revolution the European monarchs had fled "like a gang of coiners" surprised by the police, but within two years of the uprising in France, Louis Napoleon ruled the Second Empire with the support of the Catholic church, and French bayonets reinforced the position of Pope Pius IX, who in 1846 had donned the Papal tiara as a "reforming Pope." Largely because their conception of it was strongly colored by previous historical experience, the 1848 revolution had seemed to many observers the "great decisive struggle." Even after the setbacks of 1849, according to Engels, "vulgar democracy expected a renewed outbreak from day to day." He and Marx, however, believed that the "first chapter of the revolutionary period was closed and that the next phase could only begin with a new world crisis." As Marx put it, parodying the ritual formula for monarchist succession, "*The Revolution is dead!—Long live the revolution!*"[15]

In his own separate way Carlyle had arrived at a similar conclusion. By 1850, he saw that some "remounting,—very temporary remounting,—of the old machine, under new colours and altered forms," would soon ensue in most countries:

> Kings will be admitted back under . . . "Constitutions," with national Parliaments, or the like fashionable adjuncts; and everywhere the old daily life will try to begin again. But there is now no hope that such arrangements can be permanent; that they can be other than poor temporary makeshifts, which, if they try to fancy and make themselves permanent, will be displaced by new explosions, recurring more speedily than last time.[16]

New "street-barricades, and new anarchies, still more scandalous if still less sanguinary, must return and again return, till governing persons everywhere know and admit" that "universal *Democracy*" had "declared itself as an inevitable fact."[17] The hastily restored European order could not endure, and did not deserve to, and its restoration meant only that the need for change had been postponed. In England, too, Carlyle predicted "sore times" ahead and judged that the "trade of governor will not long be possible as poor Lord John [Russell] and the like of him are used to manage it."[18] For although England would resist the introduction of democracy "in the form of street-barricades and insurrectionary pikes," the "tramp of its million feet is on all streets and thoroughfares, the sound of its bewildered thousandfold voice is in all writings and speakings, in all thinkings and modes and activities of men."[19]

It seemed for a time as if revolution on the European model might enter England through the back door of Ireland or spontaneously erupt in the ranks of the Chartist movement which reached its peak in April 1848. The legitimate outrages which had moved Carlyle to write his essay on *Chartism* in 1839 had not been redressed, and now almost a decade later some 200,000 chartist petitioners were expected to demonstrate in London. In *Chartism* Carlyle had also condemned English misrule of Ireland and in the "hungry forties" conditions were even worse after the successive failure of the potato crops which brought Irish refugees streaming into English industrial towns in the north.

The Irish giant "despair" was to be seen everywhere "blue-visaged, thatched in rags, a blue child on each arm; hunger-driven, wide-mouthed, seeking whom he may devour."[20] Carlyle did not join in the popular outcry against the Irish nomads nor even against the landlords supposedly responsible for pauperizing them. England, through long neglect and misrule, deserved the army of Irish beggars now laying waste to its towns. But he did see that the Irish pauper parading his "rags and hunger, and sin and misery" was an "irrepressible missionary" to "our own people . . . heralding to us also a doom like his own."[21] For this destitute Irish army was bound to transform not only the political institutions of England but the structure of society itself.

Ireland seemed a great social laboratory where the social ills of England existed in magnified form, and where, particularly, organic government had broken down. In the summer of 1849, Carlyle decided to visit the "huge suppuration" that was Ireland to study conditions for himself. It was immediately apparent that revolutionary forces were gathering. John Mitchel, whom Carlyle had met in 1846, had come to believe that a peasants' revolt was imminent, and having left both the *Nation* and the Young Ireland Party, was readying the country for a rebellion openly advocated in his new journal *The United Irishman*. The *Nation,* too, though not radical enough for Mitchel, also appealed to Irishmen to throw off the English yoke. One such appeal, by the lady who was to become the mother of Oscar Wilde, called for a bold, decisive move against the English garrison "and the land is ours."[22] These revolutionary aspirations began to be taken seriously in England when, after the fall in February 1848 of the French government, Irishmen danced round bonfires in the certain hope that Ireland's turn to be free had now come. The Government of Westminster judged the moment had arrived to suppress the public preaching of sedition and dispatched additional troops to Ireland while arming itself with the provisions of the Treason Felony Act. Carlyle considered these moves unsympathetically, for while he approved the putting down of rebellion, without strong constructive measures to accompany it, he regarded such a policy as bankrupt. When Parliament resumed after the Easter recess of 1848, Carlyle launched a stinging attack on Lord John Russell's "remedial measures" for Ireland. Russell, he told readers of the *Spectator* on May 13, had earned the applause of all sane men for suppressing "pike-rioting" and by indicating to the Irish that their wrongs were not to be redressed by "street-barricades just at present." But the urgent question arose "by what means, then, *are* Irish wrongs to be redressed?"[23]

The Government's measures made for "prohibition of Repeal treason" but they offered no cure of "the disease which produces" it.[24] Nor did the government suggest "how the Irish population is to begin . . . to live on just terms with one another and with us,—or, alas, even how it is to continue living at all." An existence based on the treacherous potato was, after the blight and the famine which followed it, no longer possible. Did the Whig administration not also realize, he asked despairingly, that some form of "real government" for Ireland was indispensable? Did it know that the French king had fled Paris and that Europe had risen behind him to declare that it was done with "sham government"? All these facts indicated that "a *new* and very ominous era, for Ireland and for us, has arrived."[25] It is obvious that Carlyle saw the situation in Ireland in terms of the revolutions in Europe. He also saw that Irish discontent had its counterpart in the Chartist movement, which had been neither remedied nor extinguished by the demonstration of April 10. With both Chartism and Ireland in mind he asked,

> does our chief governor calculate that England, with such a Chartism under deck, and such a fireship of an Ireland indissolubly chained to her, beaten on continually by an anarchic Europe and its all-permeating influences . . . can keep the waters . . . by her old constitutional methods?"[26]

The *Pamphlets* deal with many topics, but their unifying core is democracy, the "grand, alarming, imminent, and indisputable Reality" of the time. If the long-range future for democracy had seemed assured since the first French Revolution of 1789, its immediate advent was now certain after the collapse of the third.

Carlyle's objections to democracy are not particularly palatable to modern tastes, and they were bitterly opposed by many of his contemporaries, but they have not always been clearly understood. Partly because of the effect of such misunderstanding on his reputation in general, and on the neglected *Pamphlets* in particular, the grounds for his hostility to early democracy deserve wary inspection.

Carlyle's feeling about the immense explosion of democracy was more complicated than one of simple rejection. Indeed he was as much depressed by the failure of the 1848 French revolution as he was by some of the implications that would have attended its success. To the extent that revolutionary democracy had shown up imposture and corruption he applauded it as a necessary first step towards future regeneration. Thus the expulsion of sham governors had pleased him far more than their restoration in 1849. The revolutions had contained an inchoate stirring against the very shams Carlyle had hated all his life; they had proved that a longing for justice and veracity still existed on the part of the governed, and they served notice that such charlatans as Louis Philippe could found no "habitation upon lies."[27] But, on the other hand, that the world "in its protest against False Government" should find no remedy save that "of rushing into No Government or anarchy"[28] struck him as ludicrous. He favored extirpating false government as had happened in France, but he sought a different end result from those who merely wanted access to the rights and privileges seemingly guaranteed by a democratic constitution. Here, as elsewhere, a characteristic mixture of radical and reactionary strains converge in Carlyle's thinking, leaving him opposed both to the vestiges of the ancient regimes and to the new utopianism with which many hoped to replace them.

Carlyle believed in order, but it is clear that he did not wish to prop up the existing political order. He accepted even more willingly than many of his contemporaries the inevitability and the desirability of change, and in the aftermath of the revolutionary failures of 1848 he perceived that the need for change was more urgent than ever. "There must be a new world, if there is to be any world at all. . . . These days of universal death must be days of universal newbirth, if the ruin is not to be total and final."[29] The alternatives were not "Stay where we are, or change?"[30] but how change was to be brought about and whether in Britain the transition to the new era could be made "pacifically."

He was at odds, however, with the prevailing belief that "once modelled into suffrages, furnished with ballot-boxes and suchlike,"[31] the transition to democracy would be at once achieved. He was more inclined to ask with Burke, "Is it because liberty in the abstract may be classed amongst the blessings of mankind, that I am seriously to felicitate a madman, who has escaped from the protecting restraint and wholesome darkness of his cell, on his restoration to the enjoyment of light and liberty?"[32] To use his own metaphor, if the old house of Europe had partially broken down and the "front wall of your wretched old crazy dwelling" had fallen prostrate into the street, was it sane for the whole household to burst forth celebrating the "new joys of light and ventilation. . . ."[33]

This summary by no means exhausts the complexity of Carlyle's response to European democracy, but it offers an impression of its broad contours. To conclude with a general comment—the 1848 revolutions helped to stir the social thinking of both writers in ways that were profound and productive. The revolution broke Dickens' faith in the adequacy of reform and alerted him to the ongoing process of revolutionary change and the constant possibility of the fire next time. In the mid-fifties, for instance, he recognized that the "sullen, smouldering discontent" in England was "like the general mind of France before the breaking out of the first Revolution," and that any accident might touch off "a conflagration as never has been beheld since."[34] For Carlyle, the revolution led to his most penetrating thinking about democracy, and his strictures against what he saw as its dangers and distortions led to his increasing isolation as a moral teacher and to the lowering of his reputation towards the end of the century.

Despite protests against Carlyle's views in *Latter-Day Pamphlets* there were critics who saw the value of his struggle to comprehend the major political and social changes occuring in the mid-century. Emerson, for one, said of the *Pamphlets:* "it is a pretty good minority of one; enunciating with brilliant malice what shall be the universal opinion of the next edition of mankind. And the sanity was so manifest, that I felt the over-gods had cleared their skirts also to this generation, in not leaving themselves without witness."[35]

Notes

1. Reprinted in *The Dickens Critics,* George Ford and Lauriat Lane, Jr., eds. (Ithaca: Cornell University Press, 1961), pp. 126, 127, 128.
2. *Novels of the Eighteen-Forties* (Oxford: Oxford University Press, 1961), p. 157.
3. "The Present Time," in *Latter-Day Pamphlets* (London: Chapman & Hall, 1898), p. 5.
4. Ibid., p. 6.
5. Ibid.
6. James Anthony Froude, *Thomas Carlyle: A History of His Life in London 1834–1881,* 2 vols. (London: Longmans & Co., 1884), I, 429.
7. *Correspondence of Carlyle and Emerson,* ed., C. E. Norton (London: Chatto & Windus, 1883), II, 163.
8. *Life of Charles Dickens* (Boston: James Osgood, 1875), p. 404.
9. D. A. Wilson, *Carlyle at His Zenith* (London: Kegan Paul, Trench, Trubner & Co., Ltd., 1927), p. 22.
10. (London, 1881), II, 21.
11. *The Examiner,* March 4, 1848, p. 145.
12. Froude, I, 430–431.
13. Ibid., I, 435.
14. *Letters of Matthew Arnold,* ed., George Russell (London, 1895), I, 8.
15. *Class Struggles in France 1848–1850* (New York: International Publishers, 1964), p. 59.
16. "The Present Time," p. 8.

17. Ibid., pp. 8–9.
18. Froude, I, 438.
19. "The Present Time," p. 9.
20. "Downing Street," in *Latter-Day Pamphlets,* p. 94
21. *Spectator,* May 13, 1848, p. 463.
22. July 29, 1848.
23. P. 463.
24. Ibid.
25. P. 464.
26. Ibid.
27. Froude, I, 430.
28. Ibid.
29. "The Present Time," p. 2.
30. "The New Downing Street," in *Latter-Day Pamphlets,* p. 157.
31. "The Present Time," p. 14.
32. Edmund Burke, *Reflections on the Revolution in France* (Harmondsworth: Penguin, 1970), p. 90.
33. "The Present Time," p. 10.
34. Edgar Johnson, *Charles Dickens: His Tragedy and Triumph,* 2 vols. (New York: Simon and Schuster, 1952), II, 841.
35. *The Correspondence of Emerson and Carlyle,* ed., Joseph Slater (New York: Columbia University Press, 1964), pp. 497–498.

Dickens and the Catastrophic Continuum of History in *A Tale of Two Cities*

J. M. Rignall

It is not surprising that the most remembered scene in *A Tale of Two Cities* is the last, for this novel is dominated, even haunted, by its ending. From the opening chapter in which the "creatures of this chronicle" are set in motion "along the roads that lay before them," while the Woodman Fate and the Farmer Death go silently about their ominous work, those roads lead with sinister inevitability to the revolutionary scaffold.[1] To an unusual extent, especially given the expansive and centrifugal nature of Dickens's imagination, this is an end-determined narrative whose individual elements are ordered by an ending which is both their goal and, in a sense, their source. In a historical novel like this there is a transparent relationship between narrative form and historical vision, and the formal features of *A Tale*—its emphatic linearity, continuity, and negative teleology—define a distinctive vision of history. As Robert Alter has argued in his fine critical account of the novel,[2] it is not the particular historical event that ultimately concerns Dickens here, but rather a wider view of history and the historical process. That process is a peculiarly grim one. As oppression is shown to breed oppression, violence to beget violence, evil to provoke evil, a pattern emerges that is too deterministic to owe much to Carlyle and profoundly at odds with the conventional complacencies of Whig history. Instead of progress there is something more like the catastrophic continuum that is Walter Benjamin's description of the historical process: the single catastrophe, piling wreckage upon wreckage.[3] And when, in the sentimental postscript of Carton's prophecy, Dickens finally attempts to envisage a liberation from this catastrophic process, he can only do so, like Benjamin, in eschatological terms. For Benjamin it was the messianic intervention of a proletarian revolution that would bring time to a standstill and blast open the continuum of history; for Dickens it is the Christ-like intervention of a self-sacrificing individual that is the vehicle for a vision of a better world which seems to lie beyond time and history. The parallel with Ben-

J. M. Rignall, "Dickens and the Catastrophic Continuum of History in *A Tale of Two Cities*." *English Literacy History* 58, no. 3 (1984): 575–87. © 1984. Reprinted by permission of The Johns Hopkins University Press.

jamin cannot be pressed beyond the common perception of a pernicious historical continuum and the common desire to break it, but the coexistence of these two elements in *A Tale* is, I wish to argue, important for an understanding of the novel, lending it a peculiarly haunted and contradictory quality as Dickens gives expression to a vision of history which both compels and repels him at the same time.

In Carton's final vision of a world seemingly beyond time, the paradigm of the apocalypse mediates between what is known of history and what may be hoped for it.[4] That hope is not to be dismissed as mere sentimentality, whatever the manner of its expression. However inadequately realized Carton's prophecy may be in imaginative terms, it is significant as a moment of resistance to the grimly terminal linearity and historical determinism of the preceding narrative. That resistance is not confined to the last page of the novel, for, as I shall show, it manifests itself in other places and in other ways, creating a faint but discernible counter-current to the main thrust of the narrative. This is not to say that Dickens presents a thorough-going deconstruction of his own narrative procedures and version of history in *A Tale,* for the process at work here is more ambiguous and tentative than that. There is a struggle with sombre fears that gives rise to contradictions which cannot be reduced to the internal self-contradictions of language. What the novel presents is, rather, the spectacle of an imagination both seized by a compelling vision of history as a chain of violence, a catastrophic continuum, and impelled to resist that vision in the very act of articulation, so that the narrative seems at the same time to seek and to shun the violent finality of its ending in the Terror. The nightmare vision is too grim to accept without protest, and too powerful to be dispelled by simple hopefulness, and the work bears the signs of this unresolved and unresolvable contradiction.

In his preface Dickens maintains that the idea of the novel had "complete possession" of him, and the state of imaginative obsession in which *A Tale of Two Cities* was written can be sensed in two rather different aspects of the work: in the way that it presses on relentlessly toward its violent ending, and in the way that particular scenes take on a visionary intensity, seemingly charged with obscure and powerful emotions that are neither fully controlled nor comprehended. The scenes of frenzied collective violence are the most striking examples of this kind of writing, but there are other moments, less obviously related to the main track of the story, when images and ideas erupt into the text with a spontaneous energy that arrests rather than furthers the momentum of the narrative. The first-person meditation on the death-like mystery of individuality which opens Chapter Three ("The Night Shadows") is just such an intervention:

> A wonderful fact to reflect upon, that every human creature is constituted to
> be that profound secret and mystery to every other. A solemn consideration,
> when I enter a great city by night, that every one of those darkly clustered

houses encloses its own secret; that every room in every one of them encloses its own secret; that every beating heart in the hundreds of thousands of breasts there, is, in some of its imaginings, a secret to the heart nearest it! Something of the awfulness, even of Death itself, is referable to this. No more can I turn the leaves of this dear book that I loved, and vainly hope in time to read it all. No more can I look into the depths of this unfathomable water, wherein, as momentary lights glanced into it. I have had glimpses of buried treasure and other things submerged. It was appointed that the book should shut with a spring, for ever and for ever, when I had read but a page. It was appointed that the water should be locked in an eternal frost, when the light was playing on its surface, and I stood in ignorance on the shore. My friend is dead, my neighbour is dead, my love, the darling of my soul, is dead; it is the inexorable consolidation and perpetuation of the secret that was always in that individuality, and which I shall carry in mine to my life's end. In any of the burial-places of this city through which I pass, is there a sleeper more in- scrutable than its busy inhabitants are, in their innermost personality, to me, or than I am to them? (44)

Both the form and the substance of this meditation set it clearly apart from the surrounding narrative. The brooding first-person voice is never heard again in the novel, even though the same sombre note is struck by the imper- sonal narrator. The directness and urgency of the first-person utterance invite us to look for a significant relationship between these reflections and the main themes of the novel, but it is not easy to find one. The passage is only awk- wardly related to the scene on the Dover road which it punctuates, since its insistence on the essential, metaphysical mystery of individuality is out of proportion to the condition of the passengers in the coach. Their mutual sus- picion and ignorance are occasioned simply by the hazards of the journey. Nor can it be said to illumine the general condition of life as it appears in this novel. Although there is some connection between the separateness of indi- viduals and the characters and fates of Dr. Manette and Carton, Dickens's handling of character is basically at odds with such an absolute assertion of impenetrable otherness. His imperious command of his characters is never subject to epistemological uncertainty, and even the most estranged figures, like Dr. Manette and Carton, are in the end not mysterious but knowable and known. Except in its tone the excursus is altogether out of place: Dickens here steps out of his own fiction to generalize about character and individual- ity in life rather than in books, while paradoxically using the metaphor of the book to do so.

This reflection on character and the metaphor that it employs cast a sig- nificant light on Dickens's own practice in the novel. By implication, both his presentation of character and his use of an ending are identified as simply matters of literary convention. To see death in terms of the premature closing of a book is to raise the possibility of different relationships among death, narrative, and endings from those presented by A Tale itself. Discontinuity is a fact of life and, implicitly, a narrative possibility, and to imply as much is to challenge both the conventional structure of this particular narrative and the vision of historical determinism that it projects. The challenge is only momentary and implied, but the moment is not entirely isolated. Although Dickens primarily uses the death of Carton and the ending of the novel to complete a pattern of meaning rather than to effect a premature closure, there are occasions in the novel when the desire for such a closure surfaces in the text as if in reaction to the chain of violent events that leads relentlessly to the guillotine. The first-person plural dramatization of the Darnays' flight from Paris (386–7) provides, for instance, a kind of alternative premature ending for those privileged characters who are allowed to escape the logic of the historical process. The scene is both related and opposed to the "Night Shadows" meditation and Mr. Lorry's journey to Dover: this time the characters in the coach are not suspicious, but united by love and shared apprehension; they are not mysterious and unfathomable, but familiar and transparent. Nevertheless, the "awfulness of death" threatens them from without, and, as the narrative assumes the urgency and immediacy of the first-person plural and the present tense, the scene comes to suggest a flight of the imagination from the foredoomed finality of the guillotine and the novel's preordained ending. It is a flight which necessarily carries the characters beyond the boundaries of the novel, which is headed to only one conclusion, and they never again appear directly in it. Pursued not by the Revolution but, as it turns out, only by a reflection of their own fears, they may be said to be escaping from history: "the wind is rushing after us, and the clouds are flying after us, and the moon is plunging after us, and the whole wild night is in pursuit of us; but, so far we are pursued by nothing else" (387). In fleeing the ending of the novel they have fled beyond the process of history.

There is a less direct and more complex suggestion of flight from the grim logic of the historical process in the scene of the mob around the grindstone, observed by Mr. Lorry and Dr. Manette. What they witness is an appalling spectacle of bestial violence and moral degradation as Dickens lets his wildest and deepest fears rise to the surface. The chain reaction of violent oppression and violent rebellion has passed beyond human control, and in this mass frenzy all distinctions of individuality and even sex are submerged:

> The eye could not detect one creature in the group free from the smear of blood. Shouldering one another to get next at the sharpening-stone, were men stripped to the waist, with the stain all over their limbs and bodies; men in all sorts of rags, with the stain upon those rags; men devilishly set off with spoils of women's lace and silk and ribbon, with the stain dyeing those trifles through and through.

Then, as if appalled by the terrors he has let loose, Dickens, in John Gross's words, "reaches for his gun":[5]

And as the frantic wielders of these weapons snatched them from the stream of sparks and tore away into the streets, the same red hue was red in their frenzied eyes;—eyes which any unbrutalised beholder would have given twenty years of life, to petrify with a well-directed gun.

All this was seen in a moment, as the vision of a drowning man, or of any human creature at any very great pass, could see a world if it were there. They drew back from the window, and the Doctor looked for explanation in his friend's ashy face. (291–2)

Clearly signalled as the vision of a drowning man, the scene is the product of an imagination *in extremis*. It is a bourgeois nightmare of anarchy unleashed by the rebellion of the oppressed.[6] Even if it is the logical culmination of the violent oppression that has preceded it, the violence is, when it eventuates, too great to bear. The "well-directed gun," with its sudden change of focus from dramatic scene to violent, judgmental reaction, looks like an authorial intervention aimed at terminating the nightmare. The curious insistence on the eyes of the frenzied crowd emphasizes that vision is the vital element, and the urge to "petrify" those eyes can be read as the expression of a desire to put an end to that vision. The action is transposed from subject to object: it is not their eyes that Dickens the narrator wishes to close, but his own. For a moment he seeks to retreat from his own vision of the historical process.

There is, then, a form of resistance here to the catastrophic continuum of history, but at the same time Dickens reveals something about the emotional dynamics of that historical process in a way that is more penetrating than the melodramatic simplifications of Madame Defarge and her desire for vengeance. The violent reaction of the "well-directed gun," an answering of violence with violence, implicates the writer himself in the very process he is presenting. This is characteristic of the open and unguarded nature of his procedure in *A Tale:* violent fears and violent reactions are given direct, unmediated expression, so that unwitting parallels emerge between the reflexes of the author/narrator and those of the fictional characters. In this case there is an obvious affinity between the "well-directed gun," with what has been aptly termed its "true ring of outraged rate-paying respectability,"[7] and the response of the blustering bourgeois Stryver to news of the Revolution:

Among the talkers, was Stryver, of the King's Bench Bar, far on his way to state promotion, and, therefore, loud on the theme: broaching to Monseigneur, his devices for blowing the people up and exterminating them from the face of the earth, and doing without them: and for accomplishing many similar objects akin in their nature to the abolition of eagles by sprinkling salt on the tails of the race. (267)

The reaction of the character is held firmly in focus and identified by means of irony as excessive and senseless, while the author/narrator in the grindstone passage repeats that reaction without the containing frame of any critical awareness. And both reactions have the function—the one deliberate, the other involuntary—of revealing the emotional resources that drive the catastrophic continuum of history. Dickens thus does more than simply project a deterministic vision of history; he shows how that determinism is rooted in commonplace and familiar emotions, how the potential for violence is not confined to a savage past and an alien setting, but lies very close to home. The effect is to detach history from the safety of the past and to suggest that its violent continuum may not have expired with the Revolution.

The persistence of that violence is amply demonstrated by Dickens's own susceptibility to the kinds of powerful emotions that are at work in the novel. As a caricature of the conquering bourgeois, the figure of Stryver belongs as much in the nineteenth century as the eighteenth, and Dickens himself could display distinctly Stryverish leanings in his response to contemporary events. In the same letter to Forster in which he outlines his intentions in *A Tale of Two Cities* and which he must have written about the same time as the grindstone passage,[8] there is a revealing outburst of verbal violence. The letter begins with a discussion of the case of the surgeon Thomas Smethurst, found guilty of poisoning his bigamous "wife." The trial judge, Sir Jonathan Frederick Pollock, strongly supported the verdict in the face of public unease and of moves to persuade the Home Secretary to quash or commute the sentence.[9] Dickens gives his fervent support to Pollock, and in doing so presents another example of an outraged, violent reaction to an act of violence:

> I followed the case with so much interest, and have followed the miserable knaves and asses who have perverted it since, with so much indignation, that I have often had more than half a mind to write and thank the upright judge who tried him. I declare to God that I believe such a service one of the greatest that a man of intellect and courage can render to society. Of course I saw the beast of a prisoner (with my mind's eye) delivering his cut-and-dried speech, and read in every word of it that no one but the murderer could have delivered or conceived it. Of course I have been driving the girls out of their wits here, by incessantly proclaiming that there needed no medical evidence either way, and that the case was plain without it. Lastly, of course (though a merciful man— because a merciful man I mean), I would hang any Home Secretary (Whig, Tory, Radical, or otherwise) who should step in between that black scoundrel and the gallows.[10]

The protestations of his mercifulness are convincing only as a respectable garment for his Stryverish pugnacity, and the emotional pattern of the passage recapitulates that of the grindstone scene so closely as to provide striking evidence for taking the "well-directed gun" as an authorial intervention. What is more interesting, however, is that the violence spills over into his account of his intentions in writing *A Tale:*

But I set myself the little task of making a *picturesque* story, rising in every chapter with characters true to nature, but whom the story itself should express, more than they should express themselves, by dialogue. I mean, in other words, that I have fancied a story of incident might be written, in place of the bestiality that *is* written under that pretence, pounding the characters out in its own mortar, and beating their own interests out of them. If you could have read the story all at once, I hope you wouldn't have stopped half way.[11]

As violent an exception is taken to conventional forms of storytelling as is taken to an alleged murderer, and when Dickens writes of "pounding" and "beating" his characters it seems that violence is not only central to his vision of history in this novel but is also inherent in his means of expressing that vision. This formal violence, which could be interpreted in one sense as the forcible subordination of character to the story of incident, is as revealingly related to the creation of a narrative and historical continuum as is the earlier emotional violence. The expressed intention is to prevent the reader from stopping halfway, to maintain a compelling momentum in the narrative, and this momentum also serves the vision of historical determinism by subjecting individuals to a sequence of violent events that is beyond their power to control.

What exactly Dickens means by beating his characters' own interest out of them is open to question. It might be taken to refer to the way in which they are forcibly harnessed to allegorical meanings, like Darnay with the "Everyman" implications of his original family name, or the sentimental equation of Lucie Manette with a "golden thread." But the only character who has any real interest to be beaten out of him, Carton, is not the object of any direct allegorizing. Indeed, in his case meaning is deliberately withheld rather than allegorically asserted, and no cogent reasons are offered for his alienation. This mystification has the effect of directing the search for significance away from the personal life towards the general condition of existence. Lukács's contention that Carton's fate is the one that least of all "grows organically out of the age and its social events"[12] is justified only if the wider historical process is ignored, for it is as a victim of general social values and forces—and hence, by implication, of the historical continuum—that interest and significance are beaten out of him. As Lukács sees, he is a marginal figure, but he can be said to be significant precisely for that reason: he has been marginalized, so to speak, by the energy and values embodied in Stryver who, more properly than Darnay, is his *alter ego*. In his gloomy estrangement Carton suggests the neurotic price that may be exacted by the aggressive pursuit of individual success; by the bourgeois ethos of individual endeavor in its most crassly careerist form. The accusation that he levels at Stryver evinces a social as much as a personal truth: " 'You were always driving and riving and shouldering and pressing, to that restless degree that I had no chance for my life but in rust and repose' " (120–1). A world dominated by the energy and purpose of such as Stryver claims its moral and psychological victims within the dominant class. The triumph of the bourgeois will creates its opposite in the aimless, drifting existence of a character whose self-image—" 'I should ask ... that I might be regarded as an useless ... piece of furniture' " (237)—betrays the marks of a reified consciousness. And to the extent that Stryver partakes of the violent spirit which is at work in the larger historical events, Carton comes to stand, too, as the victim of the catastrophic continuum of history, a role which he then, at the end, consciously assumes.

To define Carton in these terms is to spell out bluntly what is only intimated indirectly, for it is Dickens's refusal to define and explain precisely that gives Carton a greater degree of density and interest than the other characters. With Carton, indeed, Dickens comes closest to creating something like the mystery and opacity of individuality that he refers to in the "Night Shadows" meditation, but only up to a point, since in the final scenes of the character's transformation there is a movement back toward conventional coherence and transparency. If, as Benjamin argues, the meaning of the life of a character in a novel is revealed in his death,[13] then Carton could be said to constitute himself as a character by choosing to die by the guillotine. He gives himself a goal and a purpose, and in so doing gives shape and meaning to his life. What has been aimless and indefinite becomes purposive and defined, and continuity is established between beginning and end, between promising youth and exemplary death. He achieves character in both a formal and a moral sense, and in the process realigns himself with the other representatives of English bourgeois life, exhibiting reflexes reminiscent of Stryver's in sensing a desire to strike the life out of the wood-sawyer (341) and reflecting on the desirability of raising Madame Defarge's arm and striking under it sharp and deep (371).

Carton's transformation is clearly intended to be read as the redemption of a wasted life, but such a reading has to ignore the qualifying ambiguities that are involved in it. As he decides on his course of action, resolution is strangely mixed with fatalism:

> "There is nothing more to do," said he, glancing upward at the moon, "until tomorrow. I can't sleep."
> It was not a reckless manner, the manner in which he said these words aloud under the fast-sailing clouds, nor was it more expressive of negligence than defiance. It was the settled manner of a tired man, who had wandered and struggled and got lost, but who at length struck into his road and saw its end. (342)

The term "end" carries a double meaning: in one sense it has to be read as "goal," stressing Carton's new-found sense of purpose and smuggling into the novel on the level of the individual life the positive teleology that is so markedly absent on the level of history. But the stronger meaning here is that of "conclusion," and a conclusion that is approached with a sense of release rather than a sense of achievement. The "tired man" is simply seeking repose, and in his desire for an end he makes explicit that resistance to the narrative and historical continuum which has been intimated elsewhere in the novel and now surfaces as the deepest yearning of a particular character.

He wishes to escape but, significantly, the mode of escape he chooses merely confirms his status as a victim of socio-historical circumstances. The act of self-sacrifice—an idea which haunts Dickens's imagination in this novel as powerfully and melodramatically as images of revolutionary violence—cannot be seen as simply the ultimate expression of altruism, since it is obscurely rooted in the same values that have significantly contributed to Carton's estrangement in the first place. The puritan ethic of disciplined personal endeavor demands renunciation such as Carton has been neurotically making all along, and its final act is the renunciation of life itself.[14] Thus the very step which makes sense of his life is as perverse as it is noble, as much a capitulation to the uncontrollable forces that have governed his life as a transcendence of them. To seek to escape sacrifice by sacrificing oneself is the expression of a truly desperate desire for an ending.

These more questionable implications of Carton's self-chosen end are largely disguised by Dickens's narrative and rhetorical strategies in the closing chapters. The polarization and pathos of melodrama are engaged to elicit acceptance of him as an exemplary altruist, while the Christian rhetoric of death and resurrection serves to present his self-sacrifice as a positive act of redemption rather than an expression of world-weary resignation. The character is, as it were, borne along by an affective and rhetorical current which obscures contradictions, and this same current is clearly intended to carry the reader, unquestioning, from Carton's death under the Terror to the resurrection of civilized order in his prophetic vision of the future. This attempt to make the historical regeneration of France and the domestic happiness of the Darnays seem continuous with what has preceded them is, however, hardly convincing, as the only element of continuity is the continuing strain of imaginative resistance to the destructive historical continuum. That the historical process of escalating violence should issue in a benign future is scarcely conceivable in this context, and Dickens passes perfunctorily over how it could come about with a casual reference to "evil . . . gradually making expiation for itself and wearing out" (404). The suggestion of entropy in that last phrase is significant. It is not so much a vision of redeeming historical development that is bestowed on Carton as a vision of the end of time. " 'There is no Time there' " (403), he says to the seamstress of the "better" land to which both are going; and his own vision of a better land, with its "beautiful city" and "brilliant people" (404) rising from the abyss, appears similarly otherworldly, having a greater affinity with the New Jerusalem of the Apocalypse than with nineteenth-century Paris. Indeed, the apocalyptic note in this conclusion stresses finality rather than resurrection, and death haunts even the conventional pieties of the domestic happy ending: Lorry is seen "passing tranquilly to his reward" and the Darnays, "their course done, lying side by side in their last earthly bed" (404). Lives are shown passing to a peaceful end, and all this individual and historical "wearing out" is envisaged by a man who is himself gratefully embracing death as a welcome release. Even in his famous mawkish last words it is not the heroic deed but the long-sought repose, the "far, far better rest" (404), that receives the final emphasis.

Weariness, both of character and of creative imagination, is the keynote of this ending, and it betrays the intellectual and imaginative impasse in which Dickens finds himself. Since he sees revolution as just another link in the chain of violence and oppression, and presents the efforts of individuals, like Darnay's journey to Paris, as powerless to influence the course of historical events, he can conceive no possibility, to use Benjamin's phrase, of blasting open the continuum of history by social and political action.[15] Unlike Benjamin, Dickens can advance no alternative vision of time and history. The claim once made for *Middlemarch* that it replaces "the concepts of origin, end and continuity" by "the categories of repetition, of difference, of discontinuity, of openness"[16] can certainly not be applied to *A Tale of Two Cities*. Origin and end, feudal oppression and revolutionary retribution, are linked by a causal chain which affirms the predominance of continuity. Repetition, on the other hand, as Dr. Manette's recurrent trauma illustrates, is here simply the mark of a mind imprisoned in the past, not a new, liberating category of temporal experience. Even the moments of discontinuity discussed earlier only challenge the narrative and historical continuum by revealing a desire to evade it. Carton's prophecy is simply a final evasive move, and one that gives itself away by its weary insistence on death and its eschatological suggestion of the end of time. Only by turning away from the course of human history can Dickens find a refuge for hope, and to express hope in such terms is tantamount to a confession of despair. In this novel of imprisonments and burials alive the writer himself remains imprisoned in a rigorously linear, end-determined narrative and the grimly determinist vision of history which it articulates. The resistance he offers is that of a mind vainly struggling to escape and thereby confirming the power of that which holds it captive. This vision of history as a catastrophic continuum is only made more powerful by the clear indications in the text that Dickens is expressing what is deeply repugnant to, yet stronger than, all that he can hope and wish for.

Notes

1. *A Tale of Two Cities*, ed. George Woodcock (Harmondsworth: Penguin, 1970), 37. Further references to this edition are given after quotations in the text.
2. Robert Alter, "The Demons of History in Dickens' *Tale*," *Novel* 2 (1968–9): 135–142.

3. Walter Benjamin, "Theses on the Philosophy of History," *Illuminations,* trans. Harry Zohn, ed. Hannah Arendt (London: Fontana, 1973), 255–266 (257). See also *Gesammelte Schriften,* ed. Rolf Tiedemann and Hermann Schweppenhäuser (Frankfurt, 1974), 1(3): 1244: "Die Katastrophe als das Kontinuum der Geschichte."

4. Alter, 138, gives an illuminating account of apocalyptic allusions in the novel.

5. John Gross, "*A Tale of Two Cities,*" in *Dickens and the Twentieth Century,* ed. John Gross and Gabriel Pearson (London, 1962), 192.

6. Benjamin, in his opposition to the notion of historical continuity, stresses the importance of isolated moments of vision like this:

> To articulate the past historically does not mean to recognize it the way it really was (Ranke). It means to seize hold of a memory as it flashes up at a moment of danger. Historical materialism wishes to retain that image of the past which unexpectedly appears to a man singled out by history at a moment of danger. (*Illuminations,* 257).

Whereas Benjamin was thinking of the revolutionary proletariat as the subject of such a vision, recapturing the experience of its oppressed forebears, Dickens could be said to be presenting the bourgeois counterpart of such an experience, where the man singled out by history at a moment of danger relives the perennial fears of the property-owning class.

7. Gross, 192.

8. The weekly part containing the "Grindstone" chapter was published on September 24, 1859. In this letter of August 25, Dickens tells Forster that he has asked the publisher of *All the Year Round* to send him "four weeks' proofs beyond the current number, that are in type." The current number would be that of August 20: the four weeks in proof would cover the numbers up to 17 September, leaving the "Grindstone" part as not yet in type, and most probably either just completed or still being worked on. For the letter of August 25 see *The Letters of Charles Dickens,* ed. Walter Dexter (London: Nonesuch Press, 1938), 3:117–119.

9. See Philip Collins, *Dickens and Crime,* 2nd ed. (London, 1964), 246.

10. *Letters,* 3:118.

11. Although this quotation comes from the same letter as the preceding one, I have here cited the text as given by Charles Dickens the Younger in his introduction to *A Tale of Two Cities* (London: Macmillan, 1902), xx. He points out that Forster, in quoting the letter in his *Life,* alters "bestiality" to "odious stuff." Dexter, *Letters,* 3:118, follows Forster's diluted version.

12. Georg Lukács, *The Historical Novel,* trans. Hannah and Stanley Mitchell (Harmondsworth: Penguin, 1969), 292.

13. *Illuminations,* 100–101.

14. The irrational act of self-sacrifice could thus be said to point to a general irrationalism in history and society at large, as is suggested in a different context by Max Horkheimer and Theodor W. Adorno, *Dialectic of Enlightenment,* trans. John Cumming (London, 1973), 55: "The irrationalism of totalitarian capitalism . . . has its prototype in the hero who escapes from sacrifice by sacrificing himself. The history of civilisation is the history of the introversion of sacrifice. In other words: the history of renunciation."

15. *Illuminations,* 264.

16. J. Hillis Miller, "Narrative and History," in *ELH Essays for Earl R. Wasserman,* ed. Ronald Paulson and Arnold Stein (Baltimore and London, 1975), 165–183 (177).

Alternatives to Bourgeois Individualism
in *A Tale of Two Cities*

CATES BALDRIDGE

Dickens's ambivalence toward the Revolution he depicts in *A Tale of Two Cities* has been the subject of much thoughtful comment, and over the past few decades a number of differing causes for this ambivalence have been proposed. George Woodcock, for instance, sees in the "vigor" with which the author depicts the scenes of Revolutionary violence a kind of vicarious retribution against the society which betrayed him in his youth: "in one self [Dickens] is there, dancing among them, destroying prisons and taking revenge for the injustices of childhood."[1] Others have interpreted it as the result of the author's fitful attempts to work out an overarching theory of history, or to adapt Carlyle's ideas on historical necessity to the needs of his fictional genre.[2] Some critics have even pointed out parallels between the methods of the Jacquerie and the literary techniques employed by Dickens himself.[3] What I shall do here is to focus upon one particular aspect of the Revolutionary regime in *A Tale* which has received less attention than most, and attempt to put forward a largely political explanation for Dickens's ambivalence concerning it. The aspect I refer to is the Revolution's assertion that the group, the class, the Republic—and *not* the individual—comprise, or should comprise, the basic unit of society. The corollaries which spring from this belief (and which are themselves fully depicted in the text) will also be considered: that all merely personal claims must defer to those of the polity as a whole; that the minds and hearts of citizens must be laid bare to the scrutiny of the community; and that virtues and guilt, rights and responsibilities, inhere in groups rather than in individuals. My contention is that Dickens's deep dissatisfaction with the social relations fostered by his own acquisitive and aggressively individualist society leads him at times to explore with sensitivity and even enthusiasm the liberating possibilities offered by an ideology centered elsewhere than upon the autonomous self. As we shall see, what emerges is a subversive subtext to the narrator's middle-class horror at the collectivist Revolutionary ideology promulgated behind the barricades of Paris.

Reprinted by permission of *SEL Studies in English Literature 1500–1900* 30, No. 4 (Fall 1990): 633–54.

In what follows I shall be employing the interpretive strategies of neo-Marxist hermeneutics in a way which some readers may find troubling, in that it might appear that I am crediting Dickens with mounting some sort of *proto*-Marxist critique of his society. In fact, nothing of the kind is intended. Rather, I mean only to suggest that while Dickens finds much to disparage in the Revolutionary regime he depicts, he nevertheless understands at some level that it offers stark alternatives to the social relations undergirding those aspects of Victorian England that he *also* thoroughly despises, and that because of this an undercurrent of sympathy makes its way into the text despite his explicit intention to paint the Jacquerie as bloodthirsty, implacable, and deranged. Dickens, who will have no truck with schemes of social ameliora-tion which depend upon class-conflict, is far from being a cultural materialist, even when he thunders most vehemently against the abuses of industrial cap-italism. One can, however, safely credit him with comprehending a relation-ship between a society's view of the individual and the economic and inter-personal texture of its daily life. This act of understanding is all I mean to burden Dickens with by way of an "authorial intention," and surely much of the sympathy I find for the Revolution in *A Tale of Two Cities* escaped the nov-elist's conscious control. If the terminology I employ to describe all this is that of our century rather than his, this is not done in order to paint Dickens the Marxist he wasn't, but rather to bring to bear what I believe to be a rea-sonably precise and nuanced hermeneutical technique upon a text whose pol-itics is complicated by its author's peculiar set of personal ambivalences and historical limitations.

I

Clearly, we should not expect any such countervailing current of thought as the one outlined above to emerge except in thoroughly disguised and dis-placed forms, for, as W. J. Harvey long ago pointed out, the assumptions of bourgeois individualism are central to the enterprise of Victorian novelists generally and to that of Dickens in particular. Middle-class orthodoxy posits the discrete human subject as primary and inviolable, a move which Harvey declares to be the indispensable core of Classical Liberalism, that ideology which he credits both with nurturing the infant genre of the novel in the eighteenth century and assuring its triumph in the nineteenth. Broadly de-fined, Liberalism is, says Harvey, a "state of mind [which] has as its control-ling centre an acknowledgment of the plenitude, diversity and individuality of human beings in society, together with the belief that such characteristics are good as ends in themselves," and he goes on to assert that "tolerance, skepticism, [and] respect for the autonomy of others are its watchwords" while "fanaticism and the monolithic creed [are] its abhorrence."[4] Harvey's phrasing may strike some as overly laudatory, but it does help to underscore why the chronically permeable barriers of the self in *A Tale of Two Cities* constitute such a politically dangerous issue: in depicting the Revolution, the text takes pains to portray—and to roundly denounce—a counter-ideology to Classical Liberalism, in which the claims of the individual are assumed to be secondary to those of the collectivity, and in which the individual is seen as anything but sacrosanct. It should come as little surprise, then, that Dickens's most forceful statement of subversive sympathy for the Revolution's attack upon the idea of the discrete subject, his most anguished confession of ambivalence concerning the bourgeois notion of an inviolable individual, comprises what has long been considered merely an "anomalous" or "digressive" portion of the text—I refer specifically to the "Night Shadows" passage, a striking meditation upon the impenetrable barriers separating man from man which has proved perennially troublesome to readers.

> A wonderful fact to reflect upon, that every human creature is constituted to be that profound secret and mystery to every other. A solemn consideration, when I enter a great city by night, that every one of those darkly clustered houses encloses its own secret; that every room in every one of them encloses its own secret; that every beating heart in the hundreds of thousands of breasts there, is, in some of its imaginings, a secret to the heart nearest it! Something of the awfulness, even of Death itself, is referable to this. No more can I turn the leaves of this dear book that I loved, and vainly hope in time to read it all. No more can I look into the depths of this unfathomable water, wherein, as momentary lights glanced into it, I have had glimpses of buried treasure and other things submerged. It was appointed that the book should shut with a spring, for ever and for ever, when I had read but a page. It was appointed that the water should be locked in an eternal frost, when the light was playing on its surface, and I stood in ignorance on the shore. My friend is dead, my neighbour is dead, my love, the darling of my soul, is dead; it is the inexorable consolidation and perpetuation of the secret that was always in that individuality, and which I shall carry in mine to my life's end. In any of the burial-places of this city through which I pass, is there a sleeper more inscrutable than its busy inhabitants are, in their innermost personality, to me, or than I am to them? (p. 44)

The relationship of this passage to the major concerns of the novel has struck many a critic as problematic. Some have sought to link it with the rest of the text merely by pointing out its similarities to Carlyle's practice of dramatizing the miraculous hidden within the mundane, and thus to account for it as yet another example of the literary influence of Dickens's occasional mentor.[5] A more ambitious explanation of its thematic significance is attempted by Catherine Gallagher. She, claiming that Dickens depicts the Revolutionary ideology as ruthlessly inquisitive in order to make his own, novelistic invasion of the private sphere appear benign by comparison, sees the passage as a reassuring statement that novelists are needed by modern society to overcome a "perpetual scarcity of intimate knowledge," despite the lines' melancholy ring.[6] (I shall return to this argument later.) Most critics, however, follow the lead of Sylvère Monod in simply seeing it as an anomaly. Monod, who posits several distinct narrators for *A Tale,* asserts that he who speaks this address is employing "the philosopher's I" and that such a device "is used for general statements, not in order to convey any impression of the narrator as an individual person."[7] J. M. Rignall agrees, insisting that "the brooding, first-person voice is never heard again in the novel," that the passage is at best awkwardly related to the scene which immediately follows it, and that it cannot be said to illuminate "the general condition of life as it appears in the novel."[8]

It is Rignall's contention that I specifically wish to take issue with, for I believe that there is in fact a broadly thematic resonance to the passage—a resonance which is crucial to the book's attitudes concerning bourgeois individualism and its supposedly detested alternatives. To begin with, it is significant that all the above critics, whatever their varying degrees of bafflement or insight, call attention to the passage's tone, for it is that aspect of the "digression" which, I believe, can most quickly lead us into its involvement with the novel's political contradictions. While the adjectives used to describe this supposed fact concerning contemporary social relations are not explicitly derogatory, the atmosphere of the paragraph as a whole is distinctly—nay, poignantly—that of a lament. What clearly comes across is a deeply felt sadness and frustration before the impermeableness of the barriers between self and self—a despairing desire to merge the discrete and opaque personalities dictated by *Gesellschaft* and to enter a state of communal knowledge and even communal being. Reflecting upon the iron-clad separation of souls within the "great city" may indeed provoke wonder and awe—but it also clearly elicits a wish that things might be otherwise.

The imagery employed in the passage is also pertinent if we remember that the working title of *A Tale* was "Buried Alive," for the passage continually attempts to blur the distinction between life and death, presenting a portrait of urban existence as a kind of living entombment. Not only does the incommunicability of souls have "something of the awfulness, even of Death itself . . . referable" to it, but the narrator, in his quest for closer communion with his fellow beings, speaks of himself as looking into "depths" for "glimpses of buried treasure." Furthermore, the deaths of his friend, neighbor, and love are described as "the inexorable consolidation and perpetuation" of their isolated, living states—as if these people are most true to their nature only after they have ceased to breathe. The final sentence, in which the corpses in actual graveyards are declared to be "sleepers" no more "inscrutable" than the town's "busy inhabitants," completes the equation of the living community with that of the dead. What the narrator has accomplished here is graphically to portray the "great city" as a metropolis in which everyone is virtually "buried alive": to depict a condition of society in which each citizen goes about his everyday offices—and even endures his supposedly most intimate moments—enclosed in a sarcophagus of impenetrable individuality. As we shall see, this damning critique of the way we live now inaugurates the subversive subtext which runs beside and beneath the narrator's subsequent denigration of the French Revolution's insistence that collectivities must supersede the individual as the fundamental unit of social life; it is here that we can apprehend the first movement of that counter-current which dares to consider the ideology of the Jacquerie as a possible escape from the "solitary confinement" mandated by bourgeois individualism.

We should now briefly glance at the narrator's "official" condemnation of the Revolution's propensity to merge individuals together into large conglomerations, for much of what is denigrated here will appear later in altered forms which the novel will tacitly approve. One technique which Dickens employs in this regard is that of taking the Revolutionary government's organization of Paris by supposedly socially homogeneous "sections" a step further and relentlessly anthropomorphizing the district of Saint Antoine. Needless to say, the section, as a character, is almost always depicted as a villain: "The hour was come, when Saint Antoine was to execute his horrible idea of hoisting up men for lamps to show what he could be and do. Saint Antoine's blood was up. . . . 'Lower the lamp yonder!' cried Saint Antoine, after glaring round for a new means of death" (p. 249). Indeed, all the Republic's citizens seem to move from one place to another as a single entity, and the tone used to describe such occurrences is always fraught with fear and condemnation. Instances here come quickly to mind: the echoing footsteps which merge the tread of suffering individuals into the thundering of a vengeful herd,[9] the "sea" and "tide" of the Revolutionary mob breaking over the walls of the Bastille, and the dancing of the Carmagnole, during which the sexes seem to merge into a horrid androgyny and "five hundred people" become "five thousand demons" (p. 307). For our purposes the last of these is especially important, because in Dickens's assertion that the dancers' frightening communal gyrations are "types of the disjointed time" (p. 308), we can see his insistence that the morally detestable practice of subsuming the individual into the group has penetrated beyond the strictly political sphere and pervasively tainted other aspects of life. Clearly, then, the implication of all these passages is that collective action is necessarily evil action, that mass-movements by definition can give expression only to the basest instincts of the individuals who comprise them. Dickens's fear of mobs is of course a critical commonplace, but the very word "mob" only refers to a specific subclass among crowds—those inspired with violent intentions—whereas what in fact comes across from A Tale is the more blanketing notion that the moment any conglomeration of people can merit a collective label, one is already in a politically disruptive realm: after all, the "character" who sows the Revolution is the equally hydra-headed "Monseigneur." At the level of the novel's explicit rhetoric, Dickens doth protest too much.

The author also gets a good deal of mileage out of the revolutionary conspirators' habit of referring to each other by the code-name "Jacques"—indeed, when more than two plotters come together in a scene Dickens deliberately makes it difficult to remember who is speaking:

> "How goes it, Jacques?" said one of the three to Monsieur Defarge. "Is all the spilt wine swallowed?"
>
> "Every drop, Jacques," answered Monsieur Defarge. . . .
>
> "It is not often," said the second of the three, addressing Monsieur Defarge, "that many of these miserable beasts know the taste of wine, or of anything but black bread and death. Is it not so, Jacques?"
>
> "It is so, Jacques," Monsieur Defarge returned.
>
> "Ah! So much the worse. A bitter taste it is that such poor cattle always have in their mouths, and hard lives they live, Jacques. Am I right, Jacques?"
>
> "You are right, Jacques," was the response of Monsieur Defarge. (pp. 64–65).

Although some of these exchanges verge upon the comic, there is, from the Victorian standpoint, always a palpable air of threat about them, for this blurring of personality and agency always takes place amidst talk of a violent conspiracy, thereby undermining the middle-class faith that guilt and innocence can be doled out in just portions to discrete and self-responsible subjects. These plotters eventually receive numbers, but, with the exception of the overtly sadistic Jacques Three, the effect is just the opposite of endowing them with distinct personalities. At the storming of the Bastille, for instance, we get the following call to arms, ostensibly from Defarge: "Work, comrades all, work! Work, Jacques One, Jacques Two, Jacques One Thousand, Jacques Two Thousand, Jacques Five-and-Twenty Thousand; in the name of all the Angels or the Devils—which you prefer—work!" (p. 245). And, as with Monsieur Defarge's lieutenants, so with Madame's, for it has been noted that "The Vengeance" is one of several nicknames indicative of "the tendency toward generalization and abstraction" in the novel.[10] This "tendency," given the political concerns of A Tale, becomes highly subversive, for in a world of merely generic entities, the discriminations upon which bourgeois law and political economy depend simply cannot be made—the idea that "we are all equally guilty" is anathema to Victorian orthodoxy.

This brings us, of course, to Madame Defarge's attitudes concerning who deserves to suffer for the sins of the Ancien Regime, for these constitute the most sinister instance of moral collectivism the novel has to offer. When Darnay is arrested and flung into prison his defense rests upon his assertion that he is not *personally* responsible for the crimes either of the aristocracy in general or of his family in particular. This argument carries no weight with Madame, however, for her mind is simply incapable of focusing upon any moral entity so small and discrete as an individual—her roster of victims and villains being filled exclusively with the names of groups. Speaking of the

Evrémondes, she says that "for other crimes as tyrants and oppressors [she has] this *race* a long time on [her] register, doomed to destruction and extermination" (p. 370, italics mine). Halting the slaughter at those who can claim innocence only for themselves and not their class strikes her as unsound:

> "It is true what madame says," observed Jacques Three. "Why stop? There is great force in that. Why stop?"
> "Well, well," reasoned [Monsieur] Defarge, "but one must stop somewhere. After all, the question is still where?"
> "At extermination," said Madame.
> "Magnificent!" croaked Jacques Three. The Vengeance, also, highly approved. (p. 369)

Lucy—apparently intuiting the bent of Madame's mind in the heat of distress—appeals to her for mercy as a "sister-woman" as well as a wife and mother, but this bit of rhetoric, meant to mask a personal appeal in collectivist diction, fails to take in Madame Defarge: "We have borne this a long time. . . . Is it likely that the trouble of one wife and mother would be much to us now?" As Madame makes her way through the streets on her way to kill Lucy and the child, the narrator sums up that blind spot in her moral vision which the champion of bourgeois individualism cannot help but abhor: "It was nothing to her, that an innocent man was to die for the sins of his forefathers; she saw, not him, but them" (p. 391). Perhaps it is this mote, as much as the "red hue" of animalistic violence, which the narrator perceives in the eyes of the mob gathered round the bloody grindstone—eyes he wishes to "petrify with a well-directed gun." (p. 292)

II

I will now turn from *A Tale of Two Cities'* explicit rhetoric to its countervailing subtext and examine those passages in which the novel's repressed desire to escape the constraints of its own prevailing ideology can best be discerned. My argument is that the sentiments voiced in the "anomalous" Night Shadows passage do in fact recur throughout the text, but that Dickens's sincere allegiance to the commonplaces of Classical Liberalism forces him to displace them in two directions: toward the comic and toward the private. The former movement is expressed through Jarvis Lorry's at best intermittently successful suppression of his own personal claims in the interest of Tellson's Bank, a process which is rendered yet more innocuous by that institution's exaggerated traditionalism and firm allegiance to bourgeois social practices. (This despite the fact that even the musty "House" is shot through with reminders of the darker results of collectivist modes of thought brewing across the Channel.) The latter—and more important—movement manifests itself in the trajectory of Sydney Carton's career. As we shall see, Carton's progress through the text first underscores the pernicious effects of bourgeois-capitalist conceptions of individualism, then affirms the heroic potential unleashed by abandoning them, only to turn back upon itself and to reaffirm the tenets of Classical Liberalism in its last hours. Furthermore, Carton is allowed to escape the culturally dictated bounds of the self only in a manner which obfuscates the process's ideological import: for a few crucial moments he and Darnay genuinely transcend those traditional barriers which wall off the inviolable individual from all his fellow beings, but this merging of a *single* discrete self with *one* other deflects a broad social goal of the Revolution into the realm of private psychology—and then too, it is performed as part of an attempt to *thwart* the very revolutionary practices it imitates in miniature.

Throughout the novel, Jarvis Lorry fights a losing battle to deny his individuality, constantly insisting that he possesses no "buried life" whatsoever, and that all his aims and desires are perfectly congruent with those of the institution for which he labors. In his first interview with Lucy, for instance, he begs her not to "heed [him] any more than if [he were] a speaking machine" (p. 54). He then goes on to explain that all his dealings with Tellson's customers are devoid of private emotional entanglements:

> His [Manette's] affairs, like the affairs of many other French gentlemen and French families, were entirely in Tellson's hands. In a similar way I am, or I have been, trustee of one kind or other for scores of our customers. These are mere business relations, miss; there is no friendship in them, no particular interest, nothing like sentiment. I have passed from one to another in the course of my business life, just as I pass from one of our customers to another in the course of my business day; in short, I have no feelings; I am a mere machine. (p. 54)

In such capacity does Lorry claim to turn his "immense pecuniary Mangle" with "no time for [feelings], no chance of them." Goaded by Carton about the way his loyalty to Tellson's seems to take personal proclivities, the banker testily reminds him that "men of business, who serve a House, are not [their] own masters" and "have to think of the House more than [them]selves" (p. 113). Indeed, when Lorry shakes hands, he does so "in a self-abnegating way, as one who shook for Tellson and Co"—a trait "always to be seen in any clerk at Tellson's who shook hands with a customer when the House pervaded the air" (p. 172). "The House," of course, is both the shorthand name for Tellson's as a whole and the only title ever bestowed upon its director—touches which heighten the sense of the Bank as a single organism, staffed only by a host of undifferentiated cells.

Lorry's relentless assertion that he gladly subsumes his own will into that of the firm "whose bread [he has] eaten these sixty years" (p. 266)—the fact that he claims (and at times truly seems) to have no desires which can be distinguished from the collective aims of "the House"—clearly suggests a parallel with the Jacquerie. The banker, like the model citizen of the Revolutionary Republic, defines himself first and foremost as part of a collectivity, and only secondarily as an individual. Related to this is Lorry's contention that he is a completely *transparent* being, the entire contents of whose mind and heart can be effortlessly read because they are writ large upon the public aspirations of the collectivity he serves. Now as Gallagher points out, it is precisely the Revolution's adamant "demands for transparency" and its practice of the "universal watchfulness" (p. 275) needed to insure it that "the narrator finds particularly abhorrent," since, as the novel purports to demonstrate, such a state of affairs can only be guaranteed by "a whole population practic[ing] surveillance on itself, a surveillance that ultimately destroys."[11] A paradox clearly arises: the parallels enumerated above would all appear to denigrate Lorry, but of course the banker's career emerges as anything but sinister. Indeed, as Albert Hutter rightly notes, Lorry seems to gain mobility, strength, and even renewed youth from his unswerving devotion to Tellson's,[12] and no one can dispute the fact that his subsumption of self into the collective enterprise of the Bank endows his life both with a beneficent purposefulness and (for all his talk of heartlessness) an unproblematic sociality which that of A *Tale's* protagonist signally lacks. But with so many ties to the dogmas of Paris, why should this be so? The explanation, I think, can be approached by recalling the Night Shadows passage, for if Lorry's immaculate "citizenship" within Tellson's associates his service with the totalitarian aspirations of the Tribunals, it also exempts him from residence in the "great city" depicted by that striking segment. In other words, Lorry's devotion to "The House" renders him largely devoid of the terrifying and impenetrable secrets possessed by the denizens of that bourgeois metropolis of the prematurely buried, where the most significant fact about individuality is the utter opacity with which it confronts all attempts at genuine knowledge and communion. If the Revolutionaries of Paris are blind and intoxicated in their frenzied hurtlings, the inhabitants of the Night Shadows city are frozen in ice, and to the extent that the elderly banker inclines toward the practice of the former, he avoids the paralysis of the latter. The enveloping shackles of bourgeois orthodoxy thus partially cast off, Lorry is free to act as the novel's factotum of beneficence until Carton awakes from his own lethargy. Already Dickens's "digression" on the unknowable nature of his fellow citizens begins to nudge its way towards the novel's (suppressed) thematic center.

The physical depiction of Tellson's itself is likewise imbued with palpable ambivalence. On the one hand, what keeps Lorry's selfless devotion to the Bank safely within the confines of the comic is that institution's unswerving allegiance to a fusty—and exceedingly English—tradition. Indeed, its partners' unashamed pride in its "smallness," "darkness," "ugliness," and "incommodiousness" (p. 83) links Tellson's with the decidedly unreformed England of 1780 and allows it to function as a specifically Burkean counterweight to the programmatic rationalism of the Revolution. Thus while Lorry's devotion to the House may resemble the Jacquerie's commitment to the Republic, the entity he serves could not be more different. Moreover, banking is a profession which in some measure depends upon secrecy and opacity, and which often serves interests opposed to those of the state. When Lorry is sent to France late in the book, for instance, he sets about saving what he can of his clients' property from the Revolution's program of confiscation and nationalization.

Still, there are odd echoes of the Terror cheek by jowl with the comic "Olde England" trappings of Tellson's. For instance, if the single-minded business sense of Lorry and the Bank as a whole are, as claimed above, reminiscent of the Revolution's totalizing dynamic, it should come as no surprise that Lorry labors over "great books ruled for figures, with perpendicular iron bars to his window as if that were ruled for figures too, and everything under the clouds were a sum" (p. 172). More graphically still, Tellson's is linked to the Revolution by its alarming proximity to the corpses of those executed by the state and the consequent violent intrusion of the political sphere into a previously sacrosanct domestic realm:

> Your lighter boxes of family papers went up-stairs into a Barmecide room, that always had a great dining-table in it and never had a dinner, and where, even in the year one thousand seven hundred and eighty, the first letters written to you by your old love, or by your little children, were but newly released from the horror of being ogled through the windows, by the heads exposed on Temple Bar with an insensate brutality and ferocity worthy of Abyssinia or Ashantee. (p. 84)

Perhaps, though, the ambivalence with which the novel views Lorry's position can best be shown by a statement of the banker's which abuts upon two well-known Dickensian attitudes: a belief, on the one hand, in the Carlylean gospel of work and, on the other, a view of childhood as a realm to be protected at all costs from the intrusion of adult anxieties and responsibilities because it is the age when the crucial imaginative faculty is either nurtured or starved. Late in the book Lorry confesses to a resurgent Carton: "I have been a man of business, ever since I have been a man. Indeed, I may say that I was a man of business when a boy" (p. 339). No passage better illustrates the promises and costs which are implicitly weighed against one another in Lorry's comic renunciation of the "buried life" which is both his birthright and curse in Liberal society.

III

In turning our attention to Sydney Carton we must adopt a more diachronic approach, for whereas the very constancy of Lorry's relationship with Tellson's plays a part in revealing Dickens's ambivalence about Revolutionary notions of individualism, it is precisely the sudden, erratic reversals in Carton's career which do the most to illuminate *A Tales*'s subversive subtext. When we first encounter Sydney, he appears to be the very embodiment of the secretive and unfathomable individual lamented in the Night Shadows passage.[13] Darnay, his outward double, feels as if he is in "a dream" in his presence (p. 114), and indeed no one else—not Lorry, certainly, or even Stryver—has much of a clue as to what he is really about. The political implications of Carton's opaque character come to the fore as soon as we recall the work he performs, for as Stryver's "jackal" he enacts what can almost be termed a parody of the division of labor which upholds bourgeois capitalism. He and Stryver, it should be remembered, divide between them what should rightly be the labor of a single person and furthermore, this "division" is anything but equitable— Carton performs the labor, Stryver garners the credit. Moreover, the very nicknames "jackal" and "lion" seem to replicate the social practices of Victorian society at large, heaping opprobrium upon the faceless who sell their labor, lauding the famous who purchase it. As Rignall—pointing to this same connection between unreadable character and exploitative labor relations— puts it, Carton's "gloomy estrangement . . . suggests the neurotic price that may be exacted by the aggressive pursuit of individual success, by the bourgeois ethos of individual endeavor in its most crassly careerist form."[14] Carton, then, though distinctly odd, is in a real sense a typical citizen of Dicken's nocturnal city of unknowable individuals: the victim of alienated labor, he too is "buried alive." Thus, if we now recall Lorry's attitude toward his "business" at Tellson's—so fraught with Revolutionary connotations—and contrast them with Carton's view of his own labors, the following exchange between Sydney and the banker takes on a new significance:

> "And indeed, sir," pursued Mr. Lorry, not minding him, "I really don't know what you have to do with the matter. If you'll excuse me, as very much your elder, for saying so, I really don't know that it is your business."
> "Business! Bless you, *I* have no business," said Mr. Carton.
> "It is a pity you have not, sir."
> "I think so too."
> "If you had," pursued Mr. Lorry, "perhaps you would attend to it."
> "Lord love you, no!—I shouldn't," said Mr. Carton. (p. 113)

Carton possesses "no business" and further confesses that he has always "fallen into" his proper "rank," which he describes as "nowhere" (p. 120). Now, since in Lorry's case it is precisely "doing business" which beneficently makes him as one with the collectivity of the House, Carton's having *no* business can be taken as yet another marker of his perverse (but socially endemic) isolation from all larger communities, an isolation which renders his life and labor meaningless.

    With all this in mind, I would like to suggest a reading of Carton's name which will perhaps prove more useful than the various scramblings of the author's initials attempted in the past. "Carton," in nineteenth-century parlance, refers to layers of paper which have been treated and pressed until they have attained the sturdiness of cardboard or pasteboard, while the related word "carton-pierre" denotes a kind of papier-mâché used to imitate much harder materials such as stone or bronze. Even more suggestive is the term "cartonage," by which archaeologists signified the layers of linen or papyrus which were pressed and glued together to fashion the close-fitting mummy cases of the ancient Egyptians. In light of what has been said so far, it thus seems plausible to see the name as a cautiously hopeful comment upon the protagonist's enforced estrangement from his fellow beings. On the one hand, it is a label which draws attention to his predicament of isolation amidst a society whose creed of acquisitive individualism goes far towards turning all its citizens into self-enclosed enigmas—or, if you like, mummies in the nocturnal City of the Dead. Simultaneously, however, it seems to hint at the original flimsiness and permeability of those barriers, reminding us that what encloses and separates is merely a superfluity of material actually translucent, or gossamer calcified. The name then, is one which both diagnoses the protagonist's moral ailment and hints at the availability of a cure.

    As it happens, Sydney does eventually puncture the "carton" walls which close him off from the world; he does finally emerge from his sarcophagus of "cartonage." This is accomplished through his remarkable commingling with Darnay on the eve of his execution, an escape from the constraints of bourgeois individualism which is prepared for by the fact that Carton and Darnay bear a strong physical resemblance to each other. It is important to remember, however, that up until the time when the novel's main characters are all assembled in Revolutionary Paris, Sydney is at best a radically defective Doppelgänger of Charles. In fact, early on, the former's "doublings" of the latter serve merely to emphasize the distance which separates them. When first juxtaposed at the trial, they appear "so like each other in feature, so unlike each other in manner" (p. 108), and soon afterwards Carton admits that he resents a mirror-image who only serves to remind him "what [he has] fallen away from" (p. 116). In England, Darnay appears as a close-dangling but ultimately frustrating possibility, his physical resemblance suggesting that closer communion between men *should* be possible, the pair's mutual unintelligibility underscoring how difficult it is, under prevailing circumstances, to achieve. It is only later in Paris, when Sydney determines to sacrifice himself for Darnay and Lucy, that the doublings become nearly perfect. Indeed, "doubling" is too pallid a word to describe adequately what goes on, for such a term still implies two separate identities, two discrete selves, whereas what actually occurs is more properly described as a veritable *merging* of two individuals into one.

The central irony which emerges from Carton's successful commingling with Darnay in prison is that Sydney's "cure" is effected in the shadow of the novel's explicit condemnation of the very practice which heals him, for while he participates in a process whereby one man is able to transcend the suffocating barriers of the bourgeois self, the Revolution's insistence that the same is to be done for *all* men meets with nothing but scorn. And here one can anticipate an objection: the obvious fact that Sydney and the Jacquerie see the annihilation of the conventional barriers between individuals as the means to ends which are diametrically opposed does not weaken this irony to the extent that one might initially suppose. Yes, Carton abandons his personal claims for the protection of bourgeois domesticity (one might even say for the Victorian hearth, since Sydney's figurative descendents are to recount his story for generations) while the Paris Tribunal demands that the individual subsume himself into the polity in order to speed the flourishing of, as the narrator puts it, the Republic One and Indivisible of Liberty, Equality, Fraternity, or Death. But my point is that the former cause rests upon the foundation stone of bourgeois individualism while the latter is committed to its destruction, and that Carton can only ensure the safety of Liberal society (in the form of the Darnays, Manette, Lorry, and Pross) by temporarily violating one of its fundamental tenets. To put it another way, Carton can only make the world safe for discrete subjects by temporarily ceasing to be one himself and thereby blocking the plans of a regime bent on abolishing the entire concept of the discrete subject forevermore.

Before taking up Sydney's story again, though, we must once more look briefly at the novel's orthodox denigration of Revolutionary practices. As Darnay's second trial gets underway, the Tribunal's attack upon "selfish" bourgeois individualism is in full swing. When Manette protests that he would never violate his domestic circle by denouncing his son-in-law to officers of the state—on account of his "daughter, and those dear to her" being "far dearer to [him] than [his] life"—the President reminds him that his priorities are dangerously counter-revolutionary:

> "Citizen Manette, be tranquil. To fail in submission to the authority of the Tribunal would be to put yourself out of Law. As to what is dearer to you than life, nothing can be so dear to a good citizen as the Republic."
>
> Loud acclamations hailed this rebuke. The President rang his bell, and with warmth resumed.
>
> "If the Republic should demand of you the sacrifice of your child herself, you would have no duty but to sacrifice her. Listen to what is to follow. In the meantime, be silent!" (p. 346)

Later, when Manette's own testament has been read and the inevitable verdict of "guilty" delivered, the narrator's account is strangely divided between horror and understanding. With biting irony, he recounts how the

President suggests "that the good physician of the Republic would deserve better still of the Republic by rooting out an obnoxious family of Aristocrats, and would doubtless feel a sacred glow and joy in making his daughter a widow and her child an orphan" (p. 362). One can clearly hear in this passage the revulsion of a good Victorian—and yet, when explaining the scene as a whole, he calmly and fair-mindedly informs us that "one of the frenzied aspirations of the populace was, for imitations of the questionable public virtues of antiquity, and for sacrifices and self-immolations on the people's altar" (p. 362). For now, we will leave the book's conventional depiction of the Revolution with the surprising mildness of the phrase "questionable public virtues" still resonating and turn once more to Carton.

As Sydney takes his famous midnight walk the night before the second Parisian trial, his steps are dogged by religious images, and he repeats "I am the resurrection and the life" continually to himself as he wanders. At one point, though, he pauses to sleep, and, in a moment obviously fraught with symbolic meaning, awakes to find an analogue of his life in the motions of the Seine:

> The strong tide, so swift, so deep, and certain, was like a congenial friend, in the morning stillness. He walked by the stream, far from the houses, and in the light and warmth of the sun fell asleep on the bank. When he awoke and was afoot again, he lingered there yet a little longer, watching an eddy that turned and turned purposeless, until the stream absorbed it, and carried it on to the sea—"Like me!" (p. 344)

When one considers that Sydney has resolved to sacrifice himself in order to thwart the collectivist wrath of the Revolution, this passage reads curiously indeed, for cutting across the obvious message concerning Carton's lassitude giving way to action, there is the further hint that to do so involves subsuming himself in a larger entity. One could perhaps suggest that he is being "absorbed" into the greater life of humanity at large or into the Christian dispensation were it not for the quite programmatic way in which "tide" and "sea" have been associated throughout *A Tale* with the Revolutionary mob. The "strong tide, so swift, so deep, and certain" which now appears as Carton's "congenial friend" and into which his life is "absorbed" may not partake of the violence of that which breaks against the Bastille, but the provocative choice of simile cannot help but alert us to a parallel between Sydney's path to personal salvation and the Revolution's recipe for a secular utopia beyond the constraints of bourgeois individualism.

This hint of a parallel between Sydney's *desideratum* and that of the Jacquerie is reinforced as his plan of rescue gets underway. On the evening after Darnay has been condemned, Carton urges Manette to try his influence with the judges one final time. Lorry, watching the doctor depart, opines that he has "no hope" that the old man will succeed. Carton agrees, and explains why he has sent him on what must be a futile mission. What is striking about this passage is that since Sydney has already made up his mind to replace Darnay upon the guillotine, but has not told the banker of his plan, he and Lorry have two different individuals in mind when they employ the pronouns "his" and "he":

> "Don't despond," said Carton, very gently; "don't grieve. I encouraged Doctor Manette in this idea, because I felt that it might one day be consolatory to her. Otherwise, she might think 'his life was wantonly thrown away or wasted,' and that might trouble her."
> "Yes, yes, yes," returned Mr. Lorry, drying his eyes, "you are right. But he will perish; there is no real hope."
> "Yes, He will perish: there is no real hope," echoed Carton. And walked with a settled step, down-stairs. (p. 367)

This sharing of pronouns, causing momentary confusion about who is being referred to, is reminiscent of nothing so much as those passages in which Jacques speaks to Jacques. It is as if Carton had already ceased to be a discrete subject, his personality commingling with that of Darnay's as he approaches his salvational moment. This process of merging reaches its climax during the scene in Charles's cell, where the two, having already exchanged boots, cravats, coats, and ribbons, write what amounts to a joint letter to Lucy, Carton dictating as Darnay holds the pen. As the latter scribbles, Sydney gradually applies his hidden narcotic, so that we see Charles's individuality diffusing itself too, his consciousness drifting beyond its normal boundaries as he attempts to record Carton's sentiments:

> "What vapour is that?" he asked.
> "Vapour?"
> "Something that crossed me?"
> "I am conscious of nothing; there can be nothing here. Take up the pen and finish. Hurry, hurry!"
> As if his memory were impaired, or his faculties disordered, the prisoner made an effort to rally his attention. As he looked at Carton with clouded eyes and with an altered manner of breathing, Carton—his hand again in his breast—looked steadily at him.
> "Hurry, hurry!"
> The prisoner bent over the paper, once more.
> " 'If it had been otherwise;' " Carton's hand was again watchfully and softly stealing down; " 'I never should have used the longer opportunity. If it had been otherwise;' " the hand was at the prisoner's face; " 'I should but have had so much the more to answer for. If it had been otherwise—' " Carton looked at the pen and saw it was trailing off into unintelligible signs. (p. 381)

As any reader will attest, it is nearly impossible to read this passage without backtracking, for Dickens makes it especially difficult to keep the speakers straight for any length of time. And it is not only we who are confused as to who is being referred to, for soon afterwards Basard finds Sydney's unorthodox use of pronouns disconcerting:

> "Have no fear! I shall soon be out of the way of harming you, and the rest will soon be far from here, please God! Now, get assistance and take me to the coach."
> "You?" said the Spy nervously.
> "Him, man, with whom I have exchanged." (p. 382)

Although Carton exchanges literal freedom for imprisonment in this scene, he simultaneously effects his escape from Dickens's solipsistic City of Dreadful Night, for the entombing barriers surrounding the discrete subject of Liberal society have momentarily been shattered. Furthermore, the imagery and wordplay here associate Sydney with the self-subsuming Jacquerie at the very moment when he prevents the Tribunal from executing the man Madame Defarge defines as the last of the "race" of Evrémondes.

That Dickens was aware at some level of the parallels he had drawn can be deduced from the violent reaction which occurs in the novel's final pages, for there he takes pains to insist that although Carton is in one sense just another face among a crowd of the condemned—one more victim of what is essentially a mass murder—he nevertheless stands out as a distinct individual whose personality will remain intact even beyond the grave. This reaction begins as the narrator follows his protagonist from cell to guillotine. After emphasizing that the prison officials are exclusively concerned about the "count" in the tumbrils—that there be fifty-two bodies in it—he goes on to provide us with a catalogue of the condemned's deportment which makes it clear that they are all quite discrete personalities:

> Of the riders in the tumbrils, some observe these things, and all things on their last roadside, with an impassive stare; others, with a lingering interest in the ways of life and men. Some, seated with drooping heads, are sunk in silent despair; again, there are some so heedful of their looks that they cast upon the multitude such glances as they have seen in theatres, and in pictures. Several close their eyes, and think, or try to get their straying thoughts together. Only one, and he a miserable creature, of a crazed aspect, is so shattered and made drunk by horror, that he sings, and tries to dance. (p. 400)

Carton's own possibly "prophetic" speech at the foot of the scaffold gives us a taste of individualism triumphant, with Sydney personally persisting through the generations. He sees Lucy "with a child upon her bosom, who bears [his] name," a child who eventually "win[s] his way up in that path of life which once was [his]" and who in turn fathers a "boy of [Carton's] name," to whom he "tell[s] . . . [Sydney's] story, with a tender and faltering voice" (p. 404). Chris Vanden Bossche sums up the tone succinctly: "The image of self-sacrifice created by this speech puts the authenticity of that very self-sacrifice into question by envisioning a future that nearly effaces Darnay (only portraying his death) and foretelling a line of sons named for Carton."[15] Indeed, Sydney's "cartonage" of middle-class individuality seems so firmly and solidly back in place that not even the worm can worry it, and this sense of the protagonist's "haunting" both the place of his death and future generations is very much to the point, for it cancels out several passages in which the Revolution's practice of mass killing threatens to endorse their anti-individualist ideology by sheer weight of numbers and frequency. We have been told, for instance, that "before their cells were quit" of the fifty-two, "new occupants were appointed; before their blood ran into the blood spilled yesterday, the blood that was to mingle with theirs to-morrow was already set apart" (pp. 375–76). Earlier, the narrator informed us that death under the Revolutionary regime had become "so common and material, that no sorrowful story of a haunting Spirit ever arose among the people out of all the working of the Guillotine" (p. 343). Now haunting is the individualist pursuit *par excellence*— only individuals may haunt the living, not groups or classes. And thus Carton's death—and his subsequent life after death—stridently refute the collectivist ideology, insisting as they do both upon the individual's persistent influence in secular history and hinting of the spiritual indwelling which is the religious sanction for the discrete subject of Classical Liberalism, a subject conceived of as retaining its individuality even beyond the grave. As the author of *A Tale of Two Cities* was well aware, serious contemplations concerning the obscuring walls of the bourgeois self have "something of the awfulness, even of Death" about them.

IV

Dickens's novel of the French Revolution follows *Little Dorrit* in his canon, and much has been written about what attracted the author to a subject which, on the face of things, seems rather distant from his usual literary milieu. Of course we have Dickens's own words in the Preface explaining how he "conceived the main idea of the story" while acting in Collins's *The Frozen Deep*. The similarities between the central dramatic conflict of the play and the novel, however, tell us little as to why he chose to set his work mainly in Revolutionary Paris—after all, one may sacrifice oneself for a loved one and a rival in any number of possible situations. And then too, there is the problem of covering ground already pronounced upon—there is no other word for it—by his friend and mentor Carlyle. The obsequious tone of the Preface, in which he states that "it has been one of [his] hopes to add something to the popular and picturesque means of understanding that terrible time" while simultaneously assuring us that "no one can hope to add anything to the philosophy of Mr. Carlyle's wonderful book" (p. 29) betrays the awkwardness and risk inherent in his project. I would suggest that it is possible the Revolution attracted him precisely because it allowed him to study, confront—and to some extent flirt with—modes of thought which claimed to offer a solution to what he perceived to be one of the pervasive diseases of his own society. To understand how clearly he did in fact see the endemic and secretive individualism which underlay his acquisitive culture as a blighting phenomenon, we need only glance back as far as his preceding novel. As Arthur Clennam walks the streets of London, his thoughts give rise to images which, as George Levine says, "speak with remarkable appropriateness as representative both of the plot(s) of *Little Dorrit* and of the texture of its world."[16] Notice again how in this passage, as in Sydney's case, opacity of character is inseparable from acquisitive activity—how nefarious economic practices are protected by the obscuring partitions which mask self from self:

> As he went along, upon a dreary night, the dim streets by which he went seemed all depositories of oppressive secrets. The deserted counting-houses, with their secrets of books and papers locked up in chests and safes; the banking-houses, with their secrets of strong rooms and wells, the keys of which were in a very few secret pockets and a very few secret breasts; the secrets of all the dispersed grinders in the vast mill, among whom there were doubtless plunderers, forgers, and trust-betrayers of many sorts, whom the light of any day that dawned might reveal; he could have fancied that these things, in hiding, imparted a heaviness to the air. The shadow thickening and thickening as he approached its source, he thought of the secrets of the lonely church-vaults, where the people who had hoarded and secreted in iron coffers were in their turn similarly hoarded, not yet at rest from doing harm; and then of the secrets of the river, as it rolled its turbid tide between two frowning wildernesses of secrets, extending, thick and dense, for many miles, and warding off the free air and the free country swept by winds and wings of birds. (pp. 596–97)[17]

We are back in the "great city" of the Night Shadows passage, the city from which barricaded Paris, whatever its barbarous cruelties, allows Carton, his author, and us, a momentary escape. Dickens also writes in the Preface to *A Tale:* "I have so far verified what is done and suffered in these pages, as that I have certainly done and suffered it all myself" (p. 29). After tracing Lorry and Carton's well disguised escapes from the constricting confines of bourgeois individualism, one understands better just how secretly liberating the "doing" part of Dickens's enterprise must have seemed to him, and how truly he bespoke his deep frustration with Victorian culture in calling the era of the Revolution both the *best* and the worst of times.

Notes

1. George Woodcock, Introduction to *A Tale of Two Cities* (New York: Penguin. 1970). All subsequent citations from the novel refer to this edition.

2. See J. M. Rignall, "Dickens and the Catastrophic Continuum of History in *A Tale of Two Cities*," *ELH* 51, 3 (Fall 1984):575–87, and Jack Lindsay, "A Tale of Two Cities," in *Twentieth-Century Interpretations of "A Tale of Two Cities,"* ed. Charles E. Beckwith (Englewood Cliffs: Prentice Hall, 1972), pp. 52–63.

3. See Catherine Gallagher, "The Duplicity of Doubling in *A Tale of Two Cities*," *DSA* 12 (1983):125–45.

4. W. J. Harvey, *Character and the Novel* (Ithaca: Cornell Univ. Press, 1968), p. 24.

5. Richard Dunn, "A Tale for Two Dramatists," *DSA* 12 (1983):117–24, 121, and Michael Timko, "Splendid Impressions and Picturesque Means: Dickens, Carlyle, and the French Revolution," pp. 177–95, 186–87.

6. Gallagher, p. 141.

7. Sylvère Monod, "Dickens's Attitudes in *A Tale of Two Cities*," *NCF* 24, 4 (March 1970):488–505, 497.

8. Rignall, p. 577.

9. Franklin Court, in "Boots, Barbarism, and the New Order in Dickens's *A Tale of Two Cities*," *VIJ* 9 (1980–81):29–37, 34, points out that "by employing this particular stylistic device, Dickens can more convincingly present thousands of people—either the mob or the aristocracy—as a single power. The footsteps raging in Saint Antoine and echoing simultaneously in London can be viewed, therefore, as one gigantic, inanimate foot of a body that, in this instance, is the revolutionary mob."

10. Gordon Spence, "Dickens as a Historical Novelist," *Dickensian* 72, 1 (January 1976):21–29, 25, and Robert Alter, "The Demons of History in Dickens's Tale," *Novel* 2, 2 (Winter 1969):15–42, 138–40.

11. Gallagher, pp. 133–34.

12. Albert D. Hutter, "Nation and Generation in *A Tale of Two Cities*," *PMLA* 93, 3 (May 1978):448–62, 453.

13. Rignall, p. 533.

14. Rignall, p. 583.

15. Chris R. Vanden Bossche, "Prophetic Closure and Disclosing Narrative: *The French Revolution* and *A Tale of Two Cities*," *DSA* 12 (1983):209–21, 211.

16. George Levine, *Darwin and the Novelists: Patterns of Science in Victorian Fiction* (Cambridge, MA: Harvard Univ. Press, 1988), p. 166.

17. Charles Dickens, *Little Dorrit* (New York: Penguin, 1978).

Language, Love and Identity:
A Tale of Two Cities

TOM LLOYD

Thirty years ago G. Robert Stange criticized the "excessive artificiality" of Charles Dickens's *A Tale of Two Cities,* writing that "its construction constantly calls attention to itself" (74). Much has changed in the critical realm since 1957, for now this is exactly what commends the novel to the attention of those nurtured on post-structuralist ideas. A number of writers in recent years have analysed Dickens's fascination with language, including "redoubling of the theme of writing" (Baumgarten 163), closure, hidden desires (Vanden Bossche 211), and in general the strong influence of Thomas Carlyle's Romantic Irony on Dickens's work.[1] *A Tale of Two Cities* does question the value of language divorced from feeling and experience, but in the end affirms the value of the word. By stressing the act of writing throughout the novel, Dickens creates a discomfort in the reader owing to the fact that the fiction is thereby robbed of its capacity to enchant the reader into a willing suspension of disbelief. But this is not to deny meaning; instead, it calls into question the reader's command of the word. This is especially true with Carton's ambiguous "prophecy."[2] Near the end of the novel we learn that the French aristocrats were unable to read the signs of the times and see how the "powerful enchanter, Time" might turn fancy carriages into tumbrils headed for the guillotine (399). Dickens's text forces the reader to strip away the veil and explore the mysteries that lie at its heart, just as Lorry and Carton must explore their inner beings and resurrect life and language. But the difficulty which interpretation entails does not presuppose the "blankness" Dr Manette fears.

The problem with language that pervades *A Tale of Two Cities* is very similar to the one evoked by Carlyle in *The French Revolution.*[3] Like Friedrich Schlegel, Carlyle identifies a logically irreconcilable tension between words and things, interpretations and essences. He argues that in revolutionary France the Constitutionalists led by Sieyès tried to construct a "paper" constitution too far removed from social realities, while the extremists wanted to

Reprinted by permission of the author from *The Dickensian* (1992): 154–70.

"govern a France free of formulas. Free of formulas! And yet man lives not except with formulas" (4:68).[4] It is necessary that we read history, or any other text, from a neverending ironical perspective, which does not deny transcendental meaning but instead shocks us in the direction of the ineffable. Failure to do so leads to imprisonment in formulas or chaos. Thus in Dickens's novel the aristocrats are blinded by false words, while the most extreme sansculottes try to obliterate language in their vengeance against the old order. In between are those characters who, like Lorry, Carton, and Manette, must establish identities, workable "formulas" for themselves, amidst those varieties of fragmentation of self. Indeed, even M Defarge clings to language and meaning in the presence of his wife and the storming of the Bastille; she alone of the major characters seeks to obliterate everything and everyone, her incessant knitting of shrouds a parodic, non-verbal language which prefigures dissolution rather than the reconstruction of meaning.[5]

Throughout *A Tale of Two Cities* Dickens illustrates the precarious nature of identity in a world torn between decrepit language and destruction, where with varying degrees of success characters try to comprehend and name the "mystery" that lies at the centre of the self. Stripped of his reason, for instance, the dignified Dr Manette becomes an "it," throughout the novel he alternates without control between identities as a dehumanized shoemaker partially resurrected from the Bastille, and the melancholy Doctor who seeks stability through love for his daughter Lucie.[6] The fear that he will be forgotten and his place made a "blank" in the memories of others causes him to seek in Lucie a stable past that will formulate his identity.[7] The prison comes close to reducing Darnay to an "it" as well when, alone in a cell, his thoughts descend into a confused stream of consciousness, scraps of his tenuously retained selfhood "tossing and rolling upward from the depths of his mind": "Let us ride on again, for God's sake, through the illuminated villages with the people all awake! . . . He made shoes, he made shoes, he made shoes. . . . Five paces by four and a half" (287).[8]

Identities need formulas, yet words can falsify if they fail to reflect the organic nature of character. After all, the sign in itself is arbitrary; personalities change, while texts can become brittle. Thus Manette's letter of vengeance against the Evrémondes comes back to haunt him at Darnay's second Paris trial. Under Lucie's influence he has rediscovered love and sympathy, and can accept as his son-in-law the heir of the family that tormented him. But the letter, buried all those years in the Bastille until discovered by Defarge, was aimed at fixing the future, which throughout the novel is presented as mysterious and ambiguous: "I, Alexandre Manette, unhappy prisoner, do this last night of the year 1767, in my unbearable agony, denounce to the times when all these things shall be answered for. I denounce them to Heaven and to earth" (361). This is as destructive to identity, which is always in a process of change and formulation, as the superficially different sansculottic endeavour to destroy words and naming altogether.

There is an even more frightening alternative: the autobiographical word may disappear altogether, and identity may not be preserved in the memories of others. This is the significance of the second buried letter in *A Tale of Two Cities*. Darnay tells Lucie and her father about the discovery of the almost undecipherable sign "D.I.G." in a Tower of London prison. Under it, many years before, a now anonymous prisoner hid some writing, which now is reduced to ashes: "There was no record or legend of any prisoner with those initials, and many fruitless guesses were made what the name could have been" (131). Isolated from the outer world, where living memories can be generated through relations with other people, the individual must fall back on the language and memories he already has. These may be inadequate. Naturally Manette is shaken when he hears Darnay's story, not only because he recalls his own still buried writing in Paris, but because this calls to mind his old fear that, in the end, one's place may be just a "blank" (219).[9]

The partial, parodic, and transcendent resurrections that occur in *A Tale of Two Cities* have received considerable analysis in the past.[10] Less well known is the relationship between resurrected selves and the word revivified through love, represented above all in Lucie Manette. Lorry, for instance, progresses from regarding himself as a machine bereft of feeling (54), to a more insightful man who rediscovers the meaning of the heart and his childhood. This is accomplished through Lucie's agency, for she becomes the centre of a domestic realm which draws Lorry away from his imprisoned public self.[11] In his last conversation with Sydney Carton, he acknowledges a redemption through love and memory that echoes Wordsworth's poetry of loss and redemption through the "philosophic mind":

> "I travel in the circle, nearer and nearer to the beginning. It seems to be one of the kind smoothings and preparings of the way. My heart is touched now, by many remembrances that had long fallen asleep . . . by many associations of the days when what we call the World was not so real with me." (340)

Lorry's identity is not as threatened as Manette's by burial and blankness because the business institution into which he projects himself remains intact, even in Paris.[12] Furthermore, in his function as protector of Lucie, which he first assumed when he carried her as a baby across the Channel, Lorry has a perception of language denied to others. All along he can read character and comprehend the dubieties of language. Consider how he parries Stryver's assumption that he is "eligible" to marry Lucie Manette. The meretricious "striver" avoids the truth about his suitability by formulating his "verdict" to himself in legal jargon. Blinded by his own words, he is analagous to those French aristocrats who place their trust in plausible formulas that are at variance with nature.

> As to the strength of his case, he had not a doubt about it, but clearly saw his way to the verdict. Argued with the jury on substantial worldly grounds . . . it was a plain case, and had not a weak spot in it. (171)

The detachment of Stryver's language from reality is recognized by Lorry, who sardonically replies to his question whether he is "eligible" to marry Lucie: "Oh dear yes! Yes. Oh yes, you're eligible! . . . If you say eligible, you are eligible" (174). Like the dragon in Carroll's "The Hunting of the Snark," he affirms the truth of Stryver's "eligibility" by repeating it three times. The irony is lost on the portly suitor, who then asks, "Am I not prosperous?"[13]

Dickens analyses the imprisonment of Stryver, the British legal system, and above all the French aristocracy in words that deny human paradox and mystery, or quantify them in rational forms. Like the self-satisfied empiricists Carlyle lampoons in *Sartor Resartus* for thinking they have "scientifically decomposed" man's "spiritual Faculties," the court philosophers and scientists at the grand hotel of Monseigneur in Paris think they can control things by controlling language.[14] But they are as wide of the mark as Johnson's mad astronomer in *Rasselas,* who thinks he can control the movement of the planets by thinking:

> Unbelieving Philosophers who were remodelling the world with words, and making card-towers of Babel to scale the skies with, talked with Unbelieving Chemists who had an eye on the transmutation of metals, at this wonderful gathering accumulated by Monseigneur. (136)

But "belief" in words and people is the key to every genuine transmutation in *A Tale of Two Cities,* above all Carton's change from wastrel to hero.[15]

Yet these rationalists believe that they believe their words, like Carlyle's philosophers with their "dream-theorem[s]" and their "Words well bedded . . . in good Logic-mortar" (54). Dickens's analysis of the "leprosy of unreality" (137) among the French intellectuals mirrors Carlyle's quite closely. Phoney words about the "Centre of Truth" and the like are employed to justify a system that rests in fact on brute force, a situation dramatized by Carlyle in *The French Revolution.*[16] For example, immediately after the scene at the grand hotel, the Marquis runs down Gaspard's son without remorse or even the loss of his composure. His life centres around correct dress and composure; his face, like a "fine mask" (140), reflects the language that has conditioned him. The narrator refers to Madame Defarge, the arch-sans-culotte, as a "tigress" (391), and to Darnay's uncle as a "refined tiger" who wears a mask of civility, dismissing the poor as "dogs" but maintaining an "unchanged front, except as to the spots on his nose" (142). Like Madame Defarge, he is obsessed with exterminating his enemies from the earth (142, 369). In fact, they are both essentially nihilists, one basing his meaning on meaningless formulas and "repression," the other rejecting formulas altogether.

The Marquis tells Charles Darnay that his only philosophy is "repression." He enslaves those less powerful than he, and in turn lives in fear of Monseigneur and others above him. But his repression has another dimension as well. He has no "within," no healthy centre of self or heart, but instead, like Friedrich Schiller's "barbarian" in the *Aesthetic Education of Man,* has allowed culture to destroy his feelings, making him merely the inverse of the mob's "ungovernable fury" (25).[17] He and the "dogs" are equally given over to their material impulses. His refined sensibility denies nature its proper place in human emotions, but lets it run free in his egoistic philosophy of repression and his demonic "assumption of indifference." His denial of nature is evident in the fact that even his blush is not the product of an honest emotion: "a blush on the countenance of Monsieur the Marquis was no impeachment of his high breeding; it was not from within; it was occasioned by an external circumstance beyond his control—the setting sun" (144).[18] Schiller argues that the repressed rationalist and the revolutionary mob are equally the products of a loss of psychological harmony in individuals, whether brought on by false principles or an oppressive social order. But the "cultivated classes" are morally responsible for society's relapse into "the kingdom of the elements" (27). Once the poor "erupt," to cite Madame Defarge's volcano metaphor, they are "changed into wild beasts, by terrible enchantment long persisted in" (63). The Marquis represses his emotions and maintains his composure. The court rationalists also deny feeling, treating words as components of self-contained systems that adumbrate nature, rather than rise from it organically. His underlying brutality links Darnay's uncle with the sans-culottes, who seem to follow Carlyle's injunction to "gather whole hampers" of "sham Metaphors" and "burn them" like "pallid, hunger-bitten and dead-looking" rags (*Sartor Resartus* 73–4).

Madame Defarge embodies in its most absolute form the inevitable release of what Schiller terms the "crude, lawless instincts" of those repressed politically and psychologically (*Aesthetic Education* 25).[19] Based on Mlle Théroigne in Carlyle's *The French Revolution,* she is like a force of nature whose instinctual patience is indicated by the "register" she stores in her memory of who is to be saved and who executed once the energies of Saint Antoine are unleashed to sweep away the enervated aristocracy.[20] Madame Defarge seems conscious of the natural energy she represents, consistently comparing the Revolution to a natural force and denying that it can be quantified or defined.[21] For example, she tells her more conventional husband that "it does not take a long time . . . for an earthquake to swallow a town," but stresses the inadequacy of formulas in adding the question, "Tell me how long it takes to prepare the earthquake?" (207–8). She refuses to try to hurry the time of vengeance, saying that "When the time comes, let loose a tiger and a devil; but wait for the time with the tiger and the devil chained" (208).

M. Defarge retains a need for clear definitions and manifestations of things, which his wife recognizes, telling him, "you sometimes need to see your victim and your opportunity, to sustain you" (208). She regards as a weakness his desire to know when the violence will begin and end, insisting that such quantification is impossible, like trying "to make and store the lightning" (207). Psychologically in a realm beyond formulas, she cannot set limits to her philosophy of "extermination," and therefore opposes her husband's assertion that the Terror "must stop somewhere" (369). But M. Defarge seeks meanings even when he participates in the storming of the Bastille. Though no one is presently in the North Tower where Manette was imprisoned for eighteen years, he demands that one of the guards take him there so that he can understand the meaning of One Hundred and Five: "Does it mean a captive, or a place of captivity? Or do you mean that I shall strike you dead?" (246). In an environment where identities are scrambled or extinguished and people are reduced to "ghosts" of their former selves, Defarge wants a clear definition of the mystery called Manette. The "indifference" of the Marquis and the "absolute" extermination of Madame Defarge are antitypes of the endeavour to connect words with things.[22] Defarge's violent destruction of the furniture in Manette's old cell to find a written or other key to his mystery reflects a paradoxical desire to obliterate and know; we later discover that he found the manuscript in the chimney, a place of ashes as well as energy.[23] His search is normally fruitless, for he finds only a dead text which no longer reflects the spiritual essence of its author.

In *A Tale of Two Cities* there is a non-verbal communication based on vengeance, and another based on love. Madame Defarge repudiates formulas in favour of absolute violence and mysterious signs based on knitting, roses in handkerchiefs, and noncommittal allusions to natural forces. But at a time when the word is falsified and dead, such signs are more efficacious than M Defarge's futile search for definitions amidst the carnage at the Bastille. Those able to read history—Dickens places his reader in this advantaged position—can read the non-verbal message contained in the Cross of Blood drawn in the air by Madame Defarge's brother (356), or the verbal sign BLOOD Gaspard scrawls on a wall with wine (61). But there are also transcendent non-verbal signs based on love and sympathy, for instance in the eyes of Darnay's mother, which give meaning to her assertion that he must "have mercy and redress" the wrongs perpetrated by his family on the poor (154). Above all, Lucie Manette has this ability. By standing outside Darnay's Paris prison she can revitalize him, reversing his initial, precipitous slide into insanity. Madame Defarge's inability to comprehend this alternative form of communication is revealed by her plot to denounce Lucie for "making signs and signals to prisoners" (373).

Yet she is forced to effect a non-verbal communication with Miss Pross in the climactic scene where the sans-culotte comes hunting for Lucie, who is in the process of escaping from Paris. Here her energies are thwarted, and she is spent like any natural storm or earthquake. The cessation of her power through Pross's pistol shot foreshadows the retreat of the violently daemonic and the reconstitution of the word, symbolized by the power of the signed papers to get Darnay (disguised as Carton), Manette, and Lucie out of the country. Like Thomas Mann's demonic Cipolla, Defarge is suddenly rendered lifeless, as though a violent disrobing of civilized control and language have played themselves out, leaving Pross deaf but free. In this grotesque encounter the two cannot understand each other's words: "Each spoke in her own language; neither understood the other's words; both were very watchful, and intent to deduce from look and manner, what the unintelligible words meant" (395). Miss Pross dismisses her opponent's language as "nonsensical" (396). Yet they communicate non-verbally, one motivated by the "vigorous tenacity of love" (397), the other by sheer hatred. As with Darnay and his mother, and Carton and the young girl at the end of the novel, the eyes are the key to this non-rational language:

> "It will do her no good to keep herself concealed from me at this moment," said Madame Defarge. "Good patriots will know what that means. Let me see her. Go tell her that I wish to see her. Do you hear?
> "If those eyes of yours were bed-winches," returned Miss Pross, "and I was an English four-poster, they shouldn't loose a splinter of me. No, you wicked foreign woman; I am your match." (395).

Madame Defarge's attack is a parodic version of Sydney Carton's self-sacrifice in the next chapter: "if she had been ordered to the axe to-morrow," her only response would have been "a fierce desire to change places with the man who sent her there" (391); rendered "lifeless" by a pistol shot, she symbolically re-enters the unseen world when Pross locks her body in and throws the key into the same river Carton has already mentally followed to death (344).[24]

The guillotine itself symbolizes the revolutionary rage against language, for it "hushed the eloquent, struck down the powerful, abolished the beautiful and good" (302). Foulon's execution and the glee with which the sans-culottes stuff his mouth with grass likewise illustrate the affinity between revolutionary vengeance and the obliteration of words.[25] This descent into chaos is inevitable for the rulers' failure to read what Carlyle terms "importunate" words necessitates both physical and perceptual destruction before meaning can be reconstituted.

In Dante's *Inferno,* Dante-pilgrim's descent through Hell involves a series of encounters with deceptive and chaotic speech forms that mirror the collapse of identity among the damned. For instance, thieves have become endlessly metamorphosing creatures that "split words," while Satan himself inarticulately slobbers and beats his wings. Darnay has a similar experience at La Force prison, when he meets the general prison population on the way to his solitary cell. They are "ghosts," just like their brethren who "haunt" Tellson's in London, where their money used to be. Throughout France the very "names" of the aristocrats are being blotted out, and yet these prisoners, most of them bound for the guillotine, desperately try to keep up civilized appearances:

> The ghost of beauty, the ghost of stateliness, the ghost of elegance, the ghost of price, the ghost of frivolity, the ghost of wit, the ghost of youth, the ghost of

age, all waiting their dismissal from the desolate shore, all turning on him eyes that were changed by the death they had died in coming there. (285)

Obsessed with naming no less than Madame Defarge is with extermination, they first ask Darnay about his "name and condition" (285), politely echoing Farinata's fixation on learning Dante's lineage. They persist in the belief that naming, not essence, is the substance of their humanity.

Sydney Carton is also a ghost until he redeems himself; he "haunts" Lucie Manette's neighbourhood until brought to life through an "intention" to reveal his feelings to her (179). In the novel he moves from the "rust and repose" for which he rebukes himself to purposeful activity, as if to illustrate Teufelsdroeckh's Aristotelian assertion that a thought is worthless until it is translated into an action.[26] Lorry's statement that Cruncher should repent "in action—not in words" for his nocturnal activities as a "fisherman" likewise illustrates the idea that *The end of Man is an Action, and not a Thought* (*Sartor Resartus* 155). But there is an intermediary step between thought and action: belief. Just as Teufelsdroeckh must translate speculation into conviction, and into conduct (195–6), Sydney Carton must discover belief before he can proceed from self-analysis to meaningful activity. Lucie Manette provides the means:

> Will you let me believe, when I recall this day, that the last confidence of my life was reposed in your pure and innocent breast, and that it lies there alone, and will be shared by one? (182)

Like Lorry, who circles back to his childhood, he seeks to revive "old shadows" and "old voices" (181) that have nearly expired. Lucie's belief that he might be "much, much worthier" of himself inspires his statement that "I would embrace any sacrifice for you and for those dear to you" (183), and is echoed in his last words (404).

His moral crisis is like that of Tennyson's Ulysses, who knows that to stop striving for new experiences is to lose the constantly replenished pasts that are vital to identity; just as Sydney Carton would like to translate his "rust and repose" into activity, Ulysses would rather "shine in use" than "rust unburnished" (1. 23). Without mind-expanding experiences there can be no selfhood. Ulysses's statement that "I am become a name" (1. 11) is conditioned by his realization that names must be constantly redefined: without memory and experience, the name becomes a hollow shell. If he decides to remain on Ithaca and never again seek "a newer world," he will be like the "savage race" he rules, who "hoard, and sleep, and feed, and know not me" (11. 4,5).

The idea that one must constantly strive to redefine and affirm identity and avoid psychological burial is also important in *Faust*. Trapped in the "prison" of his study, and conditioned by books rather than by passionate experiences, Goethe's learned Doctor is alternatively suicidal and restless for escape into the wider world. The central tenet of his blood pact with Mephistopheles is that he will be damned if he ever ceases striving to experience more of life and love: "If I ever say to the moment, linger, you are quite beautiful, then you can put me in chains."[27] To relax would confirm Mephistopheles' cynical statement to the Lord that for all his ideals, man is "more beastly than any beast."[28] But this devil is imprisoned by words, arguing that Faust needs only a poet to create the semblance of a name, and (incorrectly) that he will remain forever what he is.[29] But the moment he sees Gretchen and falls in love he is transformed into a new Faust, having commenced the activity that will both imperil his soul and open the way to redemption.[30]

Like Gretchen, Lucie Manette embodies a principle of love that inspires belief and action, in her father as well as Sydney Carton.[31] To the Doctor she is a repository of memories, the "golden thread" that unites him "to a Past beyond his misery, and to a Present beyond his misery" (110). Possessing the stable identity he seeks, she inspires him to try to save his imprisoned son-in-law, thereby ensuring the continuity of past, present, and future: "As my beloved child was helpful in restoring me to myself, I will be helpful now in restoring the dearest part of herself to her," he tells Lorry (300). In the Bastille Manette imagined two daughters, one ignorant of his existence and the other sympathetic, yet unable permanently to free him. The second one would

> show me that the home of her married life was full of her loving remembrance of her lost father. My picture was in her room, and I was in her prayers. Her life was active, cheerful, useful; but my poor history pervaded it all. (219–20)

This second "and more real" daughter embodies the principles of love, remembrance, and story-telling that are essential to the affirmation of another's identity; activity is pointless if it does not have a human object and inspiration, and thereby the means of perpetuating a living fame. Thus at the novel's close, Carton projects his need for love and remembrance into the future, seeing his golden-haired namesake, the grandson of Lucie, being brought to his Paris gravesite to hear his story (404).

Lucie Manette is another of Dickens's childlike women, less a rounded character than a repository for certain ideas about memory and sympathy. Her imaginative antecedents are to be found in Wordsworth's celebration of the child as "best Philosopher" in the Poem "Ode: Intimations of Immortality" and the like and, beyond that, in Schiller's concept of childhood innocence:

> They are . . . not only the representation of our lost childhood, which eternally remains most dear to us, but fill us with a certain melancholy. But they are also representations of our highest fulfilment in the ideal.[32] (*Naive and Sentimental Poetry* 85)

This idealization of the idea of the child is evident in the "childlike ingenu-ousness" of Sissy Jupe in *Hard Times,* who puts the cynically manipulative James Harthouse to shame and introduces an element of fellow-feeling and imagination into the utilitarian Gradgrind household.[33] Similarly, Lucie Manette is whole and, in Schiller's terms, naive, in contrast to the artificiality and the divisions that characterize London and Paris. She inspires ghosts to become people through purposeful activity, but essentially this is a passive function.[34] The struggling males perceive in her what "sentimental" people see in nature and the idea represented by the child. "We love in them the tac-itly creative life, the serene spontaneity of their activity, existence in accor-dance with their own laws, the inner necessity, the eternal unity with them-selves" (Schiller, *Naive and Sentimental Poetry* 85).

Soon after his conversation with Lorry about memory and childhood, Sydney Carton experiences an epiphany in the Paris streets which centres around the revivification of language. The words of Jesus reverberate through his mind as he proceeds to carry out his self-sacrifice, inspired by the belief in-stilled in him by Lucie: "I am the resurrection and the life, saith the Lord: he that believeth in me, though he were dead, yet shall he live: and whosoever liveth and believeth in me, shall never die" (343). Significantly, these words come to him immediately after he carries a girl across a muddy street and asks her for a kiss.[35] By rediscovering his heart through Lucie Manette and the idea of the child she and this girl represent, he is able in his mind to transform the Biblical Word from an echo into a living symbol of his own experience, much as Lucie is able to change ghosts into people through her sympathetic influence: "the words were in the echoes of his feet, and were in the air. Per-fectly calm and steady, he sometimes repeated them to himself as he walked; but, he heard them always" (343).

Again it is helpful to turn to Carlyle for a fuller understanding of what Dickens means by a revivified word arising from belief. They both locate the transcendental experience and its symbolic language in the sympathetic mar-riage of minds; thus Teufelsdroeckh repeats Novalis's idea that "my Belief gains quite *infinitely* the moment I can convince another mind thereof" (*Sar-tor Resartus* 214). Carlyle likewise stated that words must be read symboli-cally. Thus he chided his friend, the eccentric minister Edward Irving, for bas-ing his faith in God "on a little text of *writing* in an ancient Book."[36] Furthermore, in *Sartor Resartus,* Teufelsdroeckh calls Jesus "our divinest Sym-bol," who bodies a "Godlike" that transcends any particular set of theological terms, including the Christian (224). That is, neither Jesus nor the Bible is fi-nal. His life is "a Symbol of quite perennial, infinite character; whose signifi-cance will ever demand to be anew inquired into, and anew made manifest" (224). Carlyle reflects the popular German idea that Jesus was the Highest Humanity, whose example must be replicated to affirm the ideal and bring to new life the language of renunciation and belief. Each age, indeed each person, must emulate what Goethe termed the "Worship of Sorrow" according to its own instruments and language. Jesus has to be "anew made manifest."

Carton's own Christ-like renunciation is confirmed by his declaration to Lorry that "I am not old, but my young way was never the way to age. Enough of me" (340). After this, he feels no doubts about his mission to die to save his mirror-image, Charles Darnay. Hutter writes that he follows the pattern of the "criminal-hero" of the Newgate Calendar who "marches steadily towards his own destruction," at which point his fate and his prophecy become transcendent (20–1). Beyond this, his self-sacrifice is based on Carlyle's ecstatic dramatization of Madame Roland's death in *The French Revolution*. Carton and Roland both discover a transcendental language that contrasts with the disintegration of language around them, but to do so they must exercise a renunciation that takes them out of the world; as I have argued elsewhere, Carlyle "imbues Madame Roland with Schillerian tragical traits that make hers an essentially passive and feminine ideal of conduct: he at once idealizes and dismisses his subject."[37] Sydney Carton's death bears the imprint of Schiller as well as Carlyle; since harmonious self-development and "production" cannot be said to begin on the scaffold (*Sartor Resartus* 197), we may conclude that his renunciation is not the Goethean kind enshrined in Teufelsdroeckh's declaration that "it is only with Renunciation (*Entsagen*) that Life, properly speaking, can be said to begin" (191).

Both of their deaths are described as "sublime": Carton looks "sublime and prophetic" (403), while Madame Roland is "sublime in her uncomplaining sorrow" (*Works* 4: 209). Their sublimity removes them from their chaotic environment and makes them exemplars of noble conduct in the face of inexorable historical forces. Thus Carlyle depicts his heroine as a Grecian art work, remote from her tumultuous age, nourished "to clear perennial Womanhood, though but on Logics, *Encyclopédies,* and the Gospel according to Jean-Jacques!" (4:211). Similarly, Dickens suggests the transcendental apartness of Carton by distancing his narrative perspective, switching like Carlyle to the present tense, and making his prophecy an ambiguous rumour of sublimity ("They said of him . . ."). To understand further the meaning of the sublime in these parallel death scenes, let us consider Schiller's theory of tragedy, which impressed Carlyle. In "On The Sublime" the German writes that the "morally cultivated man" is able mentally to defeat the physical forces arrayed against him "because he has by his own free act separated himself from everything that he can reach" (*Naive and Sentimental Poetry* 195). At the moment of greatest crisis a feeling of sublimity "suddenly and with a shock . . . tears the independent spirit out of the net in which a refined sensuousness has entoiled it . . . often a single sublime emotion suffices to rip this web of deceit asunder" (201–202). For instance, Schiller's Maria Stuart transcends her material and and emotional "nets" to experience a "worthy pride" and a "noble soul."[38] For the first time, upon accepting the inevitability of death, she looks beyond herself to care for others, for instance Melvil (1. 3506). As with Sydney Carton, the renunciation of self leads to the rediscovery of the heart. As a sacrificial offering, Maria Stuart sets a noble "example" for others, thus functioning the way Madame Roland and Carton do. Thus Darnay becomes "like a young child" in Carton's hands: "with a strength both of will and action, that appeared quite supernatural" (380), he forces the prisoner to change clothes with him. Carton's action is curiously like the role reversal in *Maria Stuart* that leaves Leicester passively doubting himself, while his former lover Maria Stuart exercises a moral will that leaves her "transformed" on the scaffold.

In one sense Carton is closer to Maria Stuart than to Carlyle's Madame Roland: while the first two are "sentimental" in their efforts to reconcile their mental divisions and seek the ideal, Madame Roland is a "naive" "noble white Vision" who naturally stands apart from the artificiality around her: she is "serenely complete" from her youth to her death (*Works* 4: 211). Her death is a model of renunciation and composure, but she does not have to struggle to achieve either. Unlike the deeply flawed Sydney Carton and Maria Stuart, she is consistently pure and inviolate, removed from the mire of the world in which she exerts her subtle influences on the Girondins' political affairs. She is "genuine, the creature of Sincerity and Nature, in an age of Artificiality, Pollution, and Cant" (2:46). She is static, while Sydney Carton must pursue an ideal "mirage of honourable ambition" through Lucie's inspiration before he can overcome the enervation of his will. In taking Darnay's place on the scaffold, he also steps into the shoes of Madame Roland and the childlike feminine transcendence she represents to Carlyle. He achieves something like the reconciled naive and sentimental visions Schiller postulates in an as yet unrealized "Idyllic" art form, "a free uniting of inclination with the law . . . none other than the ideal of beauty applied to actual life" (*Naive and Sentimental Poetry* 153).

In their death scenes, Dickens and Carlyle are interested in the relation between writing and the ineffable. Carlyle focuses on how Madame Roland asked in vain to be allowed "to write the strange thoughts that were rising in her . . . so in her too there was an Unnameable; she too was a Daughter of the Infinite; there were mysteries which Philosophism had not dreamt of!" (*Works* 4: 211)[39] Dickens's narrator marvels that every human being is a mystery "to every other" (44); Carton is a mystery to others, and even to himself, unable to explain to Lucie Manette the "mystery of my own wretched heart" (180). Dickens alludes to Madame Roland's request "to be allowed to write down the thoughts that were inspiring her" (404), just before the prophecy in which Carton enters a realm beyond reality but just short of ineffability. The narrator underscores the tentativeness, the mystery if you will, of his last words by stressing the "if": "if he had given utterance to his [thoughts], and they were prophetic, they would have been these:" (404). Dickens leaves his reader to ponder his incapacity fully to probe the mysteries of language and personality. That the text is moving beyond language to probe transcendental mysteries is evident in a seemingly minor change Dickens makes in Carlyle's account. Madame Roland comforts the printer and Assignat-director Lamarche, emulating Maria Stuart in showing a weaker male how easy it is to die. But Sydney Carton comforts a young girl, for the second time since his final interview with Lorry. Significantly, she feels guilty because she "cannot write," and therefore must leave her orphaned cousin ignorant about her execution (403). Their conversation while awaiting execution centres on the inefficacy of words as they prepare to enter a state where there is "no Time" (403). Carton tells her it is better she can not write; he accepts the impermanence of words compared to love and sympathy, the positive emotions that can render language transcendental, so that (to cite Schiller's description of the aesthetic state) we have the "dignity of free spirits" and mentally are freed from "the degrading relationship with matter" (*Aesthetic Education* 139). Thus Dickens stresses their eye contact and the comfort it gives: "Keep your eyes upon me, dear child, and mind no other object" (402).

There is a temptation to regard Carton's prophecy as a denial of meaning rather than an evocation of mystery, as if the reader must go away with the idea that the book's doubt is a poor thing, but its nihilism a very intense experience. Certainly it is ambiguous, but whether Carton projects his wished-for union with Lucie into the future and kills off Darnay in the process is another question. Vanden Bossche writes that "the image of self-sacrifice created by his speech puts the authenticity of that very self-sacrifice into question by envisioning a future that nearly effaces Darnay" (211). This is perhaps true. But another explanation is that Carton envisions a unity almost beyond naming, where even his desire for perpetuation through others' memories is subordinated to a vision of a future where divisions cease. He does not refer to himself, Darnay, or Lucie Manette by name. His most forceful assertion of identity is the "boy of my name" brought to his Paris gravesite to hear his story:

> I see that I hold a sanctuary in their hearts, and in the hearts of their descendants, generations hence. I see her, an old woman, weeping for me on the anniversary of this day. . . . I see that child who lay upon her bosom and who bore my name, a man winning his way up in that path of life which once was mine. I see him winning it so well, that my name is made illustrious there by the light of his. I see the blots I threw upon it, faded away. I see him, foremost of just judges and honoured men, bringing a boy of my name, with a forehead that I know and golden hair, to this place . . . and I hear him tell the child my story, with a tender and a faltering voice. (404)

As is the case when Carton comforts the young girl, sympathetic eyesight now takes precedence over writing and naming. In his prophecy, only those people who have failed to transcend naming through sympathetic acts retain their names: Barsad, Cly, Defarge, and the Vengeance (404).

In *A Tale of Two Cities* Dickens suggests that people are too mysterious to be reduced to mere names and formulas. M. Defarge's search for a key to Manette at the Bastille is fruitless because the essence of selfhood is only communicable through sympathy and memory. But the mystery at the core of the self always remains; as Manette tells Darnay concerning his daughter, "mysteries arise out of close love, as well as out of wide division" (165). But this does not presuppose an absence of ultimate meaning; to doubt is not to deny. The prophecy, like so much else in the novel reveals an insecurity on Dickens's part about our capacity to "name" and thus control the future, an even more precarious act than defining our identities against the onrush of contemporary events. Like the lives of George Eliot's characters in *Middlemarch,* life does not achieve finality even at death, "but merely ceases" at the point determined by the writer. To close the text or project it into a knowable future is meretricious, for the mutability of existence precludes its ever being authoritatively "read." At the end of *A Tale of Two Cities* Carton, like Madame Roland, enters the transcendental realm. Beyond the mystery there may be final knowledge and identity, or only blankness. But to insist on one or the other is to become no less trapped in words than Carlyle's dream theoreticians and Dickens's Paris Projectors are. To assert the absence of stable meaning is to articulate a code which denies authoritative codes.

Notes

1. There has been a flurry of scholarly activity in recent years on *A Tale of Two Cities;* what follows is a representative sampling. Gross analyses the partial resurrections in the novel and states that Carton "might just as well be committing suicide as laying down his life for Darnay" (23); but for MacKay his death represents a "transcendental achieving" and "inviolate action" (201). See also Hutter for a study of Carton's Christ-like resurrection (20) and its parodic counterpart in Cruncher's trade, the history of which he explores. Resurrection implies unburial and explosure, according to Gallagher, whose analysis of violations of the private are in the post-structuralist vein. She writes that the Terror "explicated the Revolution's insistence on transparency and its corollary of hidden plots" (134). Like Hutter, she compares Cruncher not only with Carton, but with the narrator, "in that both dig up the past and uncover buried mysteries" (137).

2. Needless to say, there are differing interpretations of Carton's ambiguous prophecy. My approach emphasizes the idea of presence rather than that of absence, owing to the dynamics of the scene leading up to the prophecy and to the idealistic tradition on which Dickens draws, primarily through Carlyle. MacKay writes that his words "are at once unspoken and yet transcendently true" (203). Baumgarten also affirms the truth of the prophecy within the terms set by the text: "his final vision is an unwritten piece of autobiographical writing, voiced beyond any imprisoning code and opening into the prophetic realm where writing is absolute and true" (163). Rignall states that this is a "vision of a better world which seems to lie beyond time and history" (575); see also Kuchich 168–77. But Vanden Bossche is less certain than the others about the authority of Carton's prophecy, noting that he effaces Darnay: his "vision of a peaceful Paris is problematic in the light of the reader's knowledge of its tumultuous history and other revolutions" (211).

3.   In his Preface Dickens states his debt to the "philosophy" of Carlyle's history.

4.   See Lloyd 43. Schlegel wrote that "it's equally deadly for the mind to have a system and not to have one. Therefore it will just have to decide to combine the two."

5.   This contrasts with the non-verbal communication based on sympathy which reaches its highest expression at the end of the novel, when Carton comforts a young girl on the way to execution. See below.

6.   Even Lucie is "afraid of it" when she first sees him cobbling in his locked room in Paris (69).

7.   Compare John Keats's assertion that identity is created by the interaction of intelligence, the human heart, and the external world.

8.   Surrounded by aristocratic "ghosts" and removed from any immediate human contact in his cell, Darnay is thrown upon his intelligence, which begins to disintegrate, and his heart, which momentarily is distracted from Lucie Manette's influence. Her presence outside his window eventually recreates a precarious psychological harmony.

9.   When the letter is read at Darnay's trial, we learn that Manette most missed "tidings of my dearest wife" during the eighteen years he was imprisoned (361). This would have filled his "blankness," just as Lucie fills Darnay's by standing below his cell window.

10.   Gross writes that in the novel "the grave gives up its dead reluctantly, and the prisoner who has been released is still far from being a free man" (20).

11.   "Crush humanity out of shape once more, under similar hammers, and it will twist itself into the same tortured forms" (*Tale* 399). In a milder form, what applies to the sansculottes applies to Lorry. Tellson's is a more benign mirror of the Bastille, including its iron bars and its air of death and suppression of personality: "putting to death was a recipe much in vogue with all trades and professions, and not least of all with Tellson's" (84). Lorry is twisted out of shape like all the others buried here: "When they took a young man into Tellson's London house, they hid him somewhere till he was old" (85).

12.   He is not even shaken by the Paris Tellson's with its whitewashed Cupid and the bloody "whirlings of the grindstone" in the courtyard (291).

13.   Compare Gradgrind's mental imprisonment in economic jargon in *Hard Times,* illustrated by his successful mediation of Bounderby's "proposal" to Louisa.

14.   Instead of becoming trapped in our "Philosophical Systems," Carlyle writes, we must learn to read the "Volume of Nature." "It is a Volume written in celestial hieroglyphs, in the true Sacred-writing: of which even Prophets are happy that they can read here a line and there a line" (*Sartor Resartus* 54, 258).

15.   Lucie comforts Carton by believing in his capacity for good, and he in turn comforts the young girl at the scaffold (182, 403). Belief is contagious: see below.

16.   Dickens's depiction of the Marquis and his family history owes much to Carlyle, who analyses how the ruling classes concealed their savagery beneath an apparent refinement. "Philosophism sits joyful in her glittering saloons . . . and preaches, lifted up over all Bastilles, a coming millennium" (*Works* 2:30).

17.   Schiller writes that "man portrays himself in his actions. And what a figure he cuts in the drama of the present time! On the one hand, a return to the savage state; on the other, to complete lethargy" (*Aesthetic Education* 25).

18.   The Marquis has no "within," but Darnay's mother does. He recalls how he read both her words and her eyes, which implored him to "have mercy and redress" his family's crimes (154).

19.   Carlyle draws on Schiller's analysis in *The French Revolution,* but is more sympathetic about the motivations of the poor for rebelling. For a study of the mob psychology in Carlyle's history, see La Valley.

20.   Compare also Carlyle's description of the Sphinx riddle of Nature in *Past And Present:* "the face and bosom of a goddess, but ending in claws and the body of a lioness" (*Works* 10: 7).

21.   Carlyle also uses natural imagery to describe the French Revolution, which he defines as the rebellion and victory "of disimprisoned Anarchy against corrupt wornout Authority" (*Works* 2: 211).

22.   Like Dickens, Carlyle and Schiller point to the difficulty of connecting words with things while affirming the need to try. Thus Carlyle writes that "words ought not to harden into things for us" (*Works* 5: 106), while Schiller points to the difficulty of finding language that can analyse, yet preserve the "living spirit" of nature (*Aesthetic Education* 5).

23.   Thus in *Hard Times*, the fire into which Louisa often stares is a reflection of the abyss as well as of her own thwarted energies. In *A Tale of Two Cities* a tipsy Lorry "digs" in the "live red coals" of the fireplace at his Dover hotel, as if unconsciously searching for his buried self. This follows his repeated dream of burial in the coach, where the essential relation between him and Manette becomes apparent (51, 47).

24.   Once again she protects Lucie's sanctuary. See Gallagher 138.

25.   Foulon told the starving poor they should eat grass; Carlyle also dwells on his execution in *The French Revolution* as a clash between false words and the rage against words. Foulon and the sans-culottes have all turned away from true language. Compare MacKay's assertion that Madame Defarge's decapitation of the governor of the Bastille "paradoxically unifies him with the group, now an 'ocean of faces' in Dickens' rhetoric of transcendence" (199).

26.   Rust is an important motif in *A Tale of Two Cities*. Cruncher licks it from his fingers, for example, suggesting the symbolic failure of his "resurrections" compared to those of Lorry and Carton. Rust and writing are connected in Manette's buried letter, which he wrote with a "rusty iron point . . . in scrapings of soot and charcoal from the chimney, mixed with blood" (348).

27.   "Werd ich zum Augenblicke sagen: / Verweile doch! du bist so schoen! / Dann magst du mich in Fesseln schlagen" (11. 1699–1701).

28.   Ein wenig besser wuerd er leben,
        Haettst du ihm nicht den Schein des Himmelslichts gegeben;
        Er nennt's Vernunft und braucht's allein,
        Nur tierischer als jedes Tier zu sein. (11. 283–86).

29.   "Du bleibst doch immer, was du bist" (1. 1809).

30.   "Armsel'ger Faust! ich kenne dich nicht mehr" (1. 2720).

31.   Lucie's power is not absolute: "she could recall some occasions on which her power had failed; but they were few and slight, and she believed them over" (110). This is reflected in Manette's statement to her that the second, sympathetic daughter he imagined while in the Bastille "could never deliver" him completely (220).

32.   Schiller writes that it is not the physical child or nature that inspires us: "It is not these objects, it is an idea represented by them which we love in them. We love in them the tactitly creative life, the serene spontaneity of their activity, existence in accordance with their own laws, the inner necessity, the eternal unity with themselves" (*Naive And Sentimental Poetry* 84–5).

33.   But unlike Lorry, Louisa Gradgrind has no childhood to which she can return in thought: "The dreams of childhood—its airy fables; its graceful, beautiful, humane, impossible adornments of the world beyond; so good to be believed in once, so good to be remembered when outgrown . . . what had she to do with these?" (150–51)

34.   Still, she seems conscious of her function and doubts her capacity to perform it. Thus she exclaims, upon being told that she will see her father, "I am going to see his Ghost! It will be his Ghost—not him!" (57)

35.   Mud is an important image in Dickens's novel: recall the mail-coach ride in the beginning, the environment of Tellson's (47), and the scramble in the mud for spilled wine outside Defarge's wine shop (43–44). Mud symbolizes a morally corrupt environment and burial, as it did for Carlyle, who recounted that he had to defeat the "foul and vile and soul-murdering Mud-gods of my Epoch" (*Reminiscences* 281).

36. Irving became obsessed with Corinthians 13 and speaking in tongues.

37. For more information about Schiller's influence on *The French Revolution,* see my article in *Prose Studies.*

38. "Die Krone fuehl ich wieder auf dem Haupt, / Den wuerd'gen Stolz in meiner edeln Seele!" (11. 3493–4).

39. Similarly, "strange" thoughts appear in the mind of Tennyson's speaker in Lyric 95 of *In Memoriam;* he can not fully communicate their essence in "matter-moulded forms of speech" (11. 25–32, 46).

Works Cited

Baumgarten, Murray, "Writing the Revolution." *Dickens Studies Annual* 12 (1983): 161–76.
Carlyle, Thomas. *The Centenary Edition of the Works of Thomas Carlyle.* Ed. H. D. Traill. 30 vols. London, 1896–99.
———— *Reminiscences.* Ed. C. E. Norton. London: J. M. Dent & Sons, 1972.
———— *Sartor Resartus.* Ed. Charles Frederick Harrold. New York: The Odyssey Press, 1937.
Dickens, Charles. *Hard Times.* New York: W. W. Norton & Company, 1966.
———— *A Tale of Two Cities.* Harmondsworth: Penguin, 1970.
Gallagher, Catherine. "The Duplicity of Doubling in *A Tale of Two Cities.*" *Dickens Studies Annual* 12 (1983): 125–45.
Goethe, Johann Wolfgang von. *Werke.* Hamburger Ausgabe in 14 Baenden. Hamburg: Christian Wegner Verlag, 1972. Vol. 3.
Gross, John. "*A Tale of Two Cities.*" *Twentieth Century Interpretations of A Tale of Two Cities.* Ed. Charles E. Beckwith. Englewood Cliffs, New Jersey: Prentice-Hall, 1972. 19–28.
Hutter, Albert D. "The Novelist as Resurrectionist: Dickens and the Dilemma of Death." *Dickens Studies Annual* 12 (1983): 1–39.
Kuchich, John. *Excess and Restraint in the Novels of Charles Dickens.* Athens: University of Georgia Press, 1981.
LaValley, Albert J. *Carlyle and the Idea of the Modern.* New Haven: Yale U. P., 1968.
Lloyd, Tom. "Madame Roland and Schiller's Aesthetics: Carlyle's *The French Revolution.*" *Prose Studies* 9 (1986): 39–53.
MacKay, Carol Hanbery. "The Rhetoric of Soliloquy in *The French Revolution* and *A Tale of Two Cities.*" *Dickens Studies Annual* 12 (1983): 197–207.
Rignall, J. M. "Dickens and the Catastrophic Continuum of History in *A Tale of Two Cities.*" *ELH* 51 (1984): 575–88.
Schiller, Friedrich von. *On the Aesthetic Education of Man.* Trans. Elizabeth M. Wilkinson and L. A. Willoughby. Oxford: Clarendon Press, 1967.
———— *Naive and Sentimental Poetry and On The Sublime.* Trans. Julias A. Elias. New York: Ungar, 1980.
———— *Saemtliche Werke.* 5 vols. Muenchen: Winkler Verlag, 1968. Vol. 2.
Stange, G. Robert. "Dickens and the Fiery Past: *A Tale of Two Cities* Reconsidered." *Twentieth Century Interpretations of A Tale of Two Cities.* Ed. Charles E. Beckwith. Englewood Cliffs, N. J.: Prentice-Hall, 1972. 64–75.
Vanden Bossche, Chris R. "Prophetic Closure and Disclosing Narrative: *The French Revolution* and *A Tale of Two Cities.*" *Dickens Studies Annual* 12 (1983): 209–21.

The "Angels" in Dickens's House:
Representation of Women
in *A Tale of Two Cities*

LISA ROBSON

I

A Tale of Two Cities is not a woman's text; indeed, there is little chance of its being mistaken for one. In his interpretation of the causes and effects of the French Revolution, Charles Dickens focusses on a patriarchal world of politics and historical development in which men dominate the scene, both privately and publicly. Yet several women characters factor rather importantly in the novel's development, and, as such, merit close scrutiny. The current body of criticism concerning *A Tale of Two Cities* concentrates mainly on the political and historical elements of the text, while conspicuously absent is a detailed examination of the female role in Dickens's representation of the Revolution. On the other hand, although various studies of the women in Dickens's fiction have been offered (for example, Michael Slater's *Dickens and Women* and Sylvia Jarmuth's *Dickens' Use of Women in His Novels*), most are general in nature and provide little more than a cursory examination of, if they explore at all, the women in *A Tale of Two Cities*. In this paper, therefore, I intend to present a detailed analysis of the women in this historical novel, particularly the two main female characters, Lucie Manette and Madame Defarge, as well as the most prominent secondary female character, Miss Pross.

Specifically, I am concerned with Dickens's manipulation of the angel in the house image as a Victorian representation which idealizes women for their femininity. In terms of this ideal, these three women form a complex triangle; each woman corresponds to the other two either as some form of double or antitype. Lucie Manette and Madame Defarge, for example, represent England and France, middle-class lady and peasant, the perfect angel and her complete opposite. Miss Pross, on the other hand, is Lucie's lower-class comic counterpart, enough like her mistress to act as substitute and do what Lucie, as a middle class woman, cannot. Finally, Madame Defarge and Miss Pross, two women of similar social standing on opposite sides of the novel's personal conflict, appear to have little in common, yet are deceivingly similar. However alike or unalike these characters may seem to be, the one quality which

Reprinted from *The Dalhousie Review* 72, no. 3 (1992): 311–33 by permission and by permission of the author.

links them all is an apparent lack of conventionality. As participants in the turbulent French conflict of 1789, these three representatives of Dickens's female characters are often seen in unconventional situations and positions, exposing social problems and exploring new spaces for women to inhabit. Yet, although Dickens appears to allow these women to adopt non-traditional female roles, he consistently reverts to granting them representation only as passive, silent, marginal figures. In fact, *A Tale of Two Cities* seems to allow women to break free from traditional sexual boundaries only to recontain them more forcefully in their traditional positions.

When discussing representations of women in Victorian literature, the angel in the house figure, of course, is far from unconventional; she is a most traditional female representation, her image largely reflecting the highly repressive conditions governing women's activity (or the lack thereof) during the period. Like so many of his contemporaries. Dickens often turns to this stereotypical figure in his fiction. Alexander Welsh explains how, while idealizing the home and hearth as alternatives to his vision of the dark and destructive nineteenth-century city, Dickens frequently reduces women to angel figures whose role is to fill the home with comfort and a sense of security (141–63). However, in *A Tale of Two Cities* Dickens moves beyond the specifically traditional metaphor to highlight the angel's supposedly innate redemptive and regenerative abilities, her capacity to function as a type of savior figure, and the consequent elevation she receives as a spiritual creature to be worshipped. In this manner, Dickens's portrayal of women as angels in *Tale* points to a progressive potential in this Victorian ideal. While the angel figure as reflected in the women in the novel adheres to convention in its insistence on the female as the gentler, purer sex, it also emphasizes women's vital role as men's redeemers. Such a focus on women's determining capacity highlights an apparent transgression of conventional assumptions concerning the relations of gender, sexuality and activity by creating a possibility of women's intervention into history as agents of redemption and regeneration, agents who may reach beyond the novel's moral to its social sphere. To this end, Dickens presents a series of "resurrections," beginning with Dr. Manette's return to England after eighteen years of incarceration in a French prison, aided by his daughter, Lucie, who is the novel's most pronounced angel in the house.

Following the initial excitement of the Doctor's escape, Lucie reclaims her father from his mental abstraction, bringing him back to life from his living death in prison. It is Lucie's feminine attributes, her trust, her kindness, her unselfish concern, her willing self-sacrifice, which gradually coax the old man to rejoin the living world. In a description of Lucie's importance to her father. Dickens defines his feminine angel. He writes:

> Only his daughter had the power of charming this black brooding from his mind. She was the golden thread that united him to a Past beyond his misery,

and to a Present beyond his misery: and the sound of her voice, the light of her face, the touch of her hand, had a strong beneficial influence with him almost always. Not absolutely always, for she could recal[l] some occasions on which her power had failed; but they were few and slight, and she believed them over. (110)

Dickens endows Lucie with "a power of charming," suggesting a sense of magic and mystery surrounding her unique restorative powers. His description renders her almost otherworldly in her capacity to transcend time, to erase the barriers of past and present for those who feel trapped within them. Although Dickens later admits that her powers of recall have limits (she is unable to reclaim her father from his relapse at the conclusion of the novel), he asserts that she "believes them [her failures] over," suggesting a religious framework of faith wherein the feminine approaches the semi-divine; in fact, by the end of the novel, Carton, her would-be lover, refers to Lucie as "Her." A woman whose very name suggests "light," Lucie's ability to redeem others depends upon her capacity to love them and sacrifice herself for them.

To reinforce her spiritual elevation and yet grant her some measure of corporeal authenticity, Dickens includes domestic and physical references in the above description. He refers to Lucie as the "golden thread" that unites, an image which gestures toward a mythic connection with the Greek Fates as the weavers of destiny. This mention of the traditionally female activities of spinning and sewing suggests the novel's metaphor of redemption, or the feminine saint image, by highlighting the domesticity of feminine figures in their roles as preservers and reconcilers of the family. Calling upon an iconographical tradition which links a woman's physical appearance with her personal and moral worth, Dickens's reference to Lucie's voice, face and hand further confirms her femininity by exposing her beauty and the healing power of her touch as outward manifestations of her inner, angelic qualities. (He also repeatedly refers to her lovely forehead as indicative of her sincerity.) Throughout the novel, Lucie appears as a dutiful daughter and wife, unwilling to marry her greatest love, should her father disapprove, standing by her husband with level-headed practicality and emotional fortitude when he faces the French Tribunal, and always maintaining a beautiful home, whether in Soho or Paris. As an idealized feminine figure, Lucie is everything to everyone; she is innocent child to her father, loving (yet pure and non-sexual) wife to her husband, and compassionate friend and moral inspiration to those who love her. Through this firm affirmation of Lucie and her redemptive capacity, Dickens offers such feminine virtue, charitable love and self-sacrifice as alternatives to the violence and inhumanity which dominate his representation of the French Revolution.

Accompanying such overt praise of Lucie, Dickens further endorses this idealized representation of women through mockery of a comical, lower-class nonconformist. Miss Pross, Lucie's faithful servant, is an ugly, wild spinster who, in the absence of a husband, has become so strong in order to survive in a patriarchal society that Mr. Lorry, the Darnays' friend and epitome of English common sense, initially takes her for a man. Lorry first encounters the bizarre woman when Lucie faints in his presence at the news of her father's survival and release. Miss Pross flies into the room like a fury, the redness of her hair and dress representative of the wildness within, and physically throws Lorry across the room. Lorry responds to Miss Pross in a typically patriarchal fashion, fascinated by her oddity but repulsed, at least initially, by her apparent masculinity. Without marriage or motherhood, supported by her strength, independence and passion. Miss Pross refuses to surrender to traditional standards of femininity, and Dickens presents her as a distortion of the feminine ideal in the novel by ridiculing the oddness of her physical appearance and her behavioral eccentricities.

Such derision, however, never becomes complete rejection because Miss Pross is masculine only in a superficial sense; in terms of her spiritual nature and moral sensitivity, she is another feminine angel. As Lorry grows to know Miss Pross, Dickens writes:

> Mr. Lorry knew Miss Pross to be very jealous, but he also knew her by this time to be, beneath the surface of her eccentricity, one of those unselfish creatures—found only among women—who will, for pure love and admiration, bind themselves willing slaves, to youth when they have lost it, to beauty that they never had, to accomplishments that they were never fortunate enough to gain, to bright hopes that never shone upon their own sombre lives. He knew enough of the world to know that there is nothing in it better than the faithful service of the heart; so rendered and so free from any mercenary taint, he had such an exalted respect for it, that in the retributive arrangements made by his own mind—we all make such arrangements, more or less—he stationed Miss Pross much nearer to the lower Angels than many ladies immeasurably better got up both by Nature and Art, who had balances at Tellson's. (126)

Dickens affirms Miss Pross's femininity by highlighting the unselfish disposition "found only among women" which she shares, her selfless, if somewhat pathetic, devotion to that which she desires but does not have: youth, beauty, accomplishment, hope. She is a woman of "pure heart," free of "mercenary taint" or self-concern, and her maternal dedication to Lucie and her untiring, sisterly support of her undeserving brother, Solomon, confirm her spiritual goodness. However distorted and masculinized she may appear to the naked eye, such feminine self-abnegation, incessant fidelity and unqualified compassion nullify the negative effect of her masculine idiosyncrasies and gain her respect and exaltation in the mind of Lorry who with his strong sense of practicality and dedicated business mind, is an apt representative of the English patriarchy.

As something of a feminine aberration. Miss Pross receives further vindication in terms of the novel's construction of class relations. References to her social position in the above quotation confirm her social acceptability. As a member of the English lower classes. Miss Pross knows her place and thus "binds" herself as a "willing slave" to Lucie, her social superior. She constrains herself to servitude without question, happily forfeiting her possible pleasures and goals, and in the end her hearing too, to fulfil her duty and save Lucie and her family. Although Miss Pross may love the younger woman like a daughter, Lucie remains, nonetheless, her employer, and in protecting the Darnays successfully while in France Miss Pross secures her own employment and financial security. In her "faithful service," even as an angel Miss Pross assumes her "station" among their "lower" ranks, confirming her moral superiority to those wealthy women who may have external beauty but lack this working woman's inner worth. It is in part because Miss Pross participates in Dickens's angelic ideal and happily accepts her status among the English servant classes that ridicule of her eccentricities stops short of repudiation.

In terms of both class and gender, then, Miss Pross valorizes the "thematics of suppression" (Kucich 130) in the novel and suggests the impossible position in which patriarchal society, with its hierarchical structure and masculine bias, places women. Despite their supposed elevation as agents with a redemptive, moral mission, women's subjugation to a patriarchal agenda frustrates their ability to act as feminine savior figures. In her examination of the woman-as-savior image, Nancy Klenck Hill explains: "the spiritual dimension of life which they [women] control is necessarily subservient to the material realm commanded by men, even though men recognize women's spiritual function as being higher than their own material one" (98–99). As second-class citizens, women are denied agency by a patriarchal order which demands passivity; however, hailed as idealistic, feminine redeemers, they are expected to effect salvation. Required to modify without governing, women in a patriarchal society cannot adequately meet such extravagant expectations. This impasse, in part, explains the dull and lifeless representation of Lucie in the text, because in order to survive under such circumstances Lucie must remain an "unconscious and happy" (227) heroine with little personality. By thus restricting his female characters within a patriarchal structure, Dickens places the women in his novel in an ambiguous, illogical position.

Although the effects of such ambiguity are largely masked by Lucie's initially secure, domestic happiness and by the predominantly comic treatment of Miss Pross, other similar figures in the lower classes who are represented in darker ways, grotesque rather than humorous, reveal some of the consequences of this unreasonable situation. As they attempt to fulfil their "duties" despite patriarchal constraints, women such as Mrs. Cruncher grow increasingly susceptible to male brutality. In his examination of Dickens's work in general, H. M. Daleski suggests that Dickens's characters are often related in complex patterns of analogy. Indeed, as already illustrated, Miss Pross, in many ways, can be viewed as Lucie's double, and a similar parallel can be drawn between the heroine and Mrs. Cruncher. Isolated from the main action except through the participation of her husband, Jerry, who works for Mr. Lorry in England and France, Mrs. Cruncher displays common feminine virtues such as domesticity, submissiveness and religiosity. In the end she helps successfully to redeem her husband through her example, so that he repents his unChristian disbelief and ill-treatment of her, but throughout the novel he abuses her emotionally, psychologically and physically for her "flopping," or prayer (184). Mrs. Cruncher, then, at least in some sense, acts as a feminine savior figure like Lucie; unlike Lucie, however, Mrs. Cruncher is brutalized by her husband for her efforts. The poor woman's experience exposes the universality of female insecurity in a patriarchal culture by demonstrating that a woman's safety and well-being largely depend upon the personality of her husband. Dickens may indirectly blame Lucie for Charles's quick return to England and partial renunciation of his title in France (he returns to be with her), but never is Lucie at risk because Charles loves her and is gentle of temperament. In contrast, Mrs. Cruncher's subordinate gentleness and subjugation to her husband's violence exposes the possibilities of victimization implicit in all feminine self-sacrifice.

Dickens forces such patriarchal oppression to an extreme in Dr. Manette's letter describing the events leading to his imprisonment: the rape and subsequent death of Madame Defarge's sister. In this letter, Dr. Manette quotes the girl's brother as he explains that, despite their father's despair for their future, his sister remained optimistic. He says:

> Nevertheless, Doctor, my sister married. He was ailing at that time, poor fellow, and she married her lover, that she might tend and comfort him in our cottage—our dog-hut, as that man would call it. She had not been married many weeks, when that man's brother [the Marquis] saw her and admired her, and asked that man [Charles's father] to lend her to him—for what are husbands among us! He was willing enough, but my sister was good and virtuous, and hated his brother with a hatred as strong as mine. (354–55)

Exhibiting a family loyalty shared by the girl, the brother, the speaker in this passage, does not reveal the girl's name, and this partial anonymity underscores her position as a typical representative of her gender and class. As a "good," "virtuous" and, as the Doctor soon discovers, pregnant young woman, she is another idealized angel who marries the man she loves despite his illness, in order to "tend" or nurse him, to save and comfort him. The reference to the cottage as a "dog-hut" points to the poverty among the lower classes, and the disrespect shown towards the husbands by the Marquis and his brother highlights a sense of callous, aristocratic indifference which helps to create the class hatred identified by the Defarge brother. Unaffected by the girl's virtue, Charles's uncle cruelly rapes her, an abusive act which symbolizes the aristocratic exploitation of and barbarity toward the lower classes. Although this rape generates the action which comprises the novel, rather than affirming women's agency, this event denies their ability to act. Regarded as an object or piece of property to be "admired" and "lent" by the aristocracy, the girl lies immobile on her deathbed, unable to speak save in mad ravings, acted upon by the Marquis and the Doctor, and spoken for by her brother. Madame Defarge's sister represents the epitome of feminine innocence thrust into a hostile, masculine world, exploited by abusive men and initiating action only through her violation and her death.

Such a depiction of severe male violence against women pointedly questions the novel's advocacy of feminine self-sacrifice as a means of redemption and the proposed importance of women's endless love, forgiveness and submission. Certain critics (such as Albert D. Hutter, who examines the relations between father and sons in "Nation and Generation in *A Tale of Two Cities*") suggest that Dickens indicts the patriarchal system in *Tale,* and it is true that Dickens levels much criticism against the hierarchical social and political world of his novel. However, any criticism of the patriarchy concerns women only in a narrow sense. Although Dickens's representation of women's exploitation indicates his recognition of some of the difficulties women face and his interest in their plight, his investigation goes no further. In fact, Dickens may expose some of the ambiguities in his feminine ideal and acknowledge some of the dangers of women's subordination within a patriarchal system, but his text offers no relinquishment of its sentimentalized perception of women; rather, the novel continues to affirm and cherish a feminine ideal according to which women continue to be victims. Dickens may emphasize the angel's redemptive powers, thereby allowing for the possibility of her effective agency, but because she cannot meet the contradictory demands placed on her within a patriarchal system, she is rendered passive and silent.

II

As Dickens rather abruptly shifts the novel's focus from England to France, from the private, relatively ordered world of the Manettes and Darnays in London to the public disorder of Paris, the accompanying contrast in nationality and class presents an opportunity for a somewhat different representation of women. Although Miss Pross and several other, more minor English characters are of a lower class, Dickens mainly focusses his attention on the middle classes in England, while he concentrates on the lower classes in France and their oppression by the aristocracy. Through depiction of these French working-class women in the Revolution, Dickens's text apparently overcomes some of the limits of the woman-as-savior ideal already described by granting women an active role in public life.

From an historical perspective, the vastly different views expressed by critics regarding the positions of working women during the period serve as some indication of the complexity of women's roles in the French Revolution. Jane Abray, for instance, in "Feminism in the French Revolution," insists on the existence of a feminist movement during France political upheaval, claiming that, "While it [revolutionary feminism] lasted it was a very real phenomenon with a comprehensive program for social change, perhaps the most far-reaching such program of the Revolution" (62). She asserts that, although revolutionary feminism began with a burst of enthusiasm, it failed as a result of tactical and strategical errors (such as the easy distraction of its members from their main concerns), political and managerial inexperience (or leaders acting in isolation from one another), and because women's general acceptance of the status quo and eighteenth-century definitions of femininity rendered feminism a minority movement (61–62). In an apparently contradictory but equally extreme view, Olwen Hufton, in "Women in Revolution 1789–1796," sees working women as responding to the Revolution solely in terms of their traditional roles as mothers and wives bereft of a feminist or political agenda, seeking involvement only when famine threatens their families with destitution (90–108).

In a sense, Hufton's conservative and chauvinistic analysis gains support from a comparative examination of women before and after the Revolution, since the minimal and often illusory gains in their social and political status seem to deny and possibility of positive feminist assessment. Mary Durham Johnson explains, for instance, that despite the rapidly changing governments and administrations from 1789 to 1796, women remained subject to persistently traditional, patriarchal values (132). Her description of women in pre-revolutionary France as economically dependent, legal minors, exploited in the workplace, control of their person and property transferred from father to husband upon marriage, existing to perform conjugal duties and bear healthy children (107–110), recalls conventional roles assigned women in any patriarchal system. Although the Revolution may have raised hopes for change in the status of women, governmental retaliation for female protests reasserted a paternalistic demand for obedience and dependence in order to reinforce traditional sex roles. When Napoleon came to power, his reversal of any legal and civic progress made during the Revolution regarding women's social position (in education and divorce laws, for example), and the implementation of even more sophisticated mechanisms for controlling women's behavior than had existed in the *ancien régime,* confirmed the continuation of patriarchal standards (Johnson 130–31). Such uninterrupted repression seems to illustrate a continuing failure of women's political influence.

Yet, despite their social subordination and lack of overt socio-political advancement, working women did have an impact during the Revolution, taking roles which were not strictly traditional. Harriet Branson Applewhite and Darline Gay Levy, for example, approach the period from women's perspectives in order to demonstrate that, while institutions may not have changed during the period, women's political awareness did. Finding a middle ground between Abray and Hufton as a basis for interpretation, Levy and Applewhite suggest that French revolutionary women "were not feminists, and their goals were often the age-old concerns of wives and mothers for the survival of their families, but they learned to use revolutionary institutions and democratic tactics to secure political influence" ("Women of the Popular Classes" 9). In the October insurrections of 1789, for instance, when they marched to Versailles in order to demand a stable supply of bread at affordable prices, women played an instrumental role in helping to topple the monarchy by bringing the king back to Paris with them (66). As the Revolution wore on, women made use of petitions, clubs and assemblies to gain a forum for their political views, they resorted to *taxation populaire,* or confiscation of merchants' goods to be sold at reasonable prices, and they even obtained a short-lived institutional base for their political influence in the form of the Society of Revolutionary Republican Women. Employing untraditional methods to voice traditional grievances, revolutionary women seemed to evolve from submissive subjects to participating citizens who had an impact on their government as they gained a new outlook toward themselves and their roles in society (Applewhite, Johnson and Levy 312). Even if such women were unaware of the political implications of their actions, their ability merely to act and influence public events within a patriarchal system confirms their untraditional social position.

Of course, such historical reconstructions of women's roles in the Revolution are quite recent. As for *A Tale of Two Cities* and the material to which Dickens might have been exposed when writing his novel, most scholarship confirms that Dickens's historical perspective was greatly informed by Thomas Carlyle's *The French Revolution.* The two main studies which explore Dickens's influences, Michael Goldberg's *Carlyle and Dickens* and William Oddie's *Dickens and Carlyle: The Question of Influence,* demonstrate that Dickens relied on Carlyle's text, as well as the resource material Carlyle used in writing it, as research for his historical novel (Goldberg 101; Oddie 61–63). (Oddie also leaves room for other sources, although he does not define these possibilities clearly.) L. M. Findlay explains, furthermore, that in his historical book, Carlyle portrays the women of the Revolution in a highly conservative and repressive manner, a representation which helps define the limits of his political radicalism (130–34). Nevertheless, Dickens's representation of revolutionary women in his version of the French insurrection appears strikingly modern; in fact, in many ways, it seems to echo Applewhite and Levy's discussion.

As the main representative of the French women in this rebellion, Dickens presents Thérèse Defarge, valued and trusted confidante of her husband, Ernest, and his circle of lower-class conspirators. Dickens removes Madame Defarge from a typical, domestic feminine realm to place her in the midst of the turbulent Revolution. Thus, because of her combative posture, she seems to renegotiate or redefine Dickens's feminine contradiction; as a dynamic revolutionary, she is neither submissive victim nor saintly savior. Madame De-farge demonstrates her capacity as a politically active woman responding to class suppression, for example, in the storming of the Bastille episode, when she stands out as a leader of women, forcefully declaring female equality in her sadistic cry, "We can kill as well as the men when the place is taken!" (245). Such determination, near-perfect self-control and consistency of pur-pose render her hateful yet admirable. Although Dickens makes no attempt to indicate Madame Defarge's political awareness, instead rendering women's involvement in the Revolution a result of hunger or a sense of personal wrong, his acknowledgement, through Madame Defarge, of women's partici-pation and what appears to be their often powerful influence, seems to recog-nize the progressive nature of their role. As a politically determined and ap-parently determining being, Madame Defarge appears to avoid some of the restrictions placed on other women in the novel.

This inclination toward decisive action, however, finally leads Madame Defarge to seek the execution of Lucie and her family, and as she travels the Paris streets on her way to realize her desire. Dickens writes:

> There were many women at that time, upon whom the time laid a dreadfully disfiguring hand; but, there was not one among them more to be dreaded than this ruthless woman, now taking her way along the streets. Of a strong and fearless character, of shrewd sense and readiness, of great determination, of that kind of beauty which not only seems to impart to its possessor firmness and animosity, but to strike into others an instinctive recognition of those qual-ities; the troubled time would have heaved her up, under any circumstances. But, imbued from her childhood with a brooding sense of wrong, and an invet-erate hatred of a class, opportunity had developed her into a tigress. She was absolutely without pity. If she had ever had the virtue in her, it had quite gone out of her.
>
> It was nothing to her, that an innocent man was to die for the sins of his forefathers; she saw, not him, but them. It was nothing to her, that his wife was to be made a widow and his daughter an orphan; that was insufficient punish-ment, because they were her natural enemies and her prey, and as such had no right to live. To appeal to her, was made hopeless by her having no sense of pity, even for herself. (390–91)

In this passage, Dickens singles out Madame Defarge as a magnified representation of the unnatural horror of revolutionary violence; he also pointedly connects her with Lucie Manette. He begins by suggesting that Madame Defarge, like the other women of the Revolution, is disfigured by the "time." This statement implies that Madame Defarge is negatively dis-torted by her environment, that, had she been exposed to different circum-stances, she might have turned out quite differently, perhaps even like Lucie herself. But the years leading to the Revolution turn her into a ruthless, strong, fearless, shrewd woman. Her readiness and determination render her wholly unfeminine, and the reference to her "beauty" secures her position as the fair, angelic Lucie's dark-haired antithesis. She substitutes her knitting needles of revenge, which she uses to denounce traitors, for Lucie's golden thread of harmony, and in lieu of the compassionate emotions to which Lucie often succumbs, Madame Defarge is utterly devoid of the "virtue" of pity. Certainly, she derives motivation from fidelity to her natural sister, but she distorts that devotion in order to seek vengeance and death rather than forgiveness and life. While Lucie gives birth to angelic creatures like herself and tends them with love and concern, Madame Defarge has no children, an absence which ironically connects her with the aristocratic women whom Dickens also criticizes for lacking maternal affection. (He suggests that, although upper class ladies give birth, peasant women raise the children and are, thus, more deserving of the exalted title of "Mother," 137). In short, Dickens depicts Madame Defarge as a women of distorted potential, a woman of powerful feelings who, as the result of a lifetime of pain and oppression, turns to destruction. Because he connects her so obviously with Lucie, Madame Defarge represents a perversion of Dickens's feminine-savior figure.

The above reference to Madame Defarge's physical appearance, furthermore, while contrasting with Lucie's comeliness, also asserts that the older woman's beauty is of a different "kind," one that imbues her with, or which she transforms into, power and violence. Because only instinct can recognize the firmness and animosity behind her beauty, and because her "brooding sense of wrong" derives from her childhood, a time of innocence and lack of worldly understanding, Dickens underscores the primal nature of her desires and her basic animality. Although Dickens grants her small personal and political justification for her "inveterate hatred" in the forms of her sister's rape and her own subjection to class suppression, Madame Defarge is a "tigress" who hunts her "natural enemies" and her "prey." The way in which she toys with Foulon, for example, letting the captured aristocrat go then pulling him back several times before he is finally executed, confirms her catlike nature. (Again, Madame Defarge is connected to the aristocracy; Dickens underscores the equally brutal and basic ferocity of the upper classes by referring to the Marquis as a "refined tiger," 156). The gender-specificity of Dickens's reference to Madame Defarge as one of the "women" rather than one of the people disfigured by the times highlights female brutality as being even more disturbing than the barbarity of male revolutionaries, since such savagery contrasts so greatly with the novel's idealized perception of women's potential as realized in Lucie.

In fact, this description of Madame Defarge recalls Nina Auerbach's monster in its horrified representation of women's latent powers let loose upon the world. In her comprehensive examination of Victorian female stereotypes, Auerbach suggests that, while Victorian men traditionally valued women for their sense of morality and purity, these men also feared the metamorphic power implicit in female spirituality (1–24). Auerbach goes on to claim that literary evidence for this fear of women directly reveals itself in the dark side of the angelic metaphor, taking, for example, the form of monsters, witches, sorceresses and demons (4). In terms of Auerbach's argument, then, Madame Defarge represents one such threatening monster. Although, as the above citation indicates, she is fully cognizant of and blindly driven by patrilineal ties, seeking restitution for "the sins of his [Darnay's] forefathers," Madame Defarge heedlessly attempts to subvert the familial bonds which help support a patriarchal system in her desire to kill Charles, an act which would render Lucie and her child defenceless widow and orphan. She dares to defy time and death through her unconcern, confirming her demon-like, irrational evil in her absolute lack of pity "even for herself." As a woman she achieves status among the revolutionaries, but she does so only at the expense of human compassion and remorse. Depicting her persistent and insatiable brutality, Dickens portrays Madame Defarge as a force of nature as well as an animal, identifying her as an elemental, and hence unconquerable presence; she says to her husband, "tell Wind and Fire where to stop . . . but don't tell me" (370). Such appeals to nature dehistoricize Madame Defarge, removing her from her culture and from the Revolution in order to render her effectively non-feminine and non-human, a mythic Fury.

As exaggerated as this description of Madame Defarge may appear to be, her representation echoes legends surrounding actual women of the Revolution. In *Carlyle and Dickens,* Michael Goldberg connects the activities of Madame Defarge with those of Théroigne de Méricourt (118), and Linda Kelly, in *Women of the French Revolution,* discusses various myths which grew around Théroigne as a revolutionary figure (11–23, 48–59). According to Kelly, Théroigne, who intoxicated the Revolution with her beauty, became famous for flashing through crowds in a blood-red riding habit with a sabre and pistol in hand, leading a mob to the Bastille. She subsequently came to personify the fury of the Revolution as well as women's desires to show solidarity and help in the Revolution's defense (90). However, although Théroigne apparently supported radical ideas such as a women's armed battalion, Kelly asserts that she did not help storm the Bastille, and that, in fact, much of her story in myth (11), since her eccentricity and exhibitionism denied her much revolutionary impact (35). Nevertheless, Théroigne's celebrity snowballed until she was imprisoned in connection with an attempted assassination of the Queen (47), only to be released for lack of evidence. Soon thereafter, she reportedly went mad (59). Other women such as Charlotte Corday (whose single act, the assassination of a radical journalist, Marat, supposedly performed with the intent of saving thousands of lives from the brutal measures he advocated, earned her legendary status, 100–102). Marie Antoinette (114) and Olympe de Gouges (who wrote *The Rights of Woman and the Citizen* in response to the omission of women's rights from the Revolutionary document, *The Rights of Man and the Citizen,* 122–6) were commonly depicted as monsters similar to Théroigne (102). According to such historical descriptions, therefore, the exaggeration with which Dickens depicts the brutality and inhumanity of Madame Defarge seems to owe a debt to legends concerning such revolutionary women.

More importantly, Dickens's treatment of Madame Defarge recalls the actual recontainment experienced by women in the Revolution. In the years following 1789, many men seemed to fear politically active women as subversive of male authority, suggesting that they were susceptible to manipulation by counter-revolutionary factions (Graham 247). In fact, government reaction to women's only organized seat of political power, the Society of Revolutionary Republican Women, acted upon such an apprehension. In response to public disturbances with which the Society was associated, Jacobin Deputy Amar of the Committee of General Security reportedly informed the Revolutionary Convention that women do not have the physical or moral strength to discuss political considerations and recommend resolutions; consequently, the government passed a law to restrict women from holding public meetings, from exercising political rights and from taking active roles in governmental affairs (Blum 213). As a first step in a series of repressive measures which multiplied through the reign of Napoleon, the government attempted to justify its actions through idealization of family cohesion and women's "natural" functions within the home. The political establishment promoted Rousseau's ideal of pregnant and nursing women as personifications of the regeneration of France, appealing to marriage and motherhood, to women's roles as educators within the home and family, in order to deny women political rights while exalting them as goddesses of reason (Graham 250). In partial demonstration of the limits of France's initial test of democracy (Applewhite and Levy, "Women, Democracy and Revolution" 64), the patriarchal government silenced women by legalizing female subservience in 1793.

By dismissing the unfeminine Madame Defarge as other than human and portraying women revolutionaries as beasts, Dickens apparently endorses this type of denial of women's moral and intellectual suitability for public affairs. Dickens impedes women's access to power in his representation of the Revolution by focussing on a disfigured monster whose influence is more primal than political. He thereby contains female subversion and denies women access to effective political agency by characterizing their social activities as aberrant rather than "natural" behavior. Furthermore, by endorsing only those women, such as Lucie, who do not disturb the patriarchal agenda or threaten men's supremacy, Dickens reconfirms women's subordinate status. As a half-French woman, Lucie serves as an example for her French "sisters" because she embodies Rousseau's ideal, constantly remaining a politically submissive complement to the patriarchy represented in her husband and father. Through this acceptance of Lucie and rejection of Madame Defarge, Dickens affirms the exclusion of women from political life and reveals a patriarchal fear of women becoming equal partners in the Revolution.

Beyond this bestial, demon-like version of women, at the height of the Revolution Dickens digresses even further from his ideal to blur sexual differentiation altogether. In "The Grindstone" chapter (287), for example, Dickens presents "men devilishly set off with spoils of women's lace and silk and ribbon" (291). As both sexes gather to sharpen their weapons, the general cover of blood and physical disguises prevents the accurate and easy determination of gender and identity. More pointedly, in his description of the Carmagnole, a musical celebration performed by the revolutionaries, Dickens writes:

> Men and women danced together, women danced together, men danced together, as hazard had brought them together. . . . No fight could have been half so terrible as this dance. It was so emphatically a fallen sport—a something, once innocent, delivered over to all devilry—a healthy pastime changed into a means of angering the blood, bewildering the senses, and steeling the heart. Such grace as was visible in it, made it the uglier, showing how warped and perverted all things good by nature were become. The maidenly bosom bared to this, the pretty almost-child's head thus distracted, the delicate foot mincing in this slough of blood and dirt, were types of the disjointed time. (307–308)

The participants in this revelry recall the French peasants who rejoice in the streets at the beginning of the novel when a wine cask is spilled; however, in the Carmagnole, these people celebrate the destructive spirit of the Revolution rather than the life-giving nourishment provided by the wine. Dickens underscores the horror of this spectacle as a perversion of a religious, Christmas dance by referring to the lack of discrimination and the irrelevance of sexual distinction in the selection of dance partners. In the fever of revolutionary passion, extremes collide to enforce a disruption of the presence, or at least of the usual importance, of sexual identity.

Nevertheless, despite this temporary disintegration into androgyny, the language of this passage identifies the Carmagnole as a decidedly feminine sport. Although men participate, a woman, La Vengeance, who is Madame Defarge's second-in-command and a personification of the revolutionary spirit in the novel, leads the "terrible" dance. Dickens represents the Carmagnole as a "fallen" sport, in a reference which suggests a traditional description of prostitutes or supposedly unchaste women as having "fallen" from grace and respectability (Hutter 457). His insistence on the transformation that occurs during the dance, a conversion of what was innocent, full of grace and "good by nature," into something warped, perverted and ugly, lends further support to this conventional image of an impure woman who has distorted and abused her feminine attributes. Moreover, Dickens's reference to the celebration as affecting the blood, senses and heart suggests that this dance appeals to human emotions rather than the mind, and such feeling is conventionally recognized as the feminine equivalent of masculine intelligence. He then reduces the dancers to types, all of whom are described in feminine terms: maidens, pretty children and dancers with "delicate" feet. Sexual difference may carry little import in the Carmagnole, but Dickens's description of the event appeals to an underlying sense of gender specificity.

In fact, Dickens seems to break down sexual barriers only to re-create a negative image of the Revolution itself as feminine. L. M. Findlay suggests that Carlyle defines femininity in *The French Revolution* in part by means of Maenadic reference, a depiction which helps to perpetuate patriarchal domination (135–40).[1] Here is a point where Dickens's and Carlyle's women begin to meet, since Dickens emulates this type of representation in his historical novel. Greek mythology characterizes Maenads, or the women worshippers of the god Dionysus, largely by their shared capacity for irrationality, for their uncontrollable, emotional, senseless, and therefore feminine, dancing and singing, and Dickens's portrait of the feminine figures in the Carmagnole echoes this description. Additionally, unreasonable and passionate French women such as Madame Defarge and La Vengeance tend to characterize most revolutionary scenes (Hutter 457), exceeding men in their savagery and strength, and dominating Dickens's representation of insurrection. It is important to note, however, that, despite their energy and fervor, and like the Maenads who depend upon their relationship to Dionysus to define their identity (Findlay 138). Dickens's women rely on men, or the circle of Jacques, to direct their activities. Therefore, while women are marginalized through denial of their independence, excessive revolutionary activity and its agents are negatively represented by reference to the feminine.

The two prevailing images which symbolize not only the effects but also the causes of the Revolution in Dickens's analysis are, accordingly, female. Dickens presents Medusa, or "The Gorgon's Head" (149), as a symbol of the corrupt aristocracy whose misrule helps to create conditions which demand retaliation on the part of the oppressed. As a mythological female figure who turns those who look at her to stone, Medusa represents the stone-like, upper class indifference to the poor, the legacy of social and personal repression which the Marquis attempts to pass on to Charles through the "Gorgon's spell" (Frank 137).[2] Of course, Dickens includes male embodiments of the mythological figure, in particular, the Marquis, who represents the evil in the French patriarchal system, but the image itself remains female. On the other hand, Dickens personifies the consequent peasant response to this exploitation in the form of an ironic feminine savior or goddess. He says that, "Above all, one hideous figure grew as familiar as if it had been before the general gaze from the foundations of the world—the figure of the sharp female called La Guillotine" (302). Dickens raises La Guillotine to near mythic status by suggesting her timelessness and universal familiarity, and clearly identities as female this symbol of the bloodthirstiness of revolutionary vengeance. Just as his extreme portrayal and rejection of Madame Defarge and his exaggerated depiction of Lucie as a desired feminine form demonstrates patriarchal anxiety about powerful women, so Dickens's use of feminine and female symbols to represent the French Revolution, its causes and effects, underscores a need for containment of such convulsion and a fear of revolution itself.

A careful examination of the women in Dickens's novel, therefore, clearly reveals the underlying patriarchal bias of his text. Thus, it seems rather ironic that, as the novel draws to a close, women instead of men take part in the final, decisive, climactic battle. In a revolution in which men govern activity even when women are participants in it, patriarchal traditions anticipate male orchestration and enactment of decisive action; yet Dickens allows Miss Pross and Madame Defarge to decide whether the Darnays' final flight to England will succeed. As their contest begins, Dickens writes:

> Miss Pross had nothing beautiful about her; years had not tamed the wildness, or softened the grimness, of her appearance; but, she too was a determined woman in her different way, and she measured Madame Defarge with her eyes, every inch.
>
> "You might, from your appearance, be the wife of Lucifer," said Miss Pross, in her breathing. "Nevertheless, you shall not get the better of me. I am an Englishwoman."
>
> Madame Defarge looked at her scornfully, but still with something of Miss Pross's own perception that they two were at bay. (395)

The potential irony involved in representing a physical battle between women rather than men is subdued by a recognition that these combatants are the two most masculine women in the novel, and Dickens reinforces this perception by restating Miss Pross's lack of beauty, her wildness and grimness which even time can neither tame nor soften. Once again, Dickens connects women with animals, indicating the primal nature of these two opponents in their powers of "perception," or their intuitive abilities to understand one another while "at bay" and despite their language barrier. In fact, Miss Pross's reference to Madame Defarge as the "wife of Lucifer," contrasting as it does with her own appeal to Heaven several paragraphs later, suggests that these two figures represent elemental forces more than individual women, symbolizing a revolutionary battle between evil and good, inhuman barbarity and selfless devotion. Certainly Lucie is the more obvious female embodiment of goodness, but as a woman of higher class and angelic purity, her participation in such barbaric activity would be inappropriate, so Miss Pross serves as an adequate stand-in. By suggesting that Miss Pross is determined "in her different way," a distinction which affirms her basic femininity in spite of her masculine eccentricities, Dickens carefully differentiates her from her opponent; thus, when the English woman kills Madame Defarge "with the vigorous tenacity of love, always so much stronger than hate" (397), through masculine agency Miss Pross is able to confirm the efficacy of feminine values in her certain victory over the non-feminine. (As an "Englishwoman," she also affirms England's superiority and dissociation from France's revolutionary violence.) Consequently, their individual fates pay homage to paternalistic demands for the pacification of women, as Madame Defarge, a woman who affronts femininity, experiences ultimate silencing in her death, while Miss Pross, whose feminine goodness cannot wholly atone for the murder she commits, must withdraw into the mute world of her own deafness. (Lucie, too, travels in a carriage to England in silence and passivity.) Dickens thereby allows two women to perform the climactic battle in the text without compromising patriarchal expectations.

Through manipulation of the angel in all of her various manifestations, then, Dickens is able to present women as representative of both solution and problem in the events surrounding the French insurrection of 1789 and the devastation which follows, as a source of redemption (Lucie and, to a certain extent, Miss Pross) and a symbol of revolutionary insanity (Madame Defarge). Through his paternalistic and chauvinistic polemics, he simultaneously exalts and denigrates women, exposing their ideal femininity, or lack thereof, as a measure of possible social amelioration. By twisting and distorting seemingly unconventional feminine images, Dickens recontains the women in his novel, restricting their movements and influence by forcing them to assume illogical and untenable positions in a patriarchal society. This circumscription of a potentially progressive depiction of women by a chauvinistic need for their repression and confinement underscores Dickens's gender bias.

Notes

1. In Book Seven, chapters four through eleven of *The French Revolution* (251–89), Carlyle describes women as Maenads in reference to the October days insurrections. He refers to them as "angry she-bees" or "desperate flying wasps" (254) who need guidance and find it in the form of a man, Maillard, around whom they cluster Carlyle paints the scene as a wild spectacle enlivened by uncontrollable women whose "inarticulate fury" Maillard miraculously manages to translate into coherent speech in order to communicate with the government and the king. In this description of the event, Carlyle displays a consistently patronizing attitude toward women and their activities, thereby somewhat restricting their revolutionary impact.

2. In "The Laugh of the Medusa," Hélène Cixous refers to the Medusa figure as a metaphor for women's uniqueness which Cixous insists needs to be expressed and released through oral and written language (245–64). As she calls for a revaluation of women's difference, she suggests that Medusa need not seem ugly or destructive; on the contrary, in her attempt to incite women to "laugh" or speak their differences. Cixous asserts that women need to explore Medusa, look at her and recognize her beauty. Cixous suggests that Medusa is traditionally rejected as a horrible creature only because men, who fear women's uniqueness and powers as a threat to their supremacy, describe and represent her as a monster (255). To apply Cixous's argument to *A Tale of Two Cities*, then, because Dickens employs the image of Medusa in its conventionally negative connotation, the "Gorgon's head" reinforces his participation in a patriarchal fear and rejection of women.

I also find it worth noting that Medusa is destroyed by a man, Perseus, who with the aid of the gods cuts off her head with a magic sickle. This proposed resolution to the myth confirms the appropriateness of Dickens's use of the Medusa image in terms of the guillotine and his affirmation of male dominance and control over threatening women.

Works Cited

Abray, Jane. "Feminism in the French Revolution." *The American Historical Review* 80.1 (Feb. 1975): 43–62.

Applewhite, Harriet Branson and Darline Gay Levy. "Women, Democracy, and Revolution in Paris, 1789–1794." *French Women and the Age of Enlightenment*. Ed. Samia I. Spencer, Bloomington: Indiana UP. 1984, 64–79.

————. "Women of the Popular Classes in Revolutionary Paris, 1789–1795." *Women, War and Revolution*. Eds. Carol R. Berkin and Clara M. Lovett. NY: Holmes and Meier, 1980, 9–35.

Applewhite, Harriet Branson, Darline Gay Levy and Mary Durham Johnson, eds. and trans. *Women in Revolutionary Paris 1789–1795*. Chicago: U of Illinois P. 1979.

Auerbach, Nina. *Woman and the Demon: The Life of a Victorian Myth*. Cambridge, Mass: Harvard UP, 1982.

Blum, Carol. "The Sex Made to Obey." *Rousseau and the Republic of Virtue: The Language of Politics in the French Revolution* Ithaca: Cornell UP, 1986, 204–215.

Carlyle, Thomas. *The French Revolution: A History*. 1839. London: Chapman and Hill. 1900. 3 vols.

Cixous, Hélène. "The Laugh of the Medusa." Trans. Keith Cohen and Paula Cohen. *Signs: A Journal of Women in Culture and Society* 1.4 (1976): 875–93.

Daleski, Herman M. *Dickens and the Art of Analogy*. NY: Schocken, 1970.

Dickens, Charles. *A Tale of Two Cities*. 1858. Ed. and intro. George Woodcock. London Penguin, 1988.

Findlay, L. M. " 'Maternity must forth': The Poetics and Politics of Gender in Carlyle's *French Revolution*." *Dalhousie Review* 66.1/2 (1986): 130–54.

Frank, Lawrence. "The Poetics of Impasse." *Charles Dickens and the Romantic Self* Lincoln: U of Nebraska P. 1984, 124–50.

Goldberg, Michael. *Carlyle and Dickens*. Athens: U of Georgia P. 1972.

Graham, Ruth. "Loaves of Liberty: Women in the French Revolution." *Becoming Visible Women in European History*. Eds. Renate Bridenthal and Claudia Koonz. Boston Houghton, 1977, 236–54.

Hill, Nancy Klenck. "Woman as Savior." *Denver Quarterly* 18.4 (1984): 94–107.

Hufton, Olwen. "Women in Revolution, 1789–1796." *Past and Present* (1971): 90–108.

Hutter, Albert D. "Nation and Generation in *A Tale of Two Cities*." *PMLA* 93.3 (1978): 448–62.

Jarmuth, Sylvia L. *Dickens' Use of Women in His Novels*. NY: Excelsior, 1967.

Johnson, Mary Durham. "Old Wine in New Bottles: The Institutional Changes for Women of the People During the French Revolution." *Women, War, and Revolution*. Eds. Carol R. Berkin and Clara M. Lovett. NY: Holmes and Meier, 1980, 107–143.

Kelly, Linda. *Women of the French Revolution*. London: Hamish Hamilton Paperback, 1987.

Kucich, John. "The Purity of Violence: *A Tale of Two Cities*." *Dickens Studies Annual* 8 (1980): 119–37.

Oddie, William. *Dickens and Carlyle: The Question of Influence*. London: Centenary P. 1972.

Slater, Michael. *Dickens and Women*. Stanford: Stanford UP, 1983.

Welsh, Alexander. *The City of Dickens*. London: Oxford UP, 1971, 141–63.

Index

◆

This is a selective index. Historical names, places, and events mentioned in the passages from historians of the French Revolution are not included here.

223

The Volume Editor

Michael Cotsell teaches in the English Department at the University of Delaware. He is the author of *The Companion to "Our Mutual Friend"* (London: Allen & Unwin, 1986) and former associate editor of The Dickens Companions series.

The General Editor

Zack Bowen is professor of English at the University of Miami. He holds degrees from the University of Pennsylvania (B.A.), Temple University (M.A.), and the State University of New York at Buffalo (Ph.D.). In addition to being general editor of this G. K. Hall series, he is editor of the James Joyce series for the University of Florida Press and the *James Joyce Literary Supplement.* He is author and editor of numerous books on modern British, Irish, and American literature. He has also published more than one hundred monographs, essays, scholarly reviews, and recordings related to literature. He is past president of the James Joyce Society (1977–1986), former chair of the Modern Language Association Lowell Prize Committee, and currently president of the International James Joyce Foundation.